FANBOYS™
vs. ZOMBIES

VOLUME FOUR
APOLLO Z

ROSS RICHIE CEO & Founder • JACK CUMMINS President • MARK SMYLIE Chief Creative Officer • MATT GAGNON Editor-in-Chief • FILIP SABLIK VP of Publishing & Marketing • STEPHEN CHRISTY VP of Development
LANCE KREITER VP of Licensing & Merchandising • PHIL BARBARO VP of Finance • BRYCE CARLSON Managing Editor • MEL CAYLO Marketing Manager • SCOTT NEWMAN Production Design Manager • DAFNA PLEBAN Editor • SHANNON WATTERS Editor
ERIC HARBURN Editor • REBECCA TAYLOR Editor • CHRIS ROSA Assistant Editor • ALEX GALER Assistant Editor • WHITNEY LEOPARD Assistant Editor • JASMINE AMIRI Assistant Editor • MIKE LOPEZ Production Designer
HANNAH NANCE PARTLOW Production Designer • DEVIN FUNCHES E-Commerce & Inventory Coordinator • BRIANNA HART Executive Assistant • AARON FERRARA Operations Assistant • JOSÉ MEZA Sales Assistant

BOOM! Studios, 5670 Wilshire Boulevard, Suite 450, Los Angeles, CA 90036-5679. Printed in China. First Printing.
ISBN: 978-1-60886-358-7, eISBN: 978-1-61398-212-9

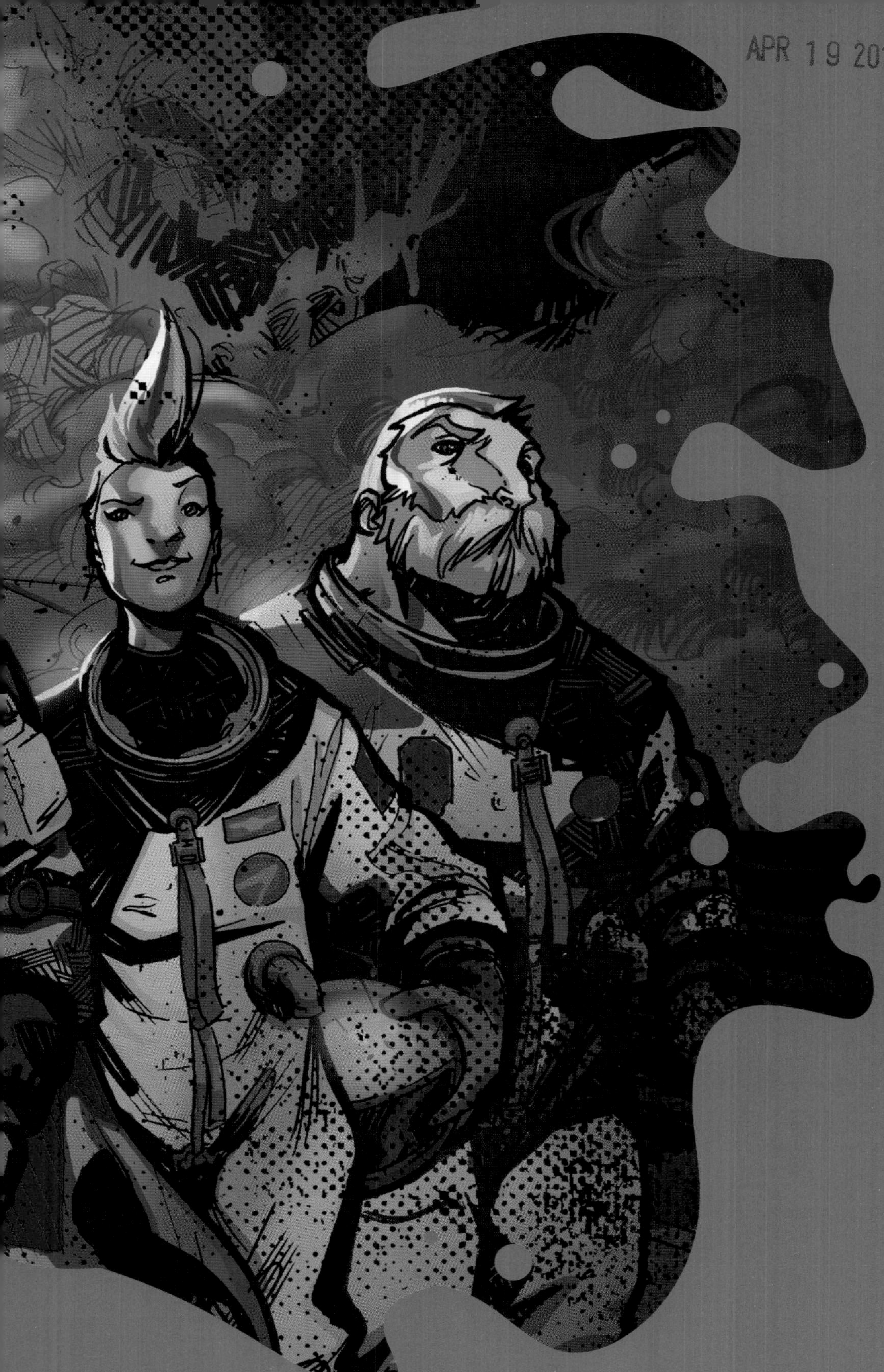

WRITTEN BY
SHANE HOUGHTON

ART BY
JERRY GAYLORD

INK ASSISTS BY
PENELOPE GAYLORD
AND
BRYAN TURNER

COLORS BY
MIRKA ANDOLFO
WITH
ANDREA DOTTA

LETTERS BY
ED DUKESHIRE

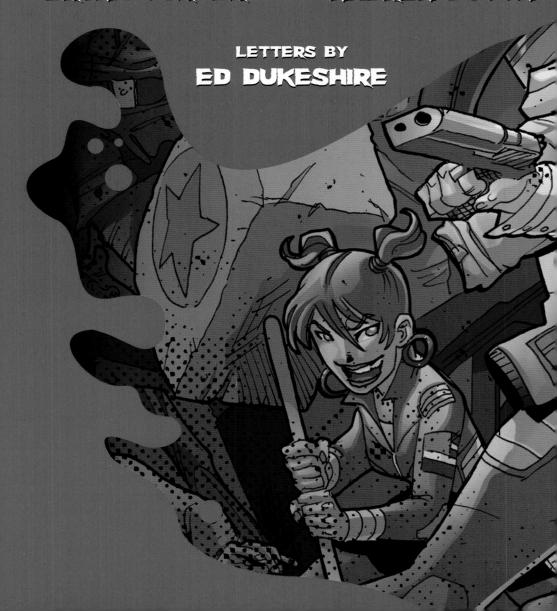

COVER BY

JERRY GAYLORD

COLORS BY **GABRIEL CASSATA**

FANBOYS VS. ZOMBIES CHARACTER DESIGNS BY HUMBERTO RAMOS AND JERRY GAYLORD

EDITOR
ERIC HARBURN

MANAGING EDITOR
BRYCE CARLSON

DESIGNER
KELSEY DIETERICH

FANBOYS VS. ZOMBIES CREATED BY BEN SILVERMAN AND JIMMY FOX

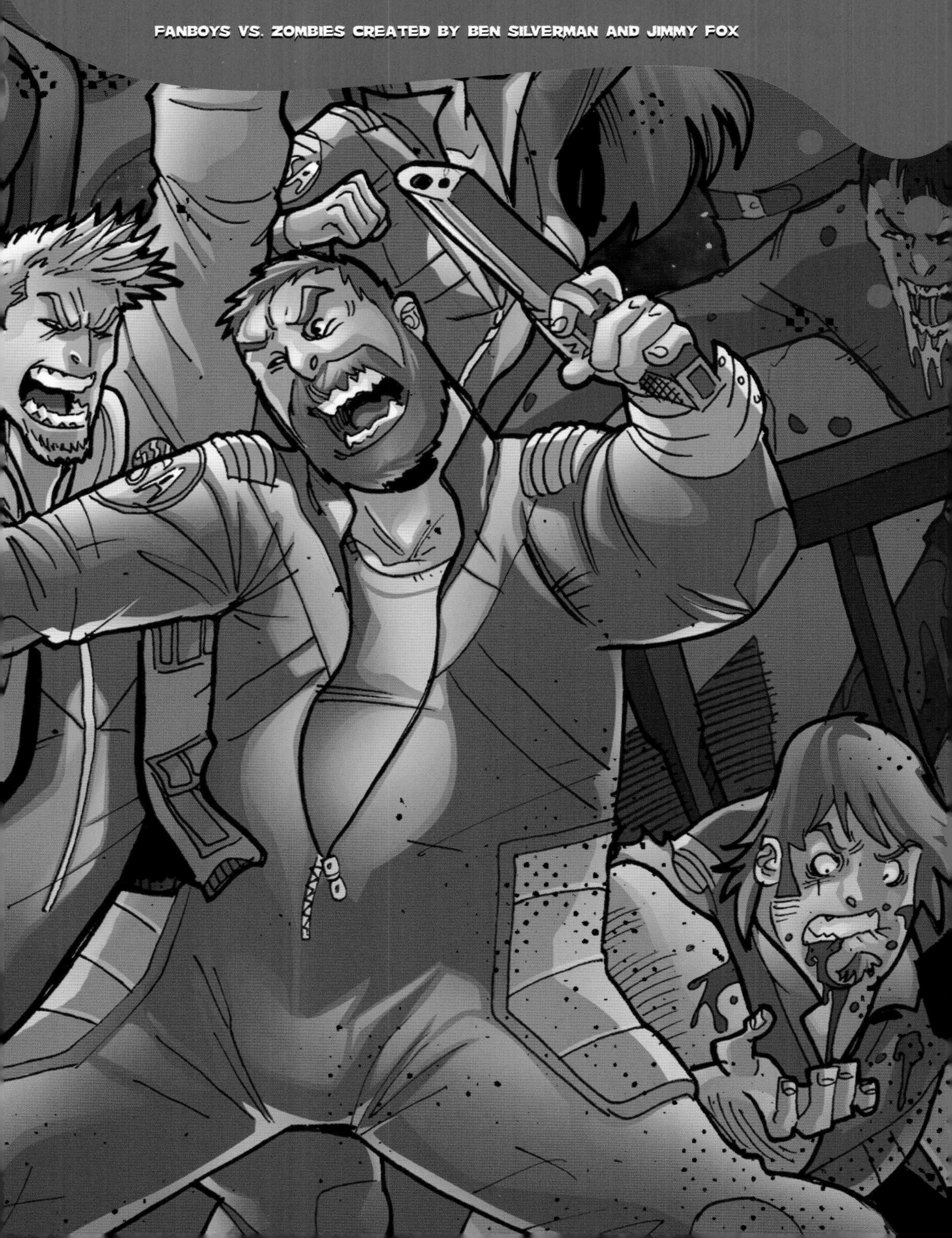

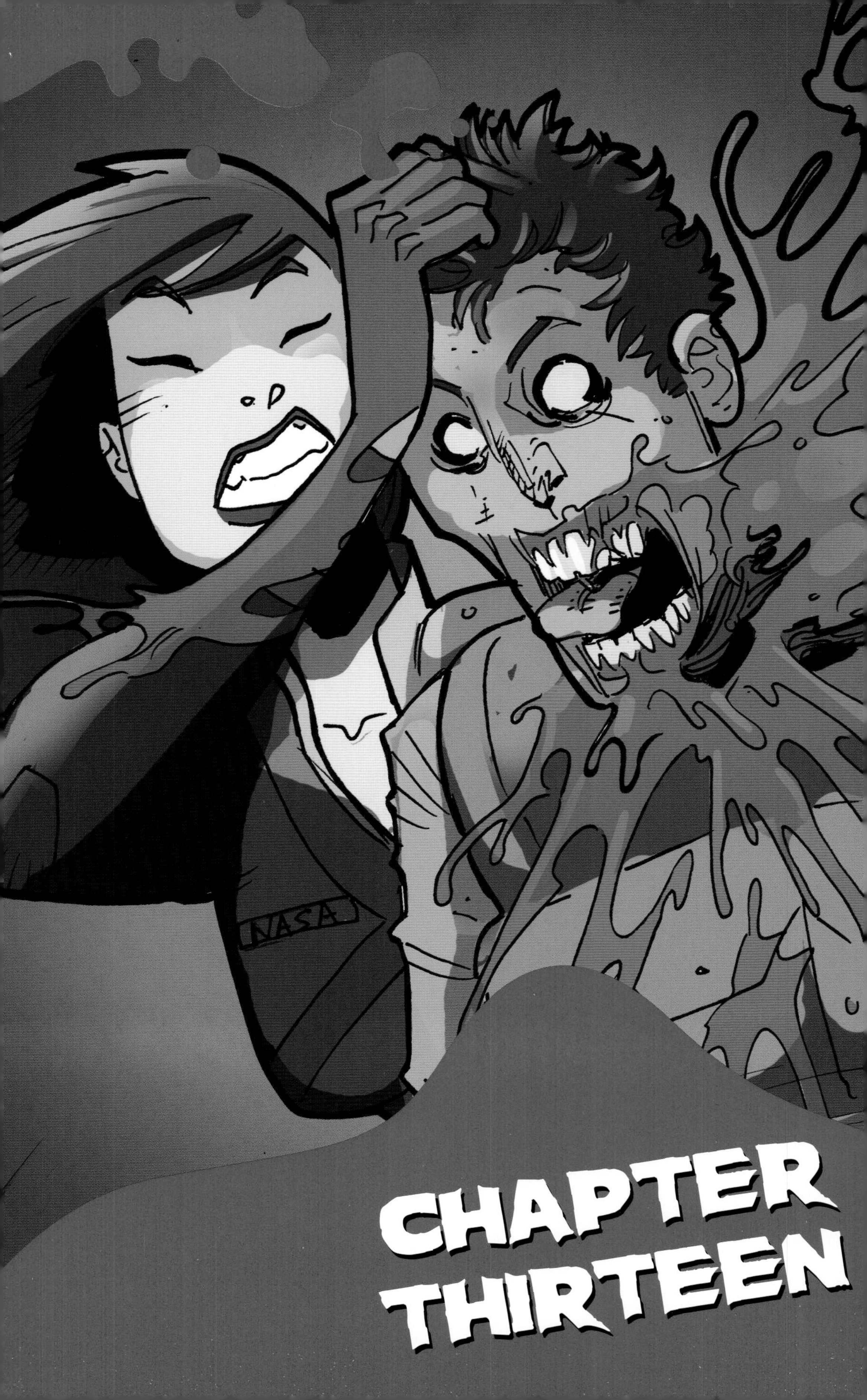
NASA

CHAPTER THIRTEEN

NOW...

GOOD MORNING, GLADYS.

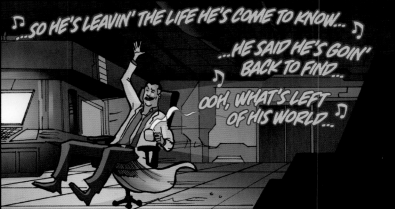

16	☑ I Keep Forgettin
17	☑ Crossroads
18	☑ Midnight Train to Georgia
19	☑ Poppa Was a Rollin' Stone
20	☑ My Girl
21	☑ 99 Problems
22	☑ ABC
23	☑ Do You Love Me
24	☑
25	☑
26	☑ I Hear a Symphony
27	☑
28	☑ Dancing in the Street
29	☑ Harlem Shake

CLK

♪ L.A. PROVED TOO MUCH FOR THE MAN... ♪

♪...SO HE'S LEAVIN' THE LIFE HE'S COME TO KNOW... ♪

...HE SAID HE'S GOIN' BACK TO FIND...

OOH, WHAT'S LEFT OF HIS WORLD... ♪

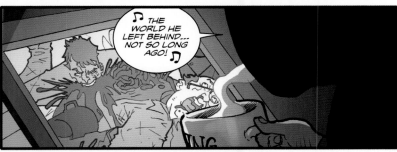

♪ THE WORLD HE LEFT BEHIND... NOT SO LONG AGO! ♪

ALERT

♪ HE'S LEAVING, ON THAT MIDNIGHT TR-- ♪

ALERT.

IT CAN'T BE...

POD APPROACHING.

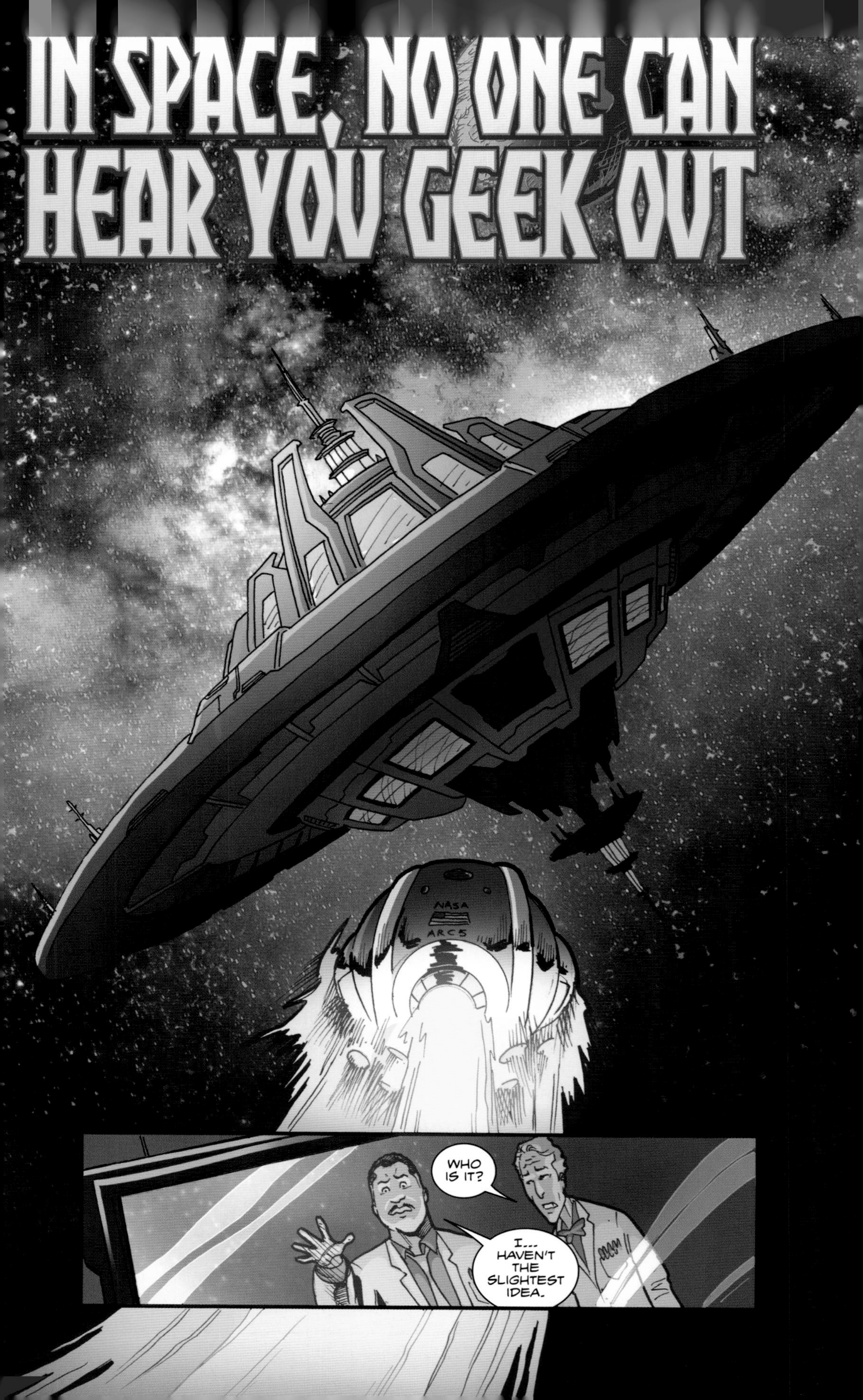
IN SPACE, NO ONE CAN HEAR YOU GEEK OUT
NASA
ARC5
WHO IS IT?
I... HAVEN'T THE SLIGHTEST IDEA.

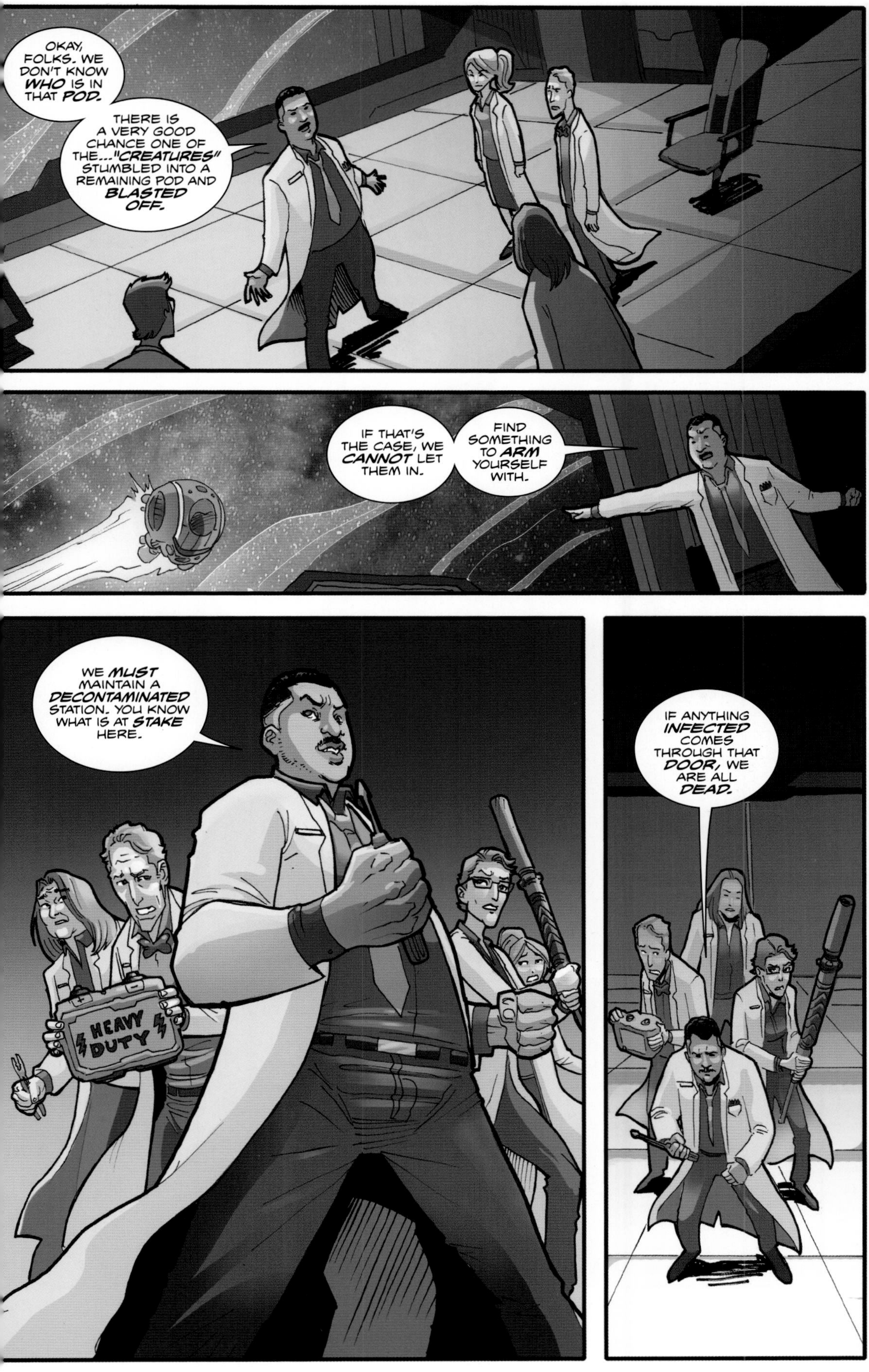
OKAY, FOLKS. WE DON'T KNOW WHO IS IN THAT POD.
THERE IS A VERY GOOD CHANCE ONE OF THE... "CREATURES" STUMBLED INTO A REMAINING POD AND BLASTED OFF.
IF THAT'S THE CASE, WE CANNOT LET THEM IN.
FIND SOMETHING TO ARM YOURSELF WITH.
WE MUST MAINTAIN A DECONTAMINATED STATION. YOU KNOW WHAT IS AT STAKE HERE.
HEAVY DUTY
IF ANYTHING INFECTED COMES THROUGH THAT DOOR, WE ARE ALL DEAD.

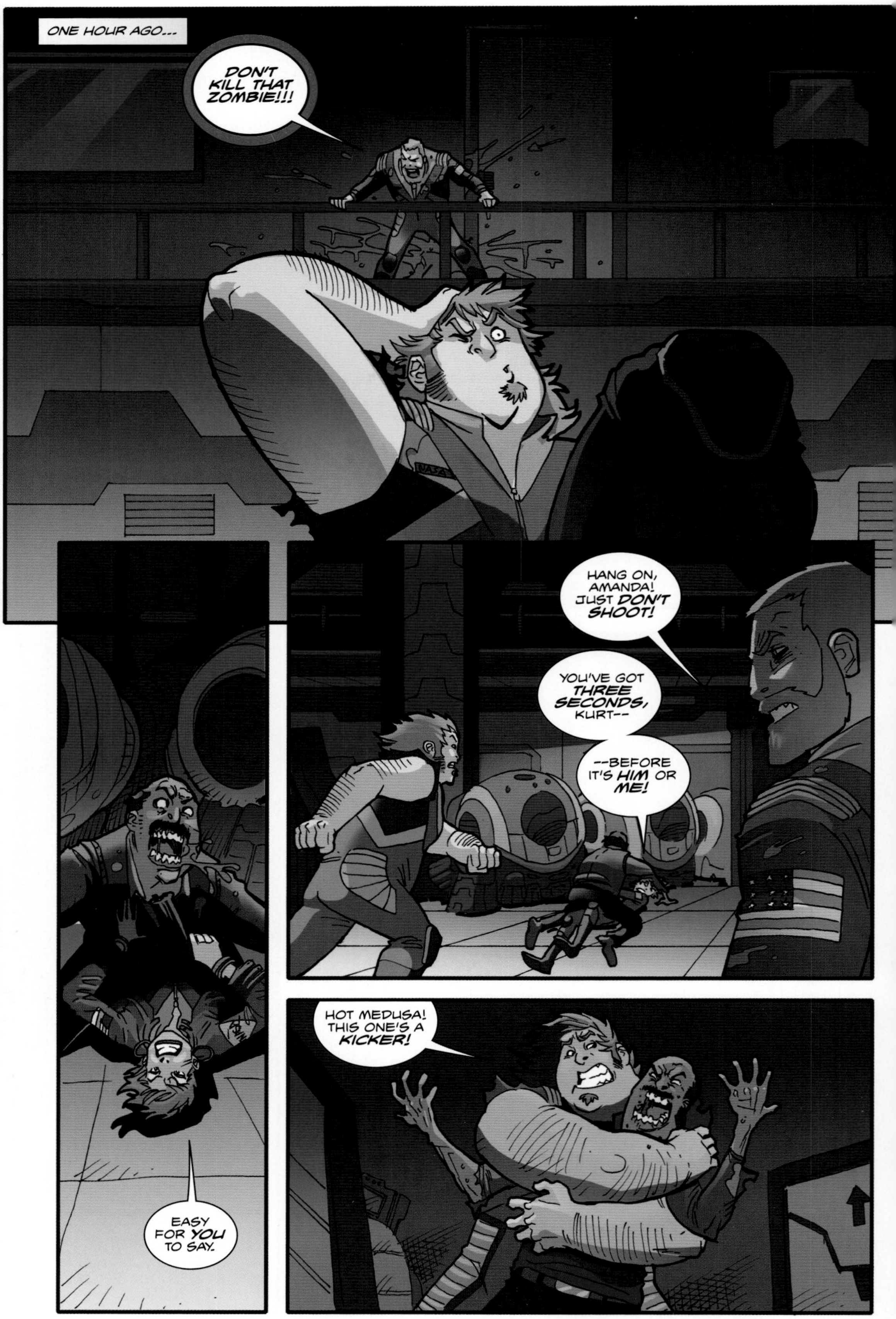
ONE HOUR AGO...
DON'T KILL THAT ZOMBIE!!!
EASY FOR YOU TO SAY.
HANG ON, AMANDA! JUST DON'T SHOOT!
YOU'VE GOT THREE SECONDS, KURT--
--BEFORE IT'S HIM OR ME!
HOT MEDUSA! THIS ONE'S A KICKER!

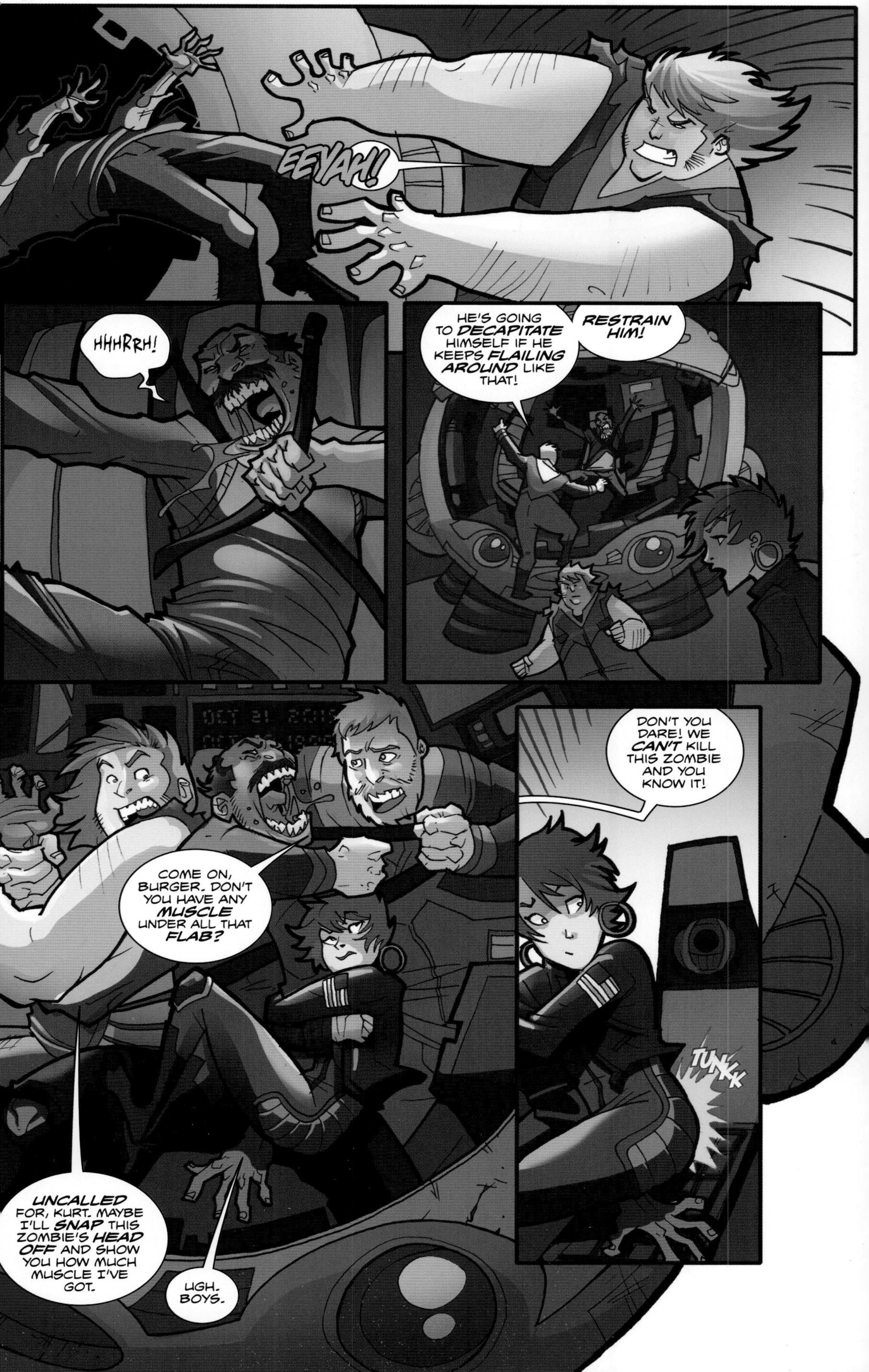
EEYAH!!
HHHRRH!
HE'S GOING TO DECAPITATE HIMSELF IF HE KEEPS FLAILING AROUND LIKE THAT!
RESTRAIN HIM!
COME ON, BURGER. DON'T YOU HAVE ANY MUSCLE UNDER ALL THAT FLAB?
UNCALLED FOR, KURT. MAYBE I'LL SNAP THIS ZOMBIE'S HEAD OFF AND SHOW YOU HOW MUCH MUSCLE I'VE GOT.
UGH. BOYS.
DON'T YOU DARE! WE CAN'T KILL THIS ZOMBIE AND YOU KNOW IT!
TUNKK

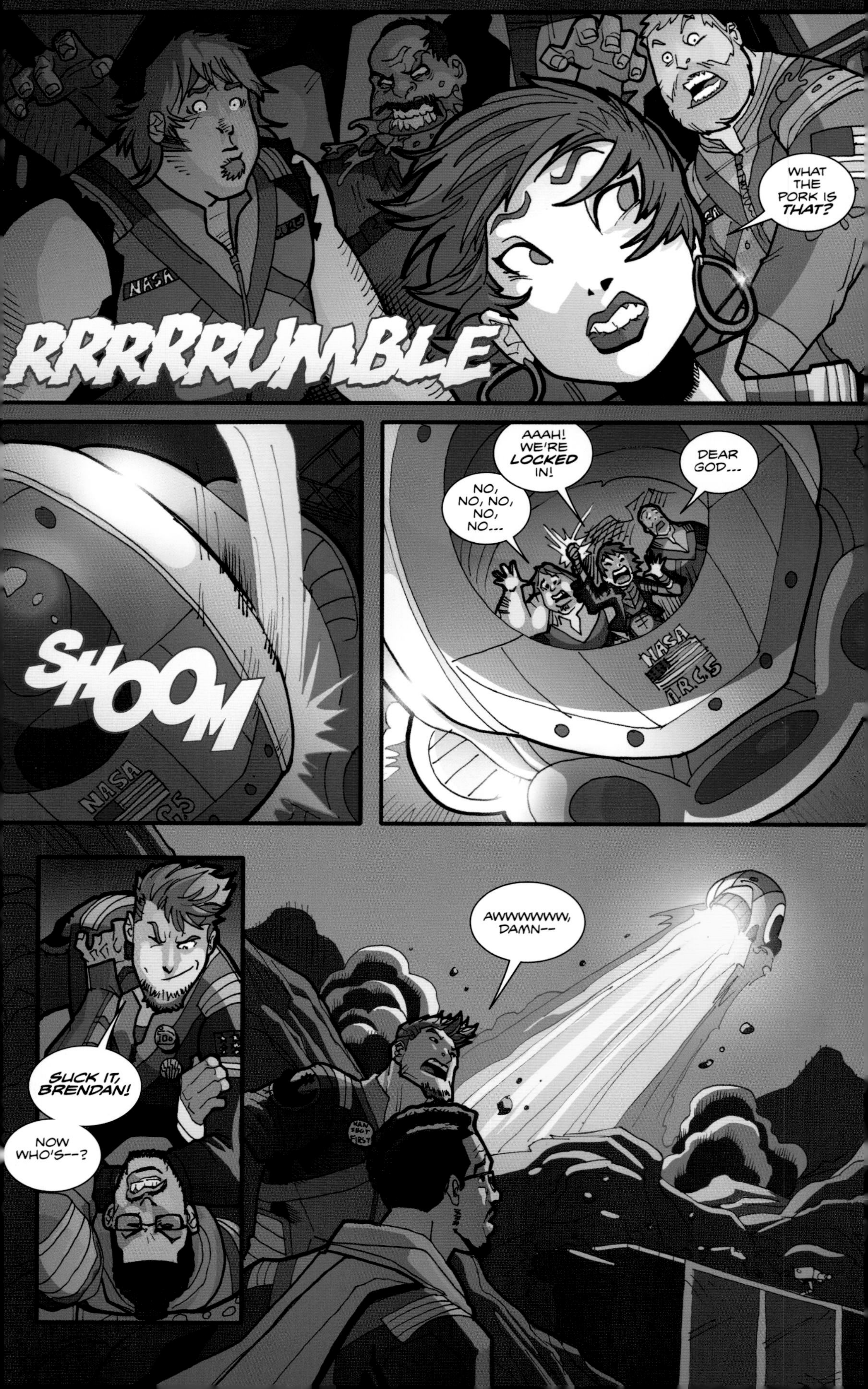
WHAT THE PORK IS THAT?
RRRRRUMBLE
SHOOM
NASA
AAAH! WE'RE LOCKED IN!
DEAR GOD---
NO, NO, NO, NO, NO---
NASA
A.R.C.5
AWWWWWW, DAMN--
SUCK IT, BRENDAN!
NOW WHO'S--?
HAN SHOT FIRST

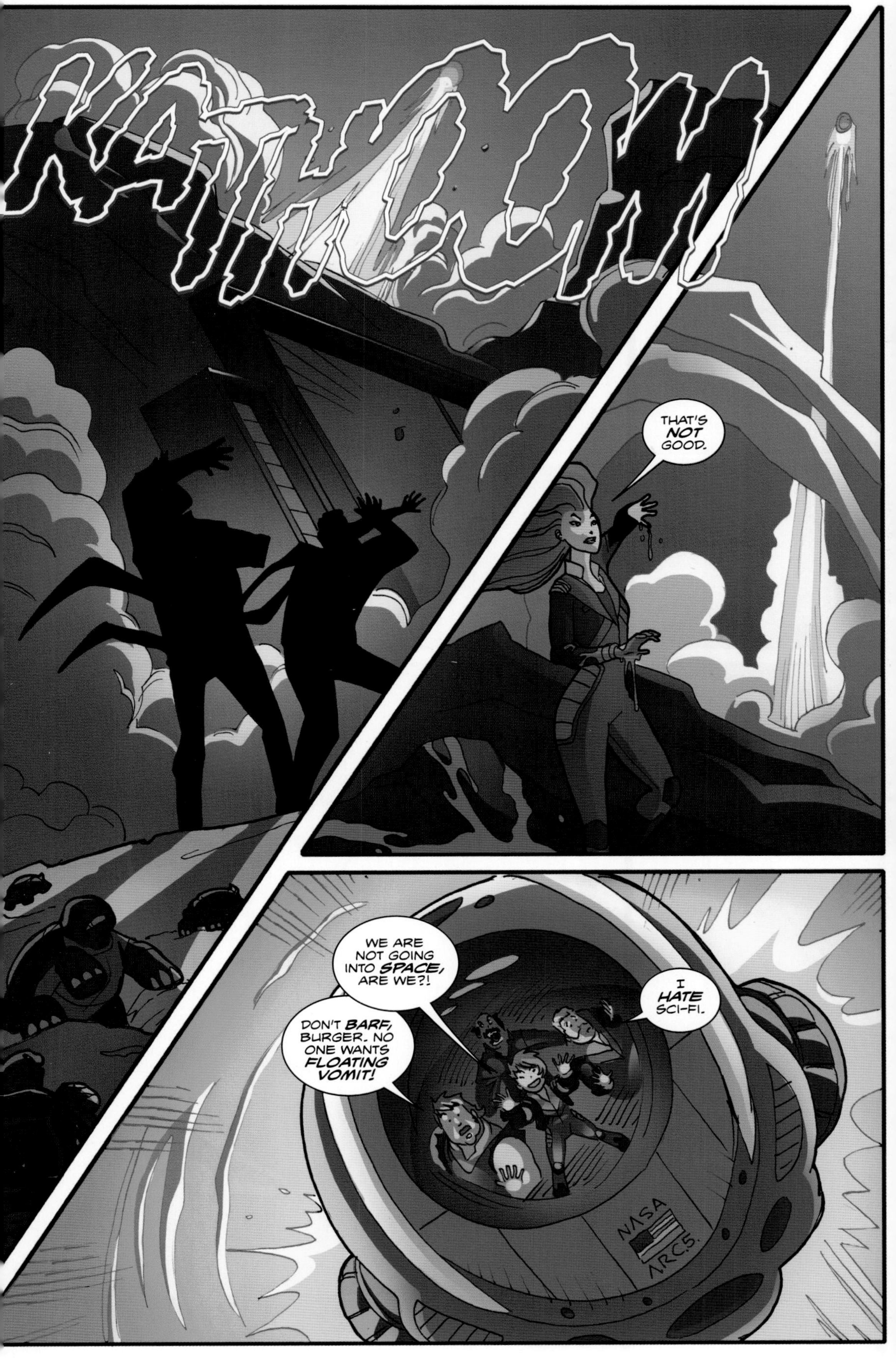
KATHOOOM
THAT'S NOT GOOD.
WE ARE NOT GOING INTO SPACE, ARE WE?!
I HATE SCI-FI.
DON'T BARF, BURGER. NO ONE WANTS FLOATING VOMIT!
NASA
ARC 5.

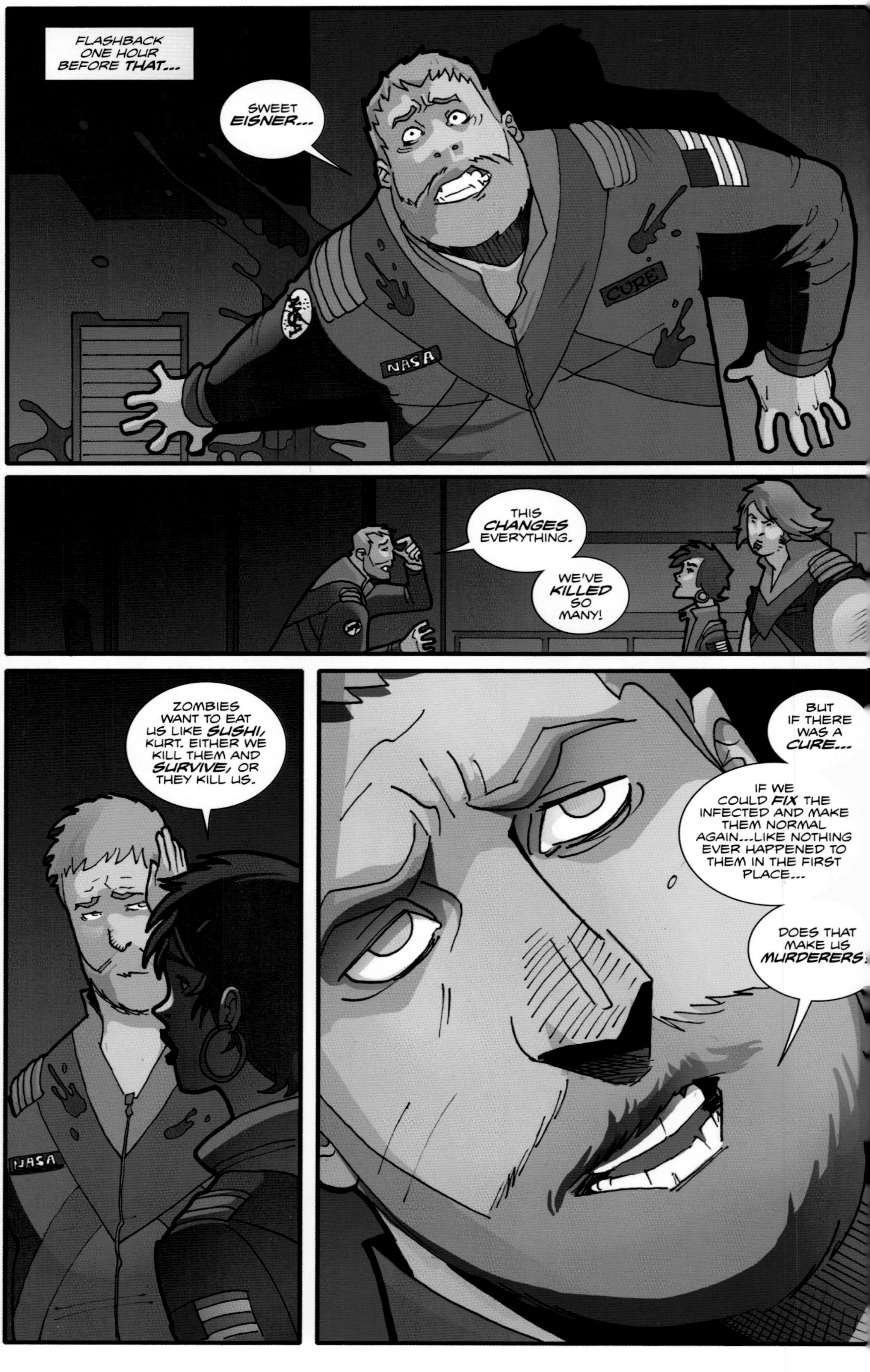
FLASHBACK ONE HOUR BEFORE THAT...
SWEET EISNER...
CURE
NASA
THIS CHANGES EVERYTHING.
WE'VE KILLED SO MANY!
ZOMBIES WANT TO EAT US LIKE SUSHI, KURT. EITHER WE KILL THEM AND SURVIVE, OR THEY KILL US.
NASA
BUT IF THERE WAS A CURE...
IF WE COULD FIX THE INFECTED AND MAKE THEM NORMAL AGAIN...LIKE NOTHING EVER HAPPENED TO THEM IN THE FIRST PLACE...
DOES THAT MAKE US MURDERERS?

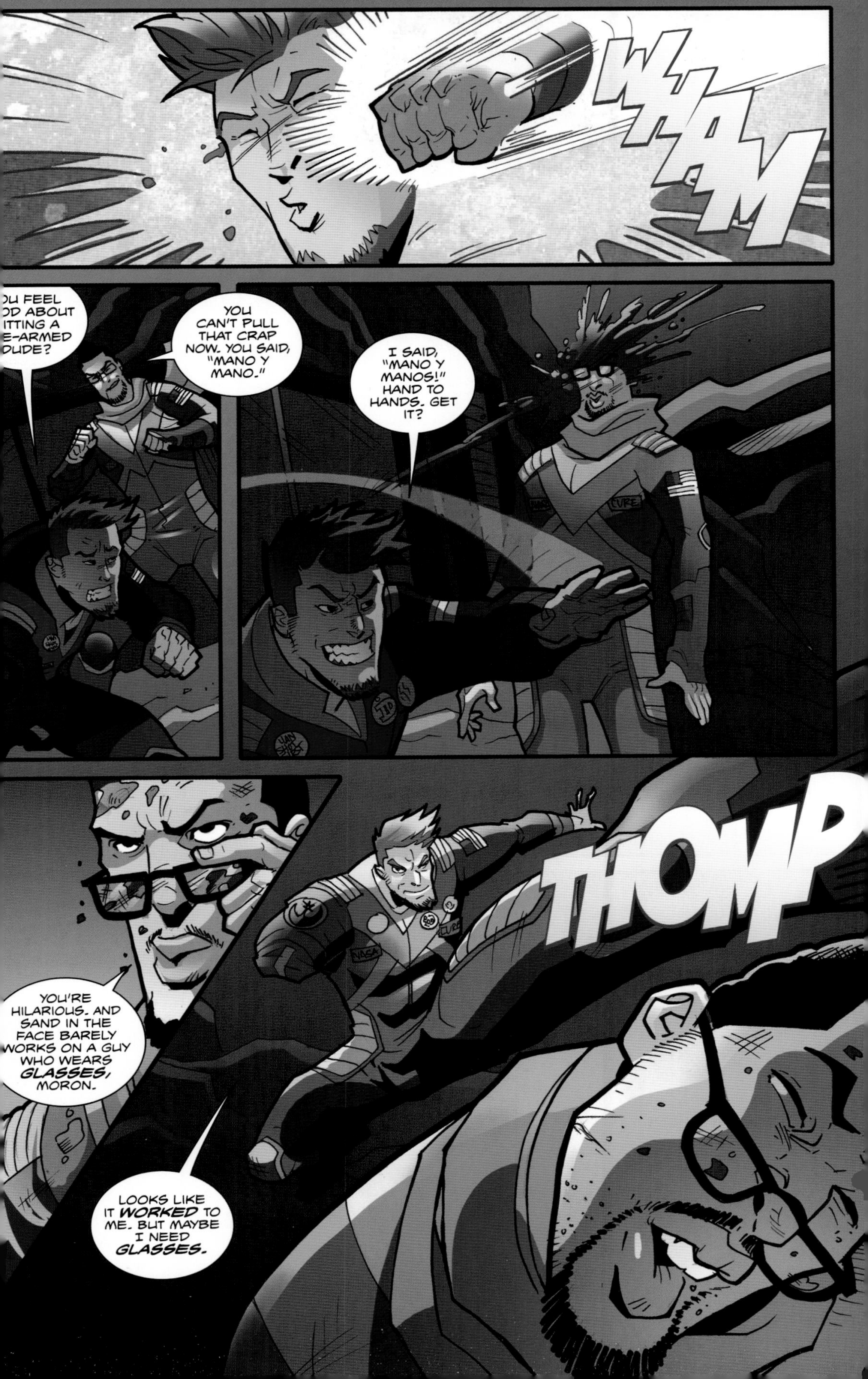
WHAM
OU FEEL OD ABOUT ITTING A E-ARMED DUDE?
YOU CAN'T PULL THAT CRAP NOW. YOU SAID, "MANO Y MANO."
I SAID, "MANO Y MANOS!" HAND TO HANDS. GET IT?
THOMP
YOU'RE HILARIOUS. AND SAND IN THE FACE BARELY WORKS ON A GUY WHO WEARS ***GLASSES,*** MORON.
LOOKS LIKE IT ***WORKED*** TO ME. BUT MAYBE I NEED ***GLASSES.***

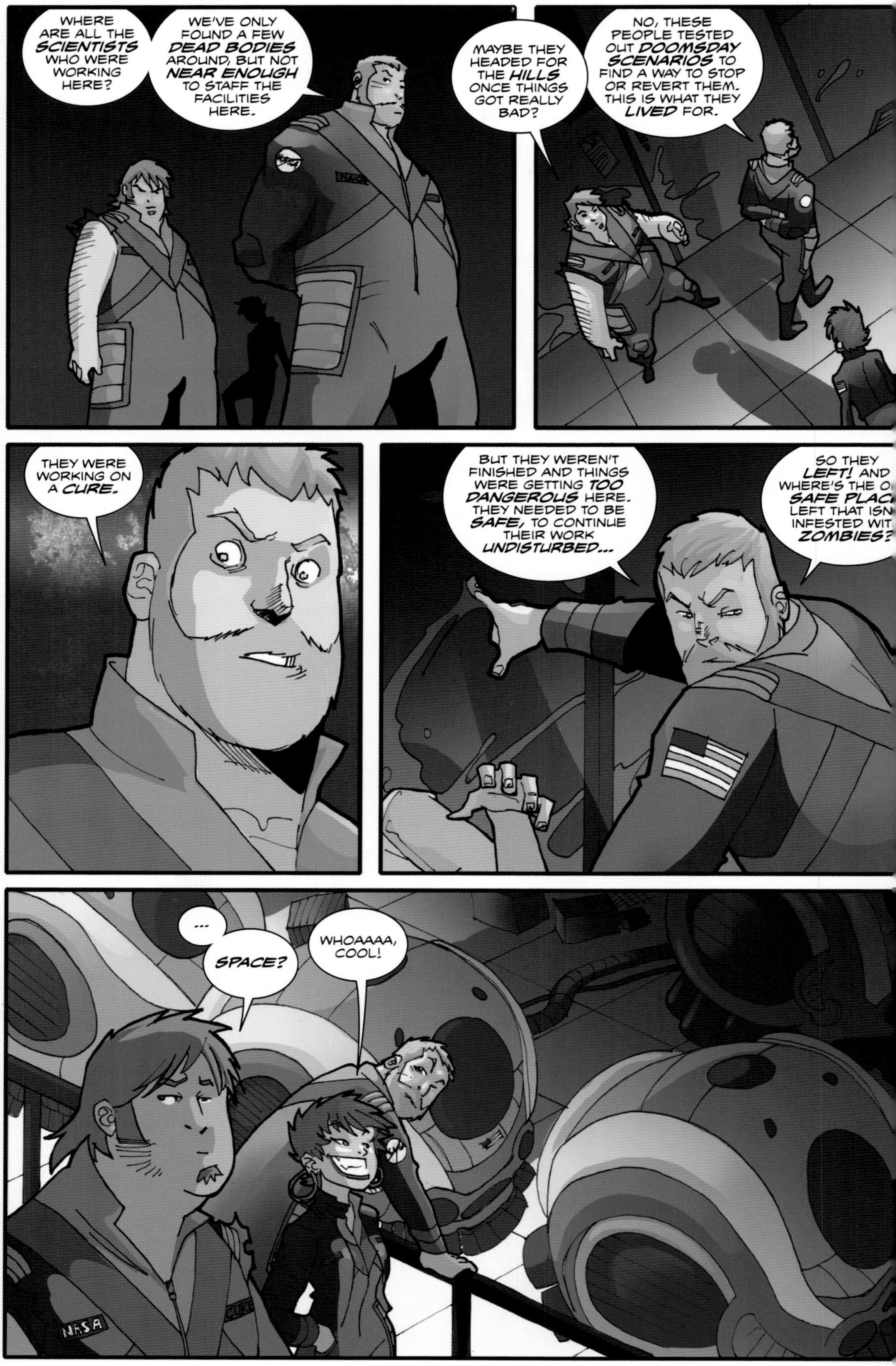
WHERE ARE ALL THE SCIENTISTS WHO WERE WORKING HERE?
WE'VE ONLY FOUND A FEW DEAD BODIES AROUND, BUT NOT NEAR ENOUGH TO STAFF THE FACILITIES HERE.
MAYBE THEY HEADED FOR THE HILLS ONCE THINGS GOT REALLY BAD?
NO, THESE PEOPLE TESTED OUT DOOMSDAY SCENARIOS TO FIND A WAY TO STOP OR REVERT THEM. THIS IS WHAT THEY LIVED FOR.
NASA
THEY WERE WORKING ON A CURE.
BUT THEY WEREN'T FINISHED AND THINGS WERE GETTING TOO DANGEROUS HERE. THEY NEEDED TO BE SAFE, TO CONTINUE THEIR WORK UNDISTURBED...
SO THEY LEFT! AND WHERE'S THE O SAFE PLAC LEFT THAT ISN INFESTED WIT ZOMBIES?
...
SPACE?
WHOAAAA, COOL!
NASA
CURE

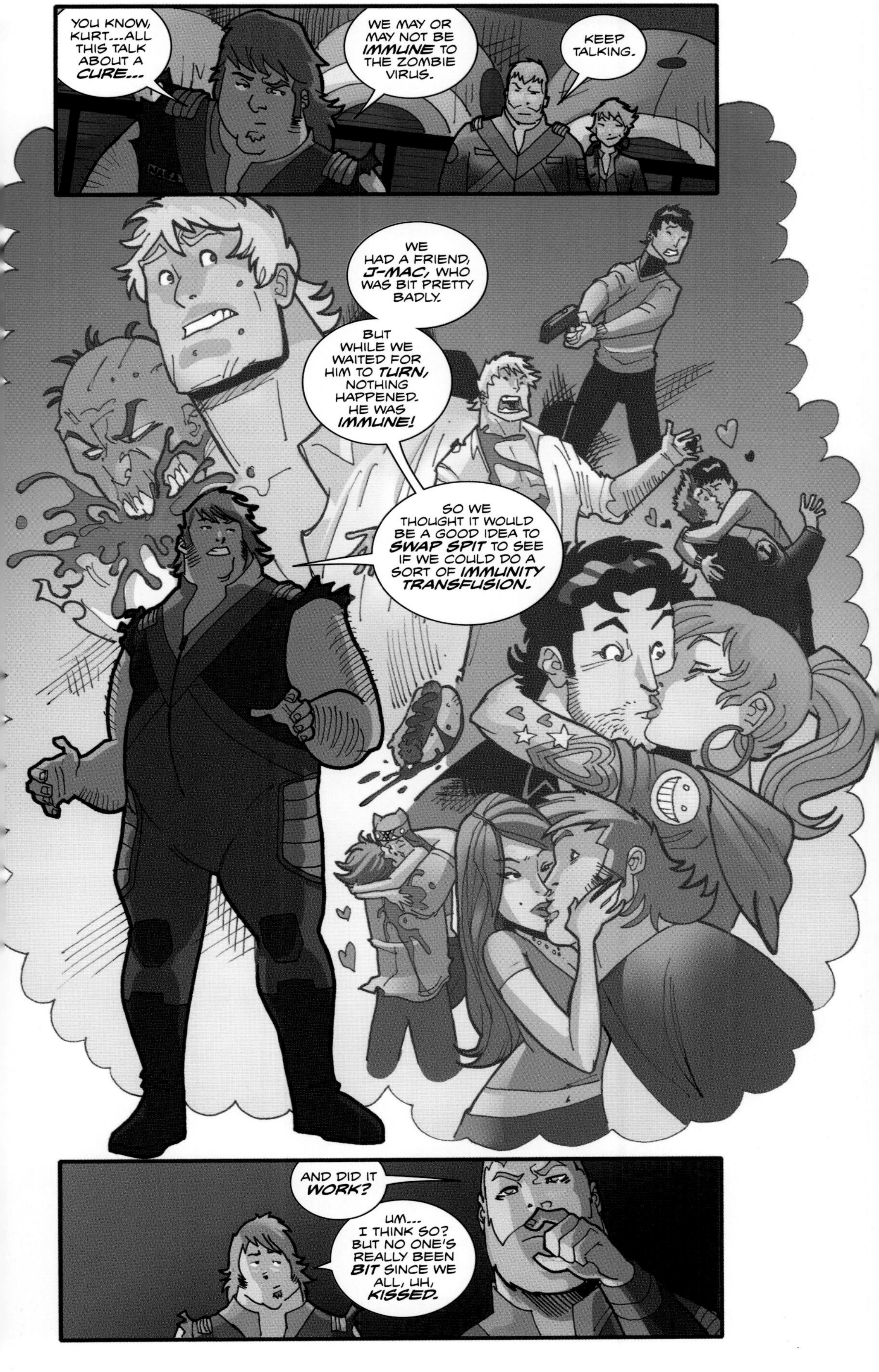
YOU KNOW, KURT...ALL THIS TALK ABOUT A *CURE*...
WE MAY OR MAY NOT BE *IMMUNE* TO THE ZOMBIE VIRUS.
KEEP TALKING.
WE HAD A FRIEND, *J-MAC,* WHO WAS BIT PRETTY BADLY.
BUT WHILE WE WAITED FOR HIM TO *TURN,* NOTHING HAPPENED. HE WAS *IMMUNE!*
SO WE THOUGHT IT WOULD BE A GOOD IDEA TO *SWAP SPIT* TO SEE IF WE COULD DO A SORT OF *IMMUNITY TRANSFUSION.*
AND DID IT *WORK?*
UM... I THINK SO? BUT NO ONE'S REALLY BEEN *BIT* SINCE WE ALL, UH, *KISSED.*

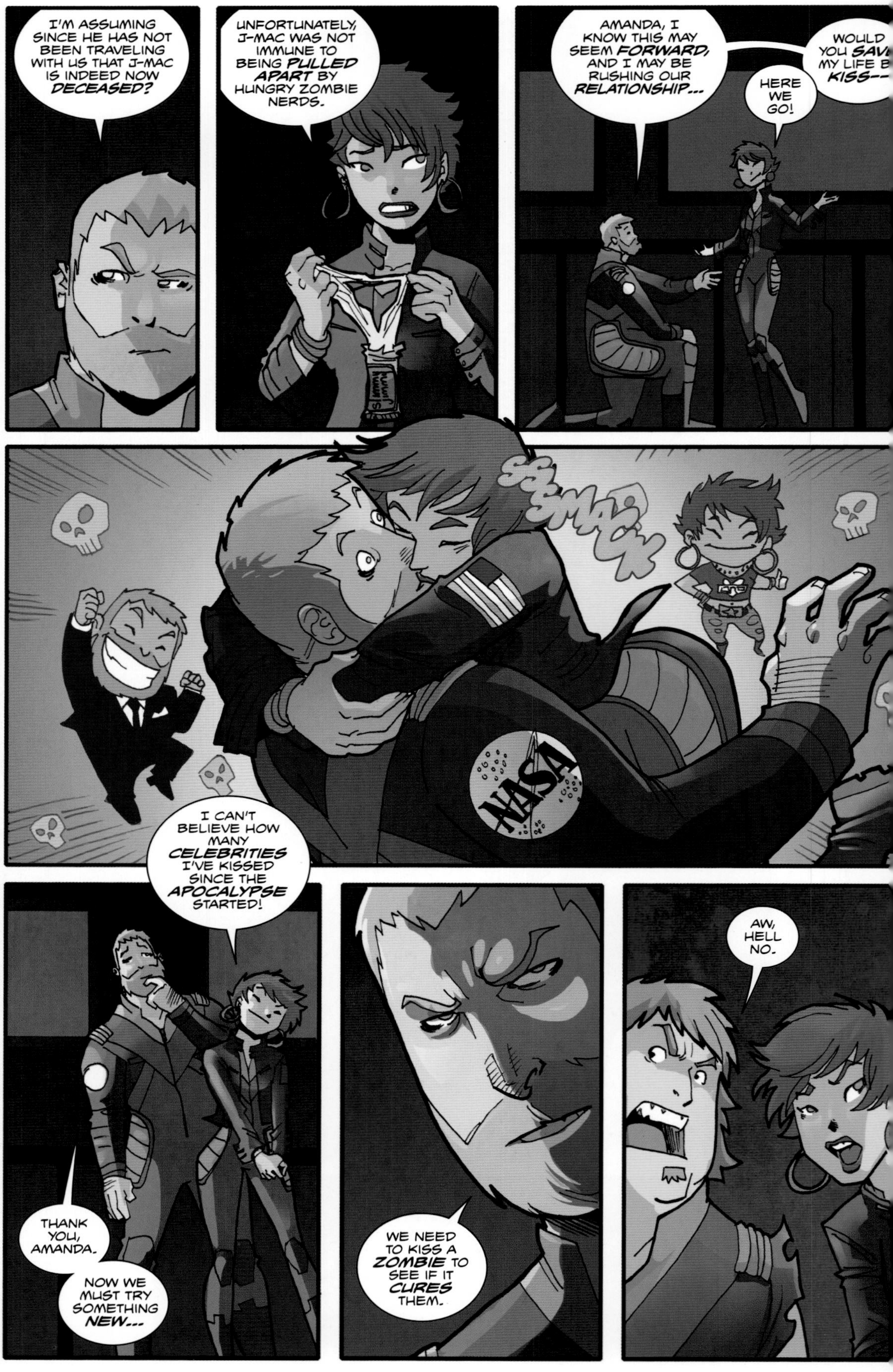
I'M ASSUMING SINCE HE HAS NOT BEEN TRAVELING WITH US THAT J-MAC IS INDEED NOW DECEASED?
UNFORTUNATELY, J-MAC WAS NOT IMMUNE TO BEING PULLED APART BY HUNGRY ZOMBIE NERDS.
AMANDA, I KNOW THIS MAY SEEM FORWARD, AND I MAY BE RUSHING OUR RELATIONSHIP...
WOULD YOU SAV MY LIFE B KISS--
HERE WE GO!
SSSMACK
NASA
I CAN'T BELIEVE HOW MANY CELEBRITIES I'VE KISSED SINCE THE APOCALYPSE STARTED!
THANK YOU, AMANDA.
NOW WE MUST TRY SOMETHING NEW...
WE NEED TO KISS A ZOMBIE TO SEE IF IT CURES THEM.
AW, HELL NO.

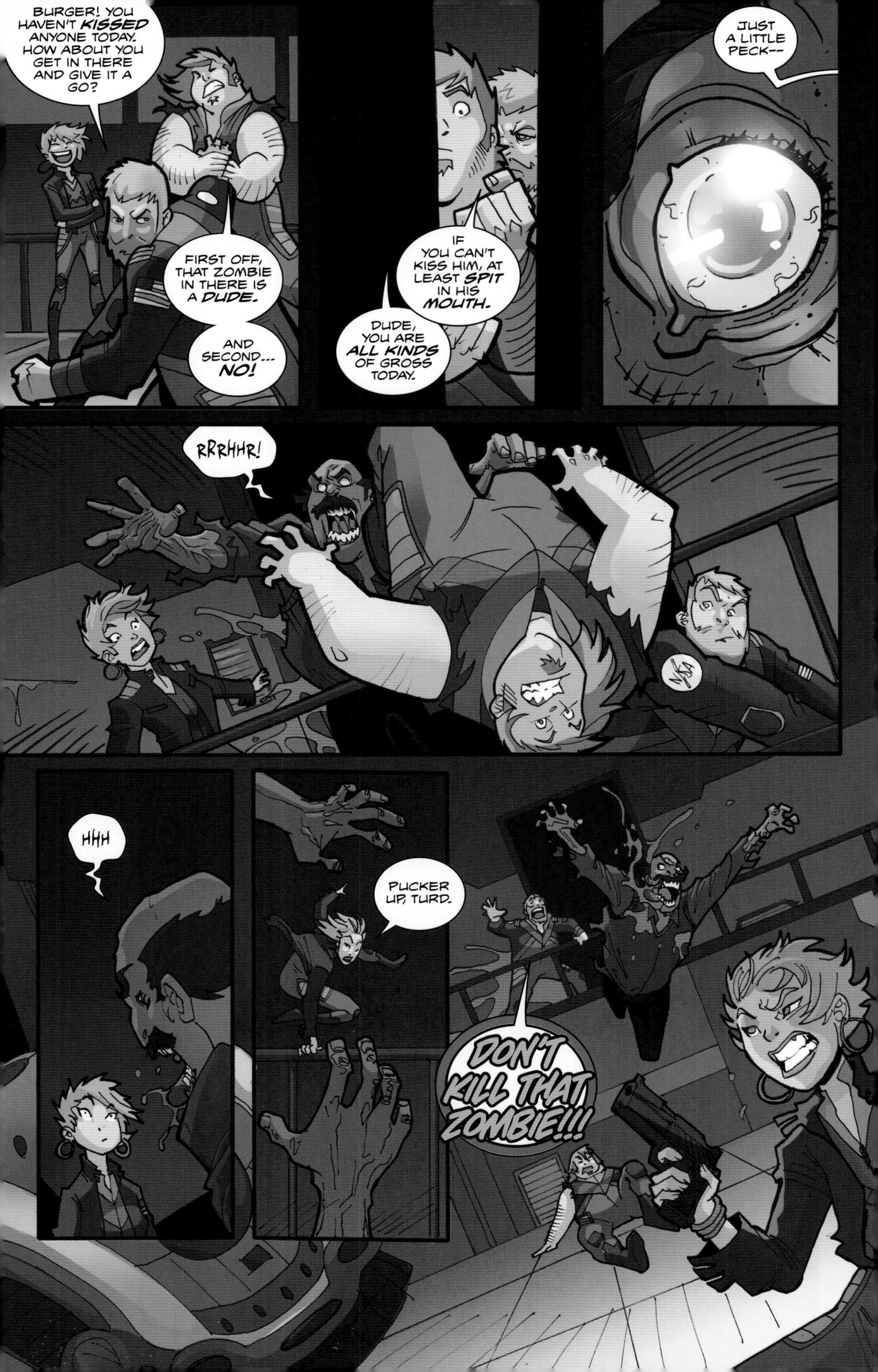

BURGER! YOU HAVEN'T KISSED ANYONE TODAY. HOW ABOUT YOU GET IN THERE AND GIVE IT A GO?
FIRST OFF, THAT ZOMBIE IN THERE IS A DUDE.
AND SECOND... NO!
IF YOU CAN'T KISS HIM, AT LEAST SPIT IN HIS MOUTH.
DUDE, YOU ARE ALL KINDS OF GROSS TODAY.
JUST A LITTLE PECK--
RRRHHR!
HHH
PUCKER UP, TURD.
DON'T KILL THAT ZOMBIE!!!

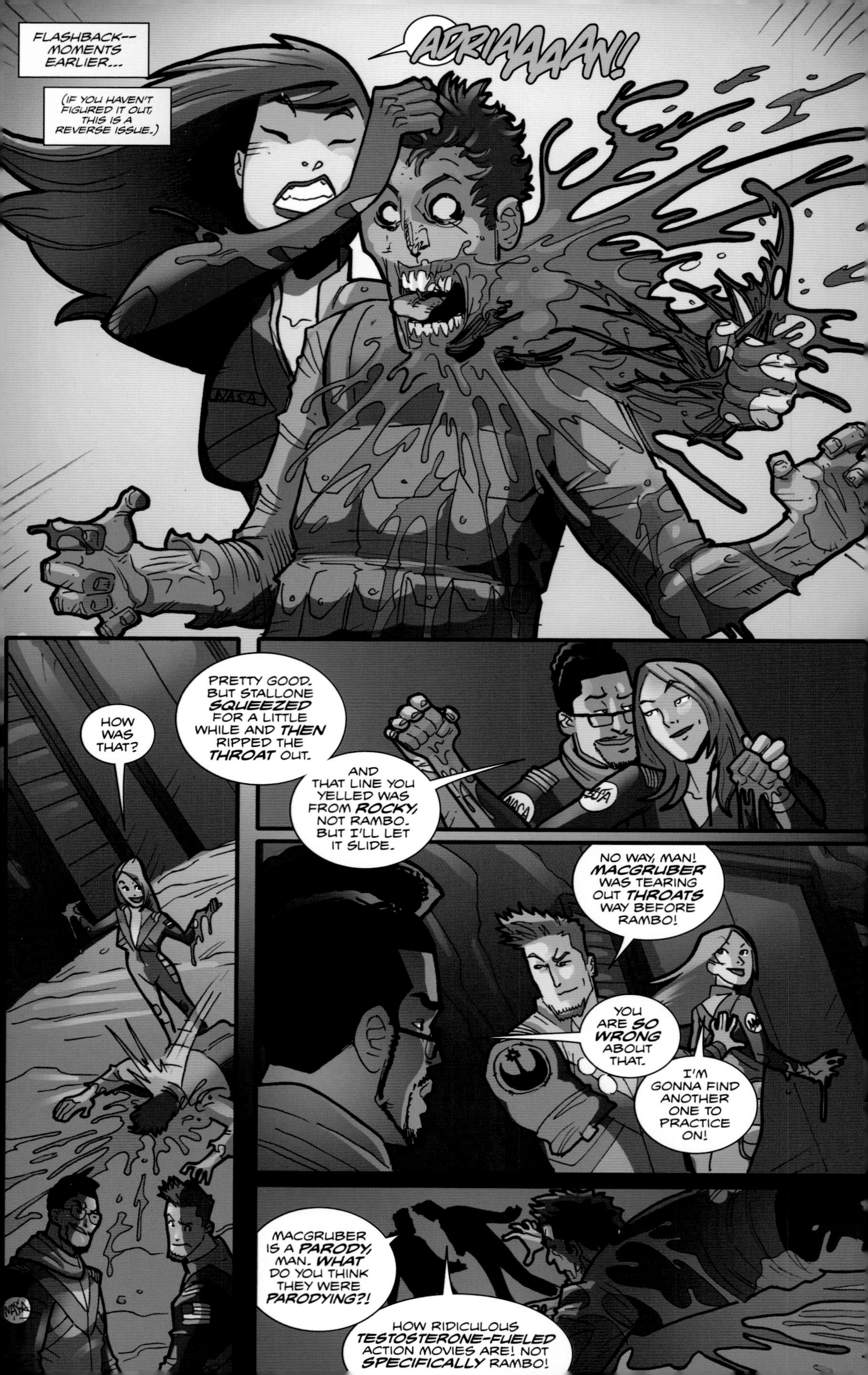
FLASHBACK-- MOMENTS EARLIER...
(IF YOU HAVEN'T FIGURED IT OUT, THIS IS A REVERSE ISSUE.)
ADRIAAAAAN!
HOW WAS THAT?
PRETTY GOOD. BUT STALLONE SQUEEZED FOR A LITTLE WHILE AND THEN RIPPED THE THROAT OUT.
AND THAT LINE YOU YELLED WAS FROM ROCKY, NOT RAMBO. BUT I'LL LET IT SLIDE.
NO WAY, MAN! MACGRUBER WAS TEARING OUT THROATS WAY BEFORE RAMBO!
YOU ARE SO WRONG ABOUT THAT.
I'M GONNA FIND ANOTHER ONE TO PRACTICE ON!
MACGRUBER IS A PARODY, MAN. WHAT DO YOU THINK THEY WERE PARODYING?!
HOW RIDICULOUS TESTOSTERONE-FUELED ACTION MOVIES ARE! NOT SPECIFICALLY RAMBO!

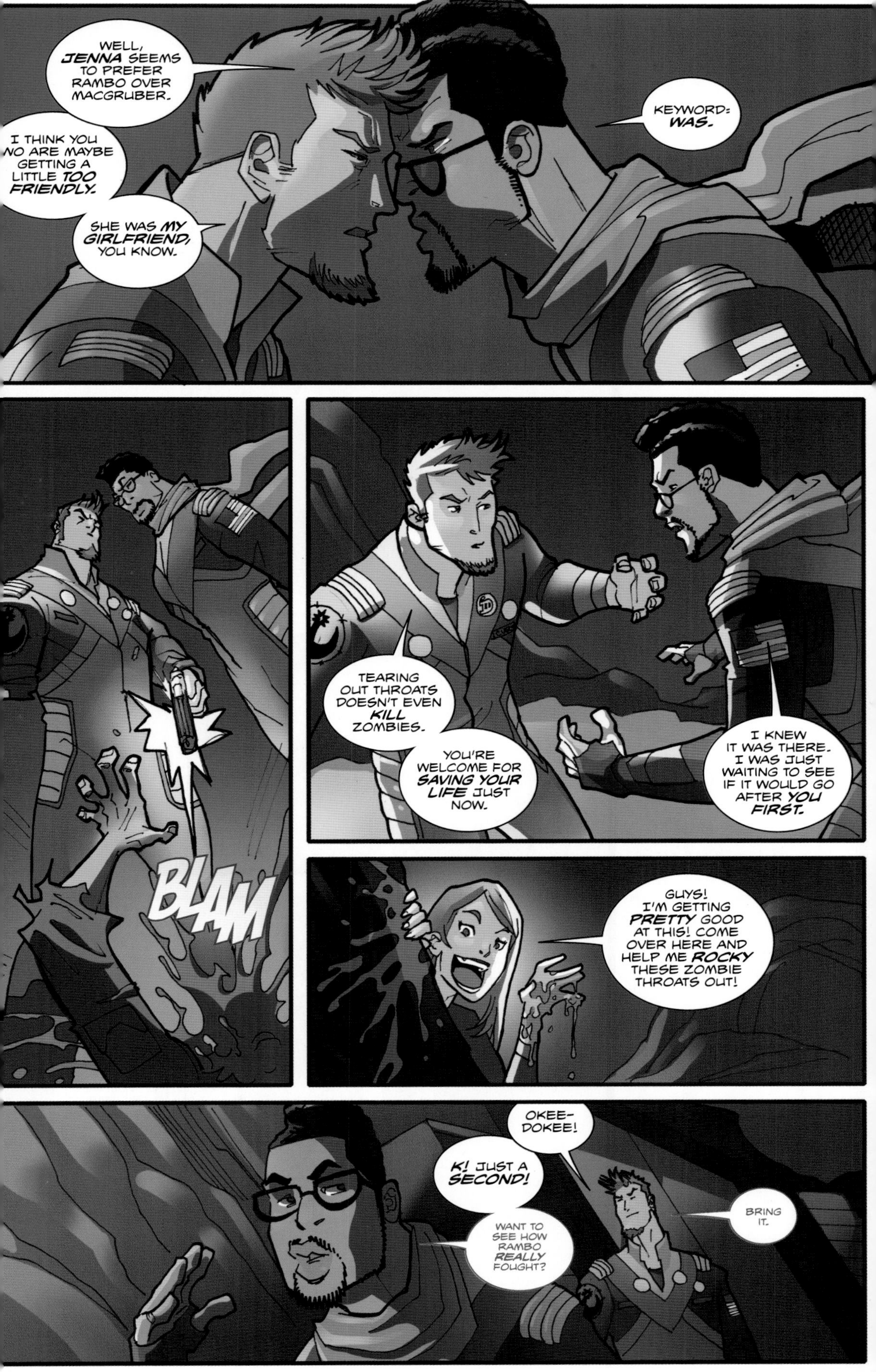
WELL, JENNA SEEMS TO PREFER RAMBO OVER MACGRUBER.
I THINK YOU NO ARE MAYBE GETTING A LITTLE TOO FRIENDLY.
SHE WAS MY GIRLFRIEND, YOU KNOW.
KEYWORD: WAS.
BLAM
TEARING OUT THROATS DOESN'T EVEN KILL ZOMBIES.
YOU'RE WELCOME FOR SAVING YOUR LIFE JUST NOW.
I KNEW IT WAS THERE. I WAS JUST WAITING TO SEE IF IT WOULD GO AFTER YOU FIRST.
GUYS! I'M GETTING PRETTY GOOD AT THIS! COME OVER HERE AND HELP ME ROCKY THESE ZOMBIE THROATS OUT!
OKEE-DOKEE!
K! JUST A SECOND!
WANT TO SEE HOW RAMBO REALLY FOUGHT?
BRING IT.

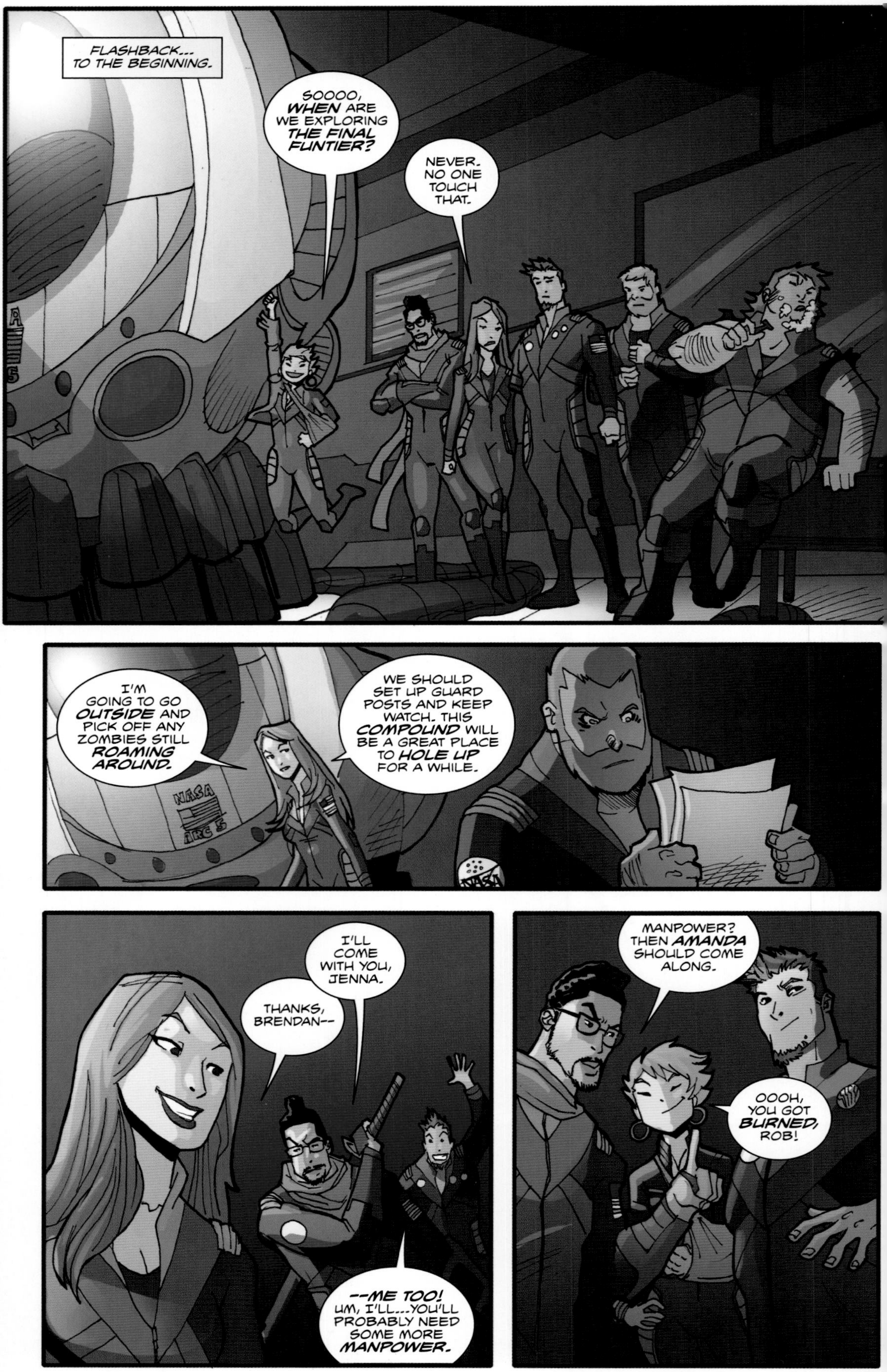
FLASHBACK... TO THE BEGINNING.
SOOOO, WHEN ARE WE EXPLORING THE FINAL FUNTIER?
NEVER. NO ONE TOUCH THAT.
I'M GOING TO GO OUTSIDE AND PICK OFF ANY ZOMBIES STILL ROAMING AROUND.
WE SHOULD SET UP GUARD POSTS AND KEEP WATCH. THIS COMPOUND WILL BE A GREAT PLACE TO HOLE UP FOR A WHILE.
NASA
ARC 5
I'LL COME WITH YOU, JENNA.
THANKS, BRENDAN--
--ME TOO! UM, I'LL...YOU'LL PROBABLY NEED SOME MORE MANPOWER.
MANPOWER? THEN AMANDA SHOULD COME ALONG.
OOOH, YOU GOT BURNED, ROB!

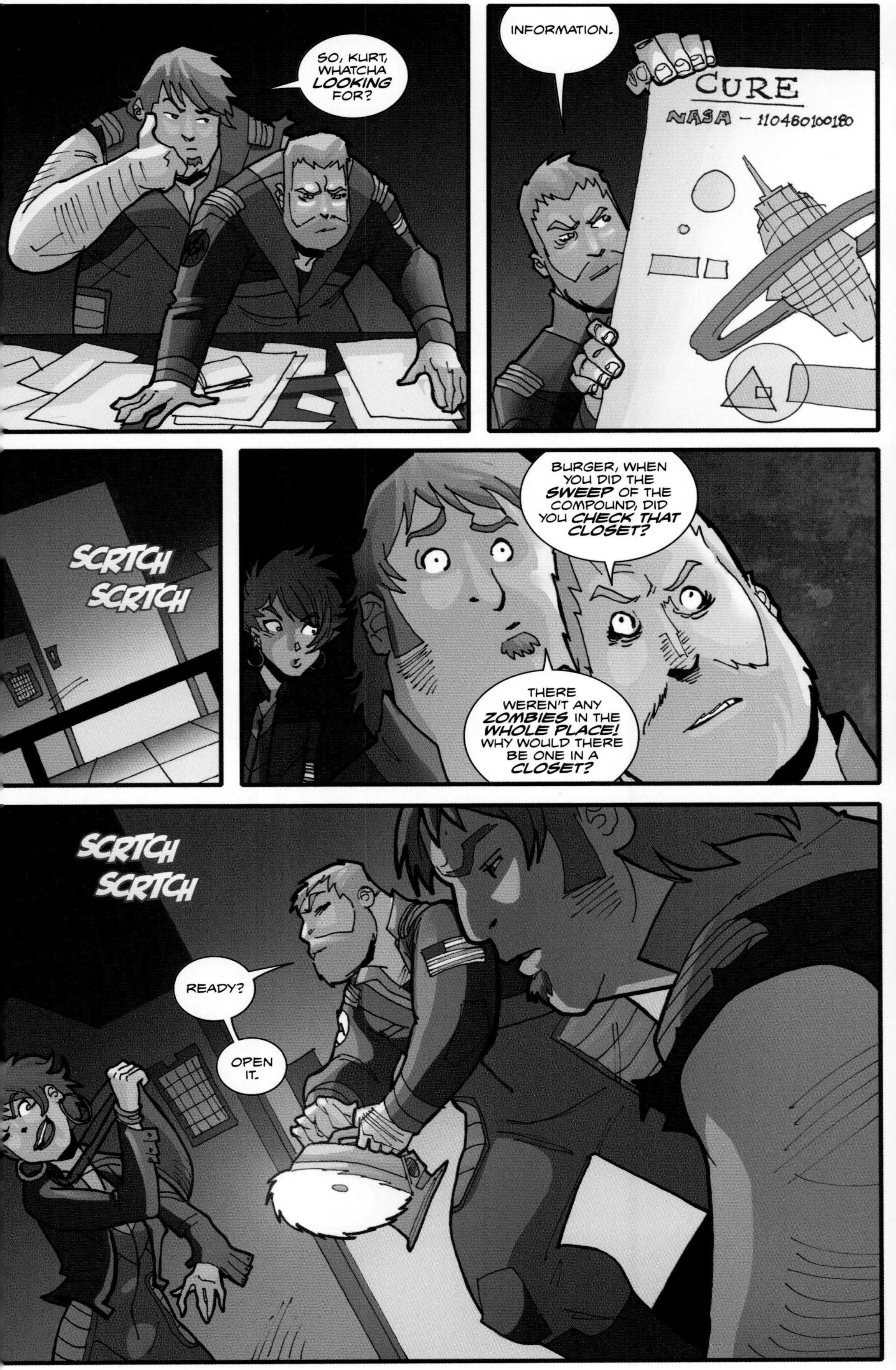
SO, KURT, WHATCHA LOOKING FOR?
INFORMATION.
CURE
NASA - 110480100180
SCRTCH SCRTCH
BURGER, WHEN YOU DID THE SWEEP OF THE COMPOUND, DID YOU CHECK THAT CLOSET?
THERE WEREN'T ANY ZOMBIES IN THE WHOLE PLACE! WHY WOULD THERE BE ONE IN A CLOSET?
SCRTCH SCRTCH
READY?
OPEN IT.

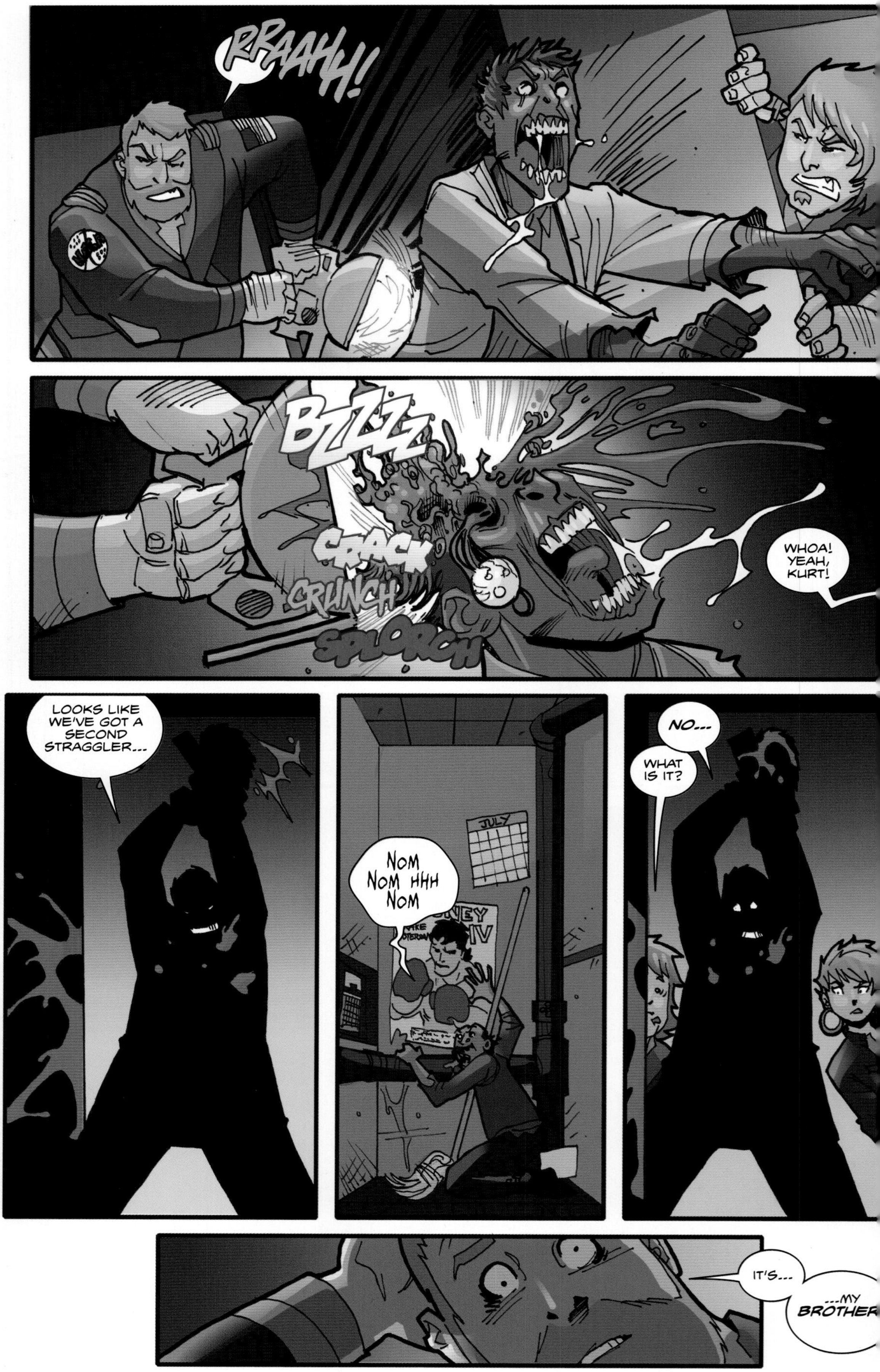
RRAAHH!
BZZZZ
CRACK
CRUNCH
SPLORCH
WHOA! YEAH, KURT!
LOOKS LIKE WE'VE GOT A SECOND STRAGGLER...
NOM NOM HHH NOM
JULY
NO...
WHAT IS IT?
IT'S...
...MY BROTHER

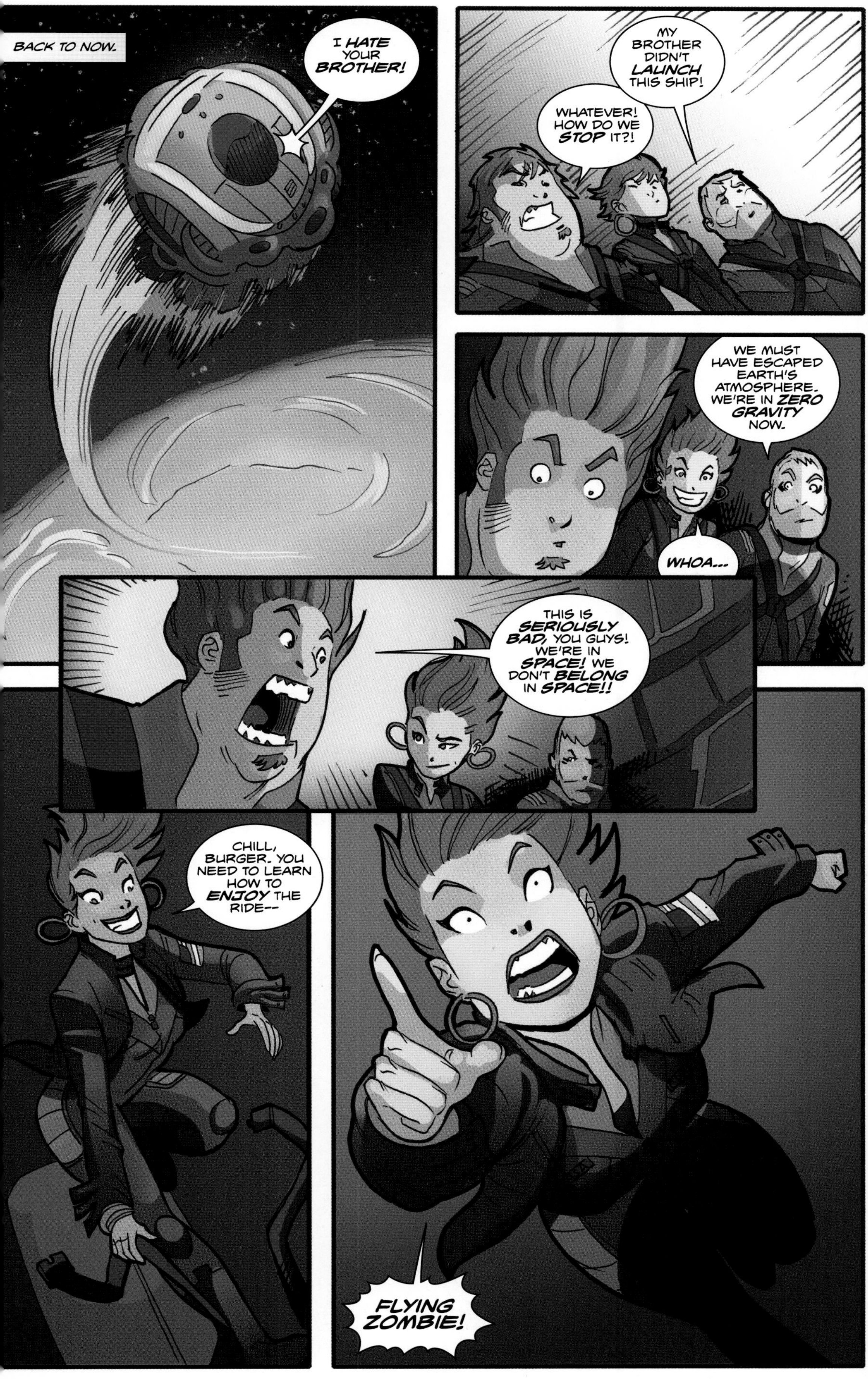
BACK TO NOW.
I HATE YOUR BROTHER!
MY BROTHER DIDN'T LAUNCH THIS SHIP!
WHATEVER! HOW DO WE STOP IT?!
WE MUST HAVE ESCAPED EARTH'S ATMOSPHERE. WE'RE IN ZERO GRAVITY NOW.
WHOA...
THIS IS SERIOUSLY BAD, YOU GUYS! WE'RE IN SPACE! WE DON'T BELONG IN SPACE!!
CHILL, BURGER. YOU NEED TO LEARN HOW TO ENJOY THE RIDE--
FLYING ZOMBIE!

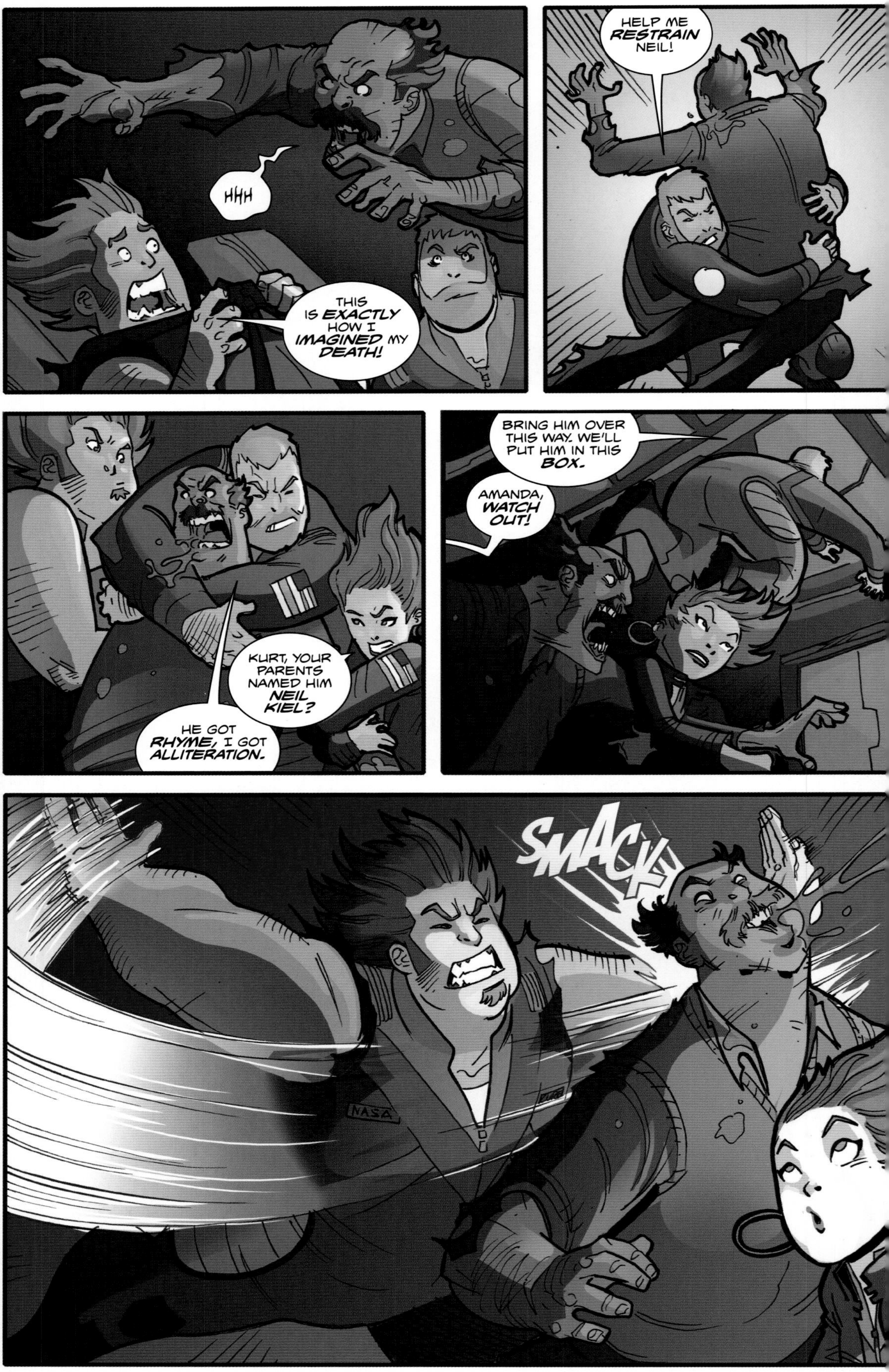
HHH
THIS IS EXACTLY HOW I IMAGINED MY DEATH!
HELP ME RESTRAIN NEIL!
KURT, YOUR PARENTS NAMED HIM NEIL KIEL?
HE GOT RHYME, I GOT ALLITERATION.
BRING HIM OVER THIS WAY. WE'LL PUT HIM IN THIS BOX.
AMANDA, WATCH OUT!
SMACK
NASA

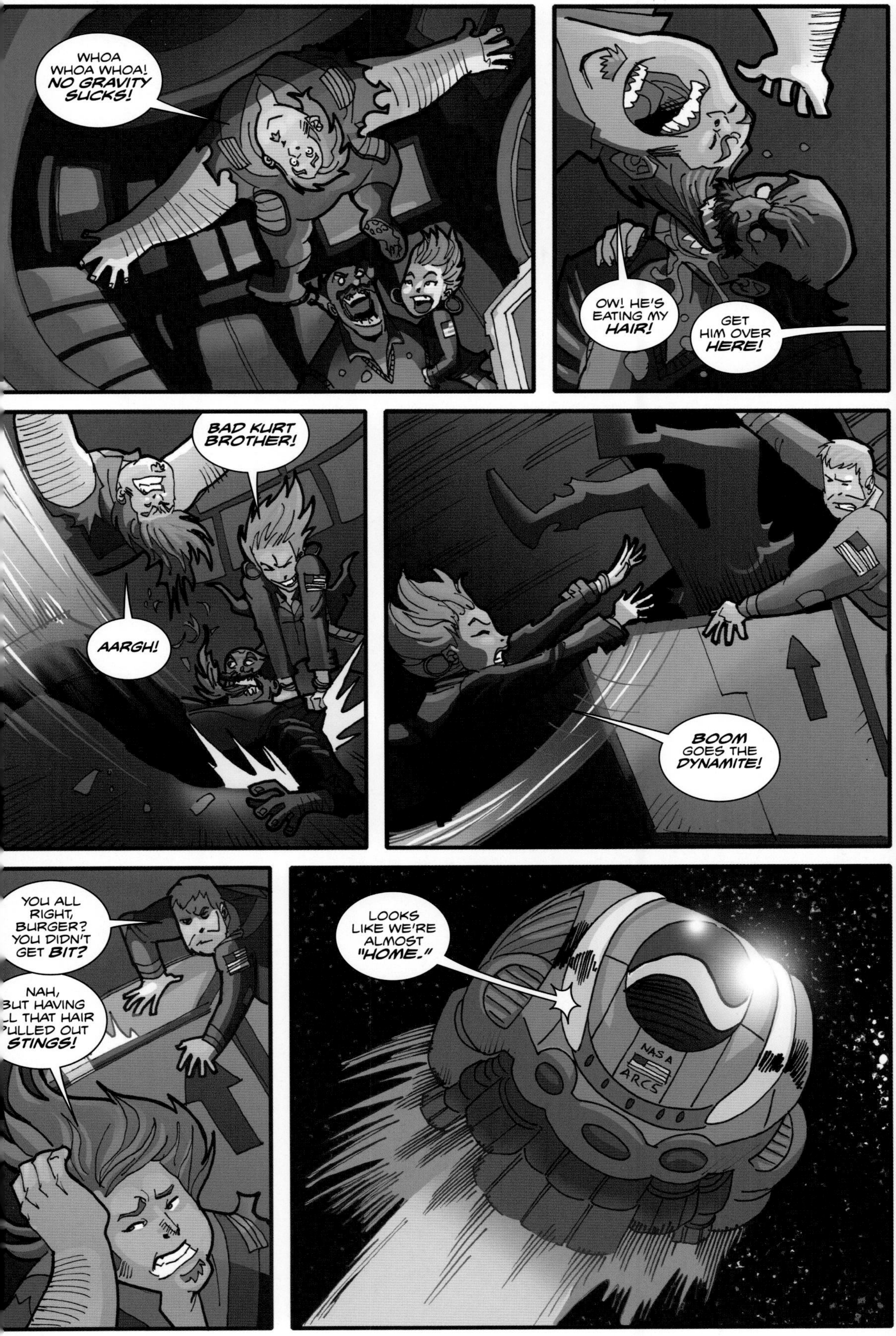
WHOA WHOA WHOA! NO GRAVITY SUCKS!
OW! HE'S EATING MY HAIR!
GET HIM OVER HERE!
BAD KURT BROTHER!
AARGH!
BOOM GOES THE DYNAMITE!
YOU ALL RIGHT, BURGER? YOU DIDN'T GET BIT?
NAH, BUT HAVING LL THAT HAIR ULLED OUT STINGS!
LOOKS LIKE WE'RE ALMOST "HOME."
NASA
ARCS

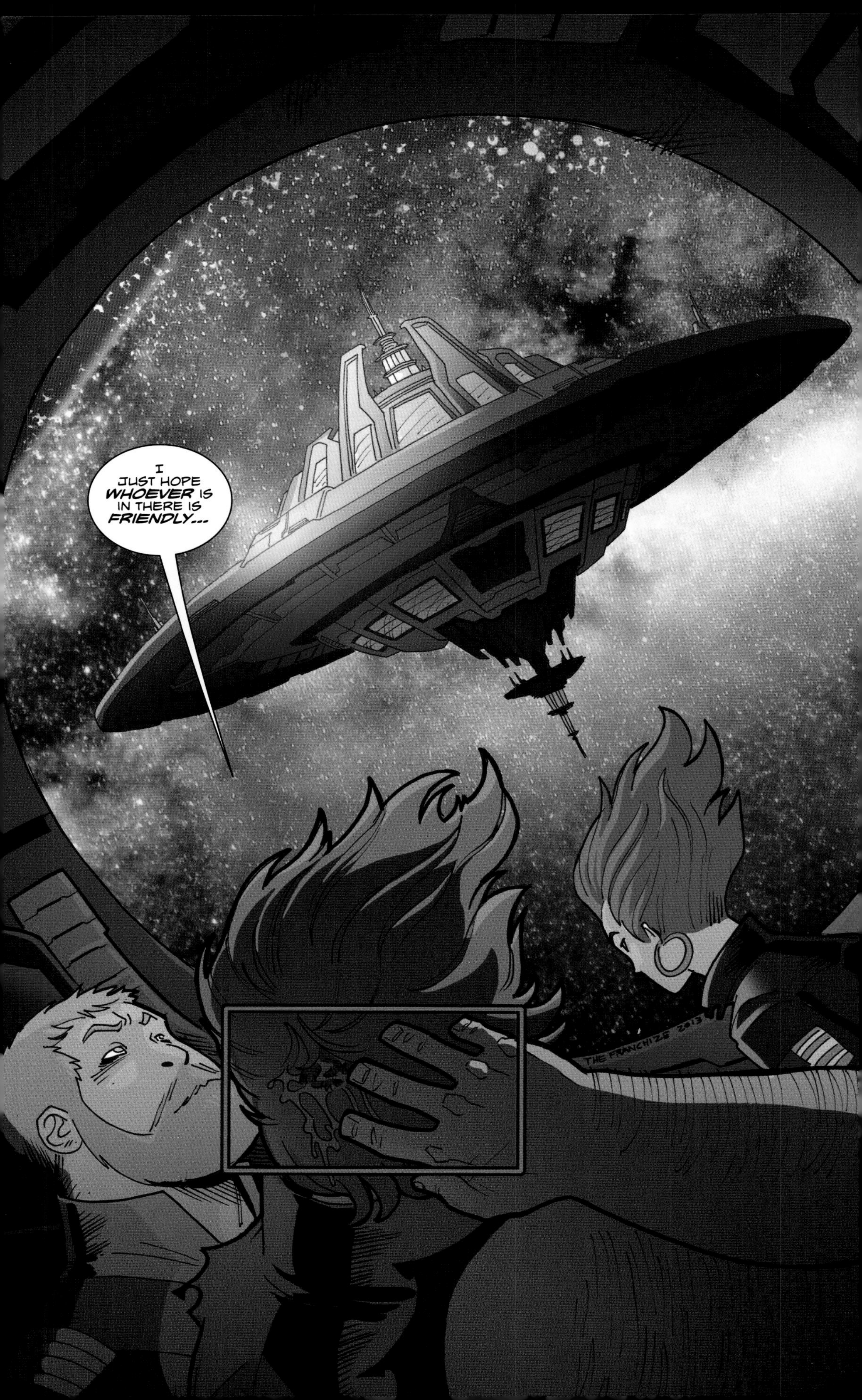
I JUST HOPE WHOEVER IS IN THERE IS FRIENDLY...
THE FRANCHIZE 2013

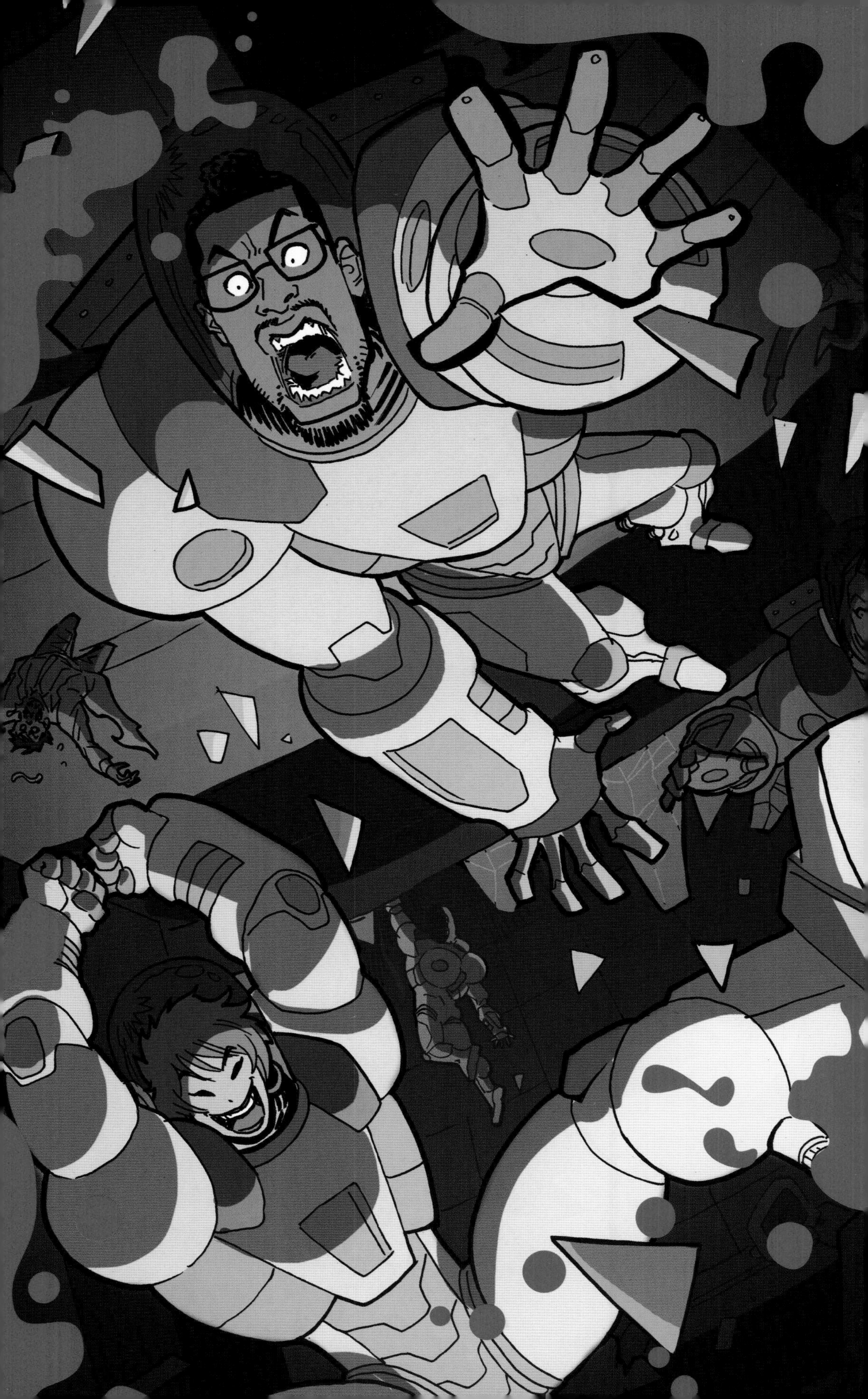

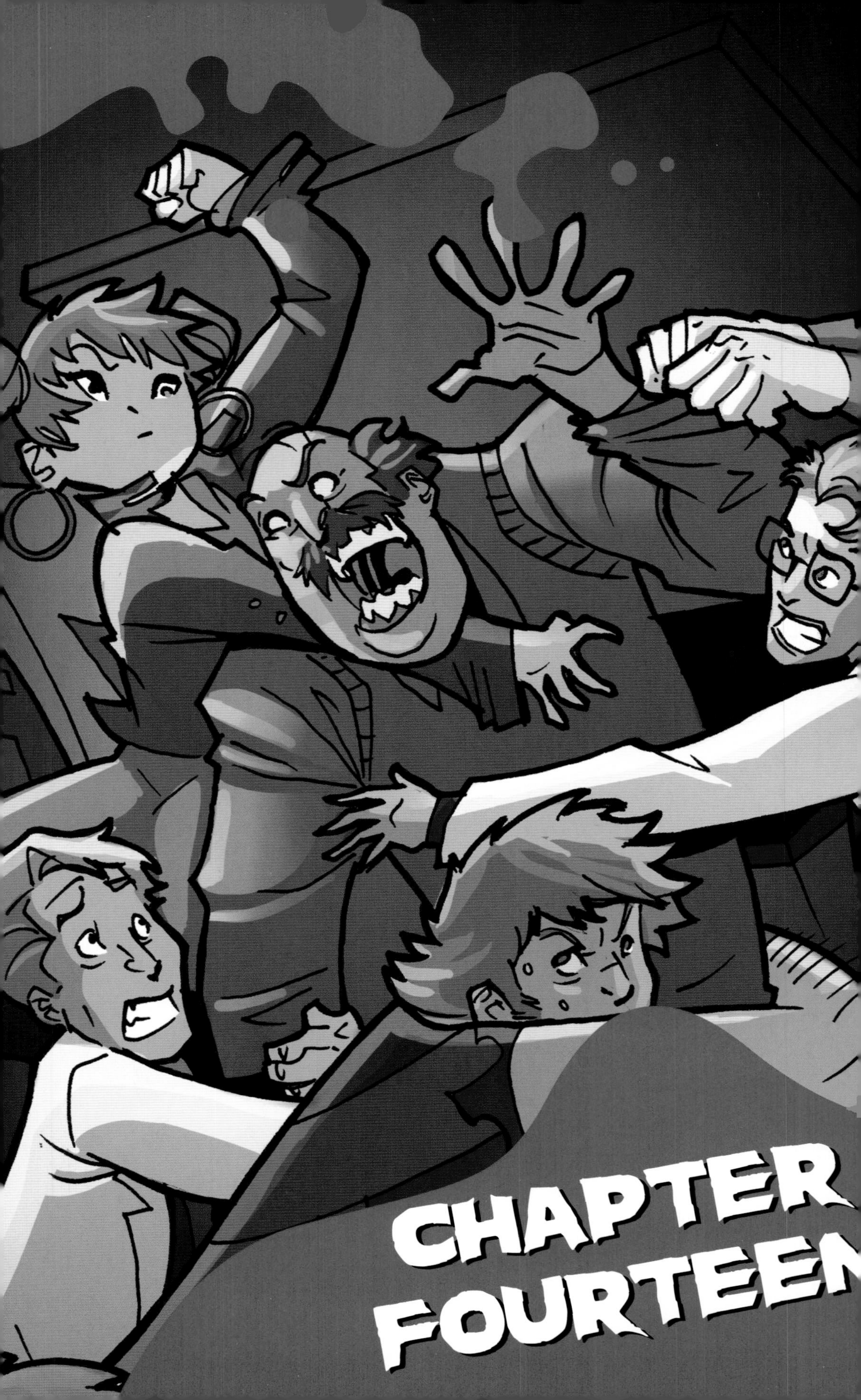

CHAPTER FOURTEEN

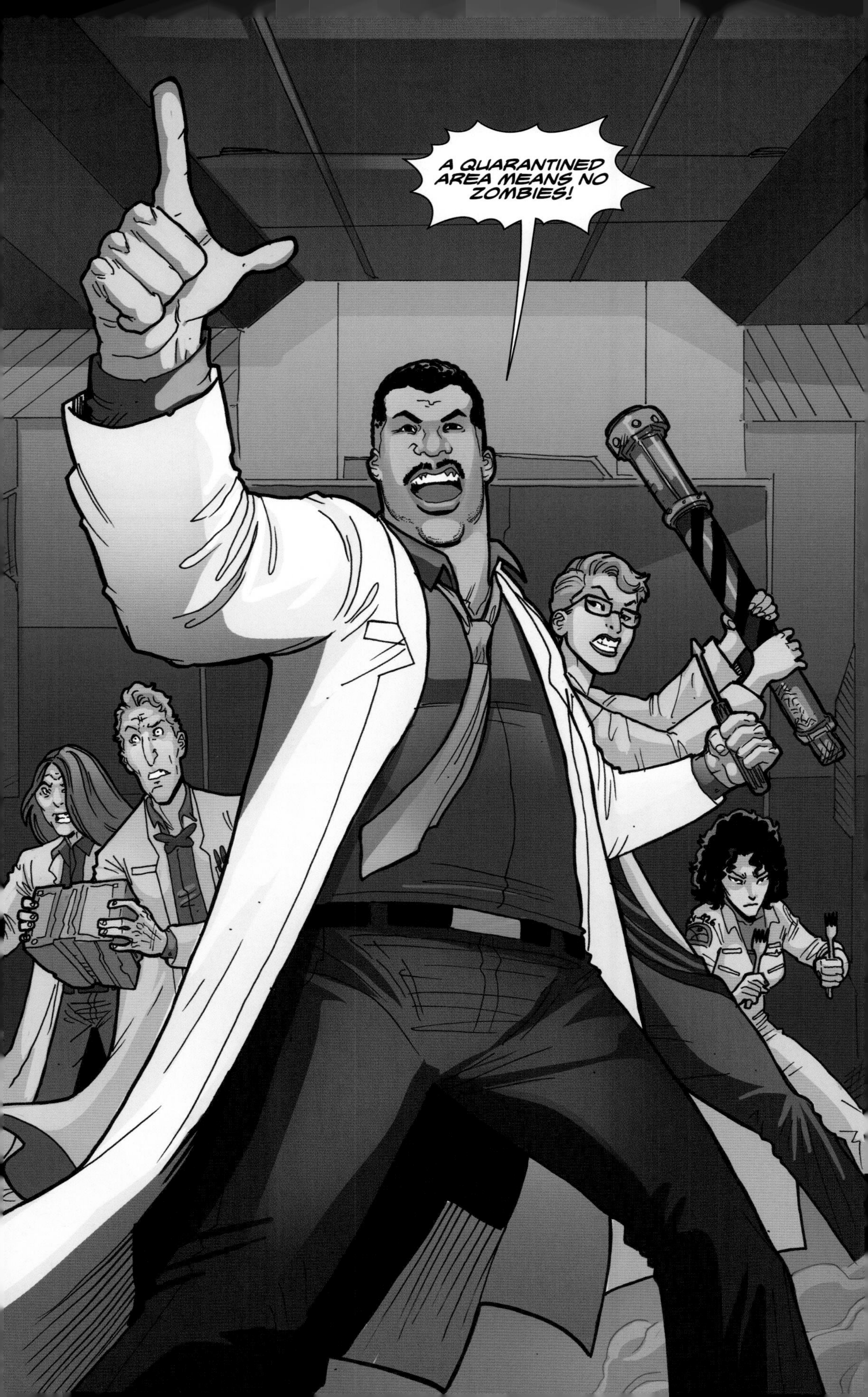
A QUARANTINED AREA MEANS NO ZOMBIES!

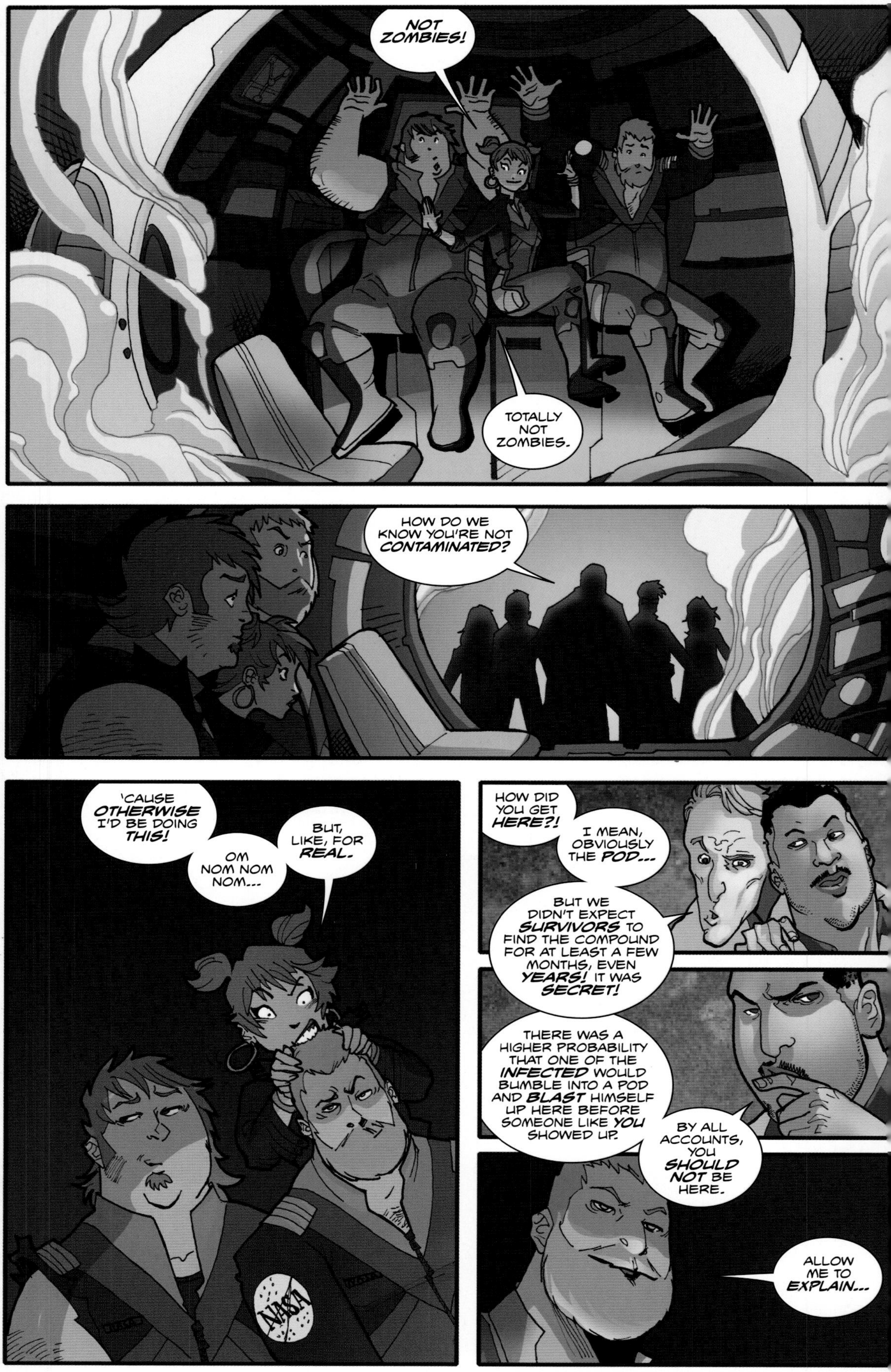
NOT ZOMBIES!
TOTALLY NOT ZOMBIES.
HOW DO WE KNOW YOU'RE NOT CONTAMINATED?
'CAUSE OTHERWISE I'D BE DOING THIS!
OM NOM NOM NOM...
BUT, LIKE, FOR REAL.
HOW DID YOU GET HERE?!
I MEAN, OBVIOUSLY THE POD...
BUT WE DIDN'T EXPECT SURVIVORS TO FIND THE COMPOUND FOR AT LEAST A FEW MONTHS, EVEN YEARS! IT WAS SECRET!
THERE WAS A HIGHER PROBABILITY THAT ONE OF THE INFECTED WOULD BUMBLE INTO A POD AND BLAST HIMSELF UP HERE BEFORE SOMEONE LIKE YOU SHOWED UP.
BY ALL ACCOUNTS, YOU SHOULD NOT BE HERE.
ALLOW ME TO EXPLAIN...
NASA

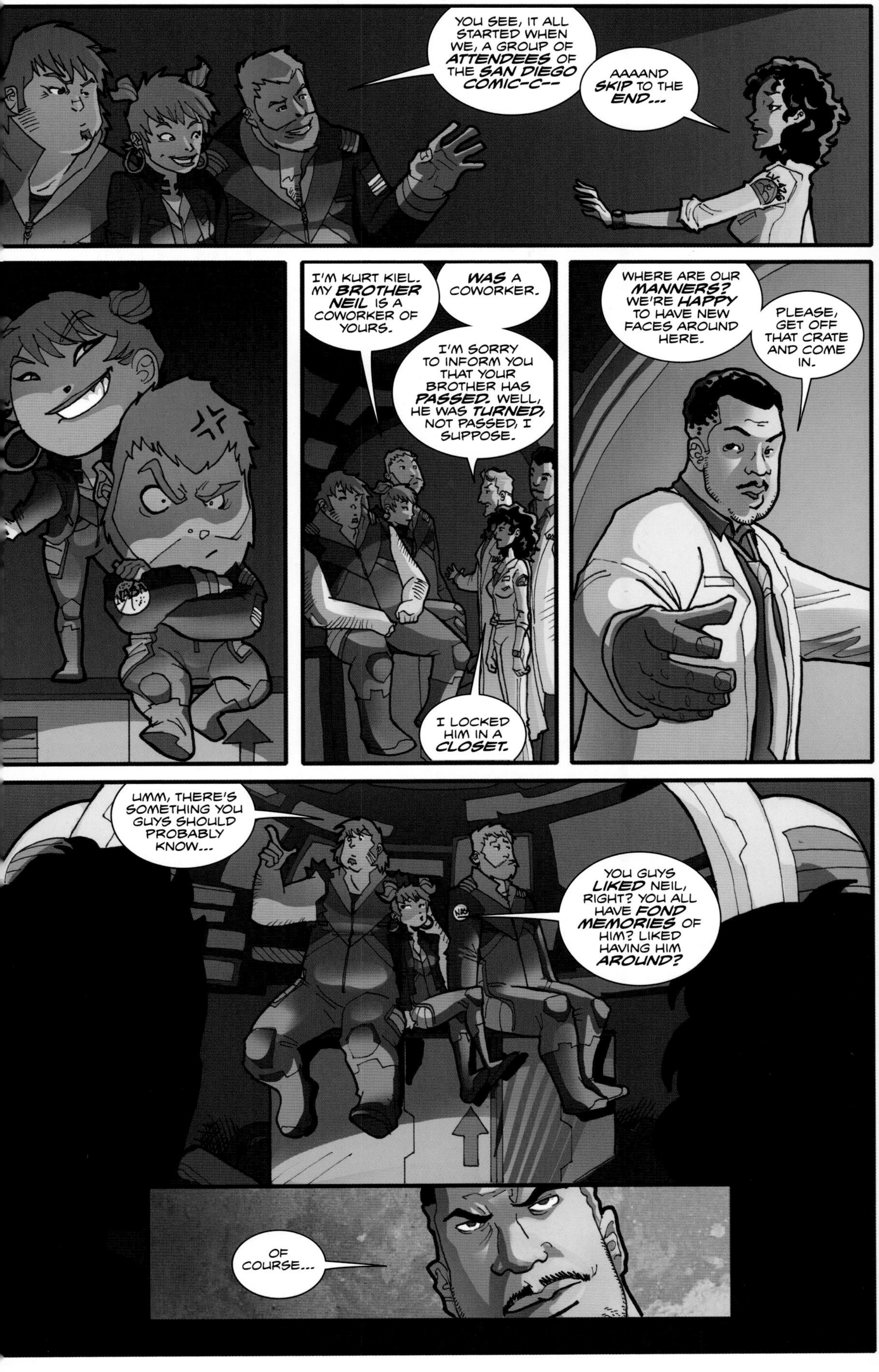

YOU SEE, IT ALL STARTED WHEN WE, A GROUP OF ATTENDEES OF THE SAN DIEGO COMIC-C--
AAAAND SKIP TO THE END...
I'M KURT KIEL. MY BROTHER NEIL IS A COWORKER OF YOURS.
WAS A COWORKER.
I'M SORRY TO INFORM YOU THAT YOUR BROTHER HAS PASSED. WELL, HE WAS TURNED, NOT PASSED, I SUPPOSE.
I LOCKED HIM IN A CLOSET.
WHERE ARE OUR MANNERS? WE'RE HAPPY TO HAVE NEW FACES AROUND HERE.
PLEASE, GET OFF THAT CRATE AND COME IN.
UMM, THERE'S SOMETHING YOU GUYS SHOULD PROBABLY KNOW...
YOU GUYS LIKED NEIL, RIGHT? YOU ALL HAVE FOND MEMORIES OF HIM? LIKED HAVING HIM AROUND?
OF COURSE...

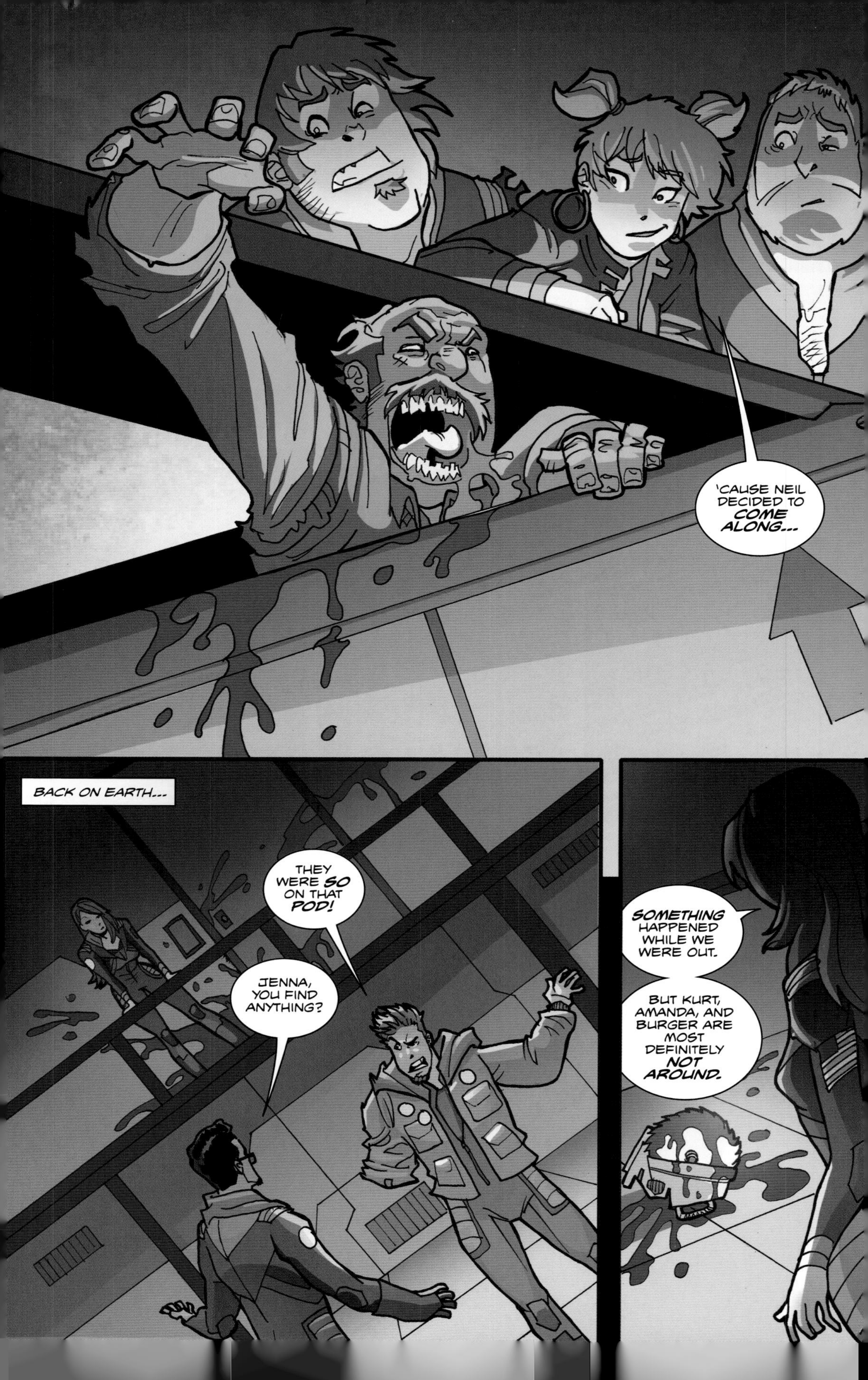
'CAUSE NEIL DECIDED TO COME ALONG...
BACK ON EARTH...
THEY WERE SO ON THAT POD!
JENNA, YOU FIND ANYTHING?
SOMETHING HAPPENED WHILE WE WERE OUT.
BUT KURT, AMANDA, AND BURGER ARE MOST DEFINITELY NOT AROUND.

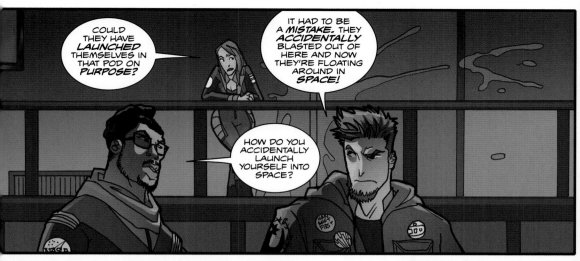

COULD THEY HAVE *LAUNCHED* THEMSELVES IN THAT POD ON *PURPOSE?*

IT HAD TO BE A *MISTAKE.* THEY *ACCIDENTALLY* BLASTED OUT OF HERE AND NOW THEY'RE FLOATING AROUND IN *SPACE!*

HOW DO YOU ACCIDENTALLY LAUNCH YOURSELF INTO SPACE?

I BET WE COULD DO IT.

WE LAUNCH *OURSELVES* INTO SPACE AND FIND OUT *WHERE* THEY WENT.

ROB, DO YOU REALIZE HOW *CRAZY* YOU SOUND RIGHT NOW?

YES. YES, I DO.

JENNA, YOU'RE NOT INSANE. WHAT DO WE DO?

IT'S A PRETTY BALLSY MOVE TO BLAST OURSELVES, COMPLETELY *UNTRAINED* AND *INEXPERIENCED,* INTO FREAKING SPACE...

SOOOO...

WE FLIP A *COIN?*

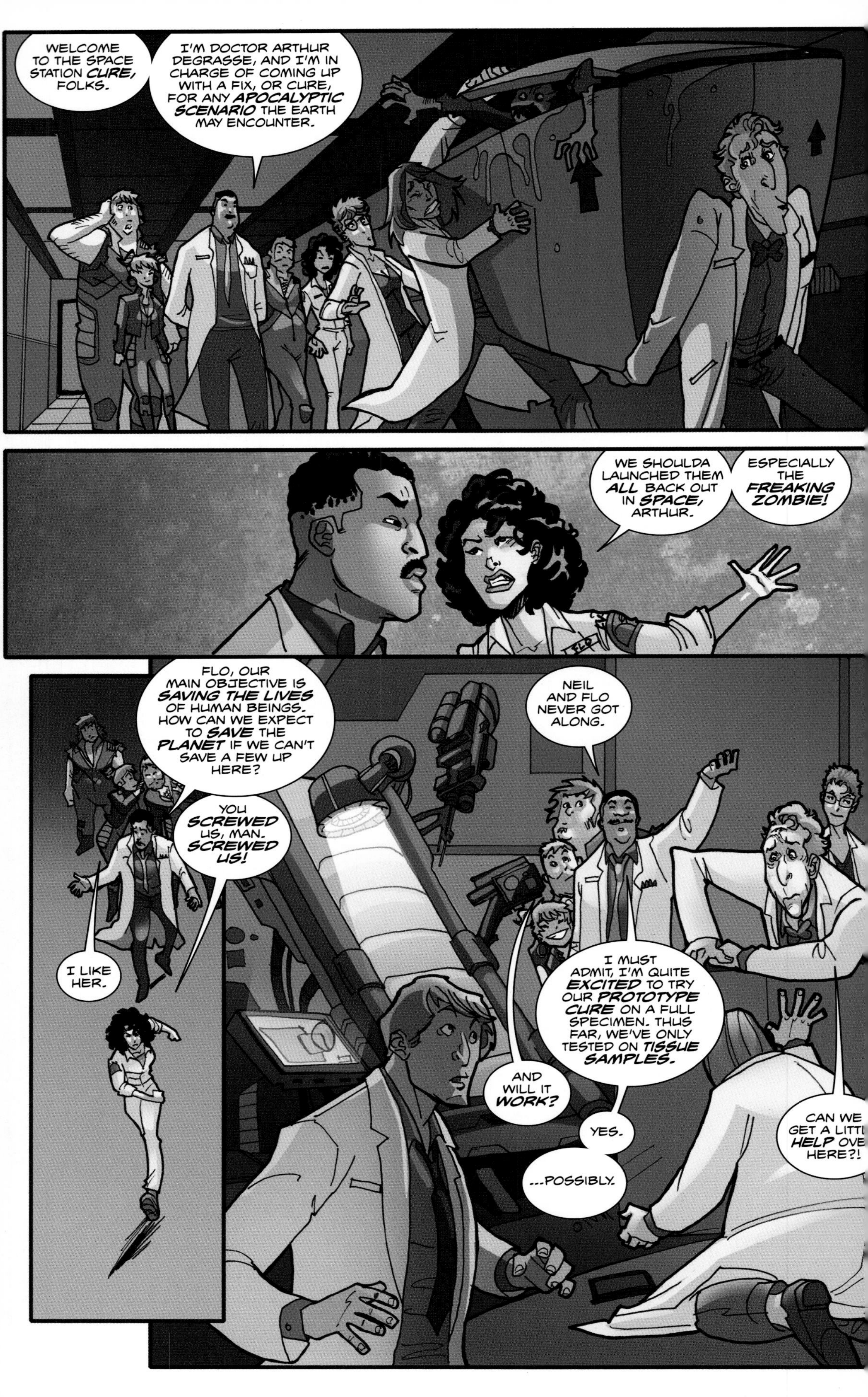
WELCOME TO THE SPACE STATION CURE, FOLKS.
I'M DOCTOR ARTHUR DEGRASSE, AND I'M IN CHARGE OF COMING UP WITH A FIX, OR CURE, FOR ANY APOCALYPTIC SCENARIO THE EARTH MAY ENCOUNTER.
WE SHOULDA LAUNCHED THEM ALL BACK OUT IN SPACE, ARTHUR.
ESPECIALLY THE FREAKING ZOMBIE!
FLO
FLO, OUR MAIN OBJECTIVE IS SAVING THE LIVES OF HUMAN BEINGS. HOW CAN WE EXPECT TO SAVE THE PLANET IF WE CAN'T SAVE A FEW UP HERE?
YOU SCREWED US, MAN. SCREWED US!
I LIKE HER.
NEIL AND FLO NEVER GOT ALONG.
I MUST ADMIT, I'M QUITE EXCITED TO TRY OUR PROTOTYPE CURE ON A FULL SPECIMEN. THUS FAR, WE'VE ONLY TESTED ON TISSUE SAMPLES.
AND WILL IT WORK?
YES.
---POSSIBLY.
CAN WE GET A LITTL HELP OVE HERE?!

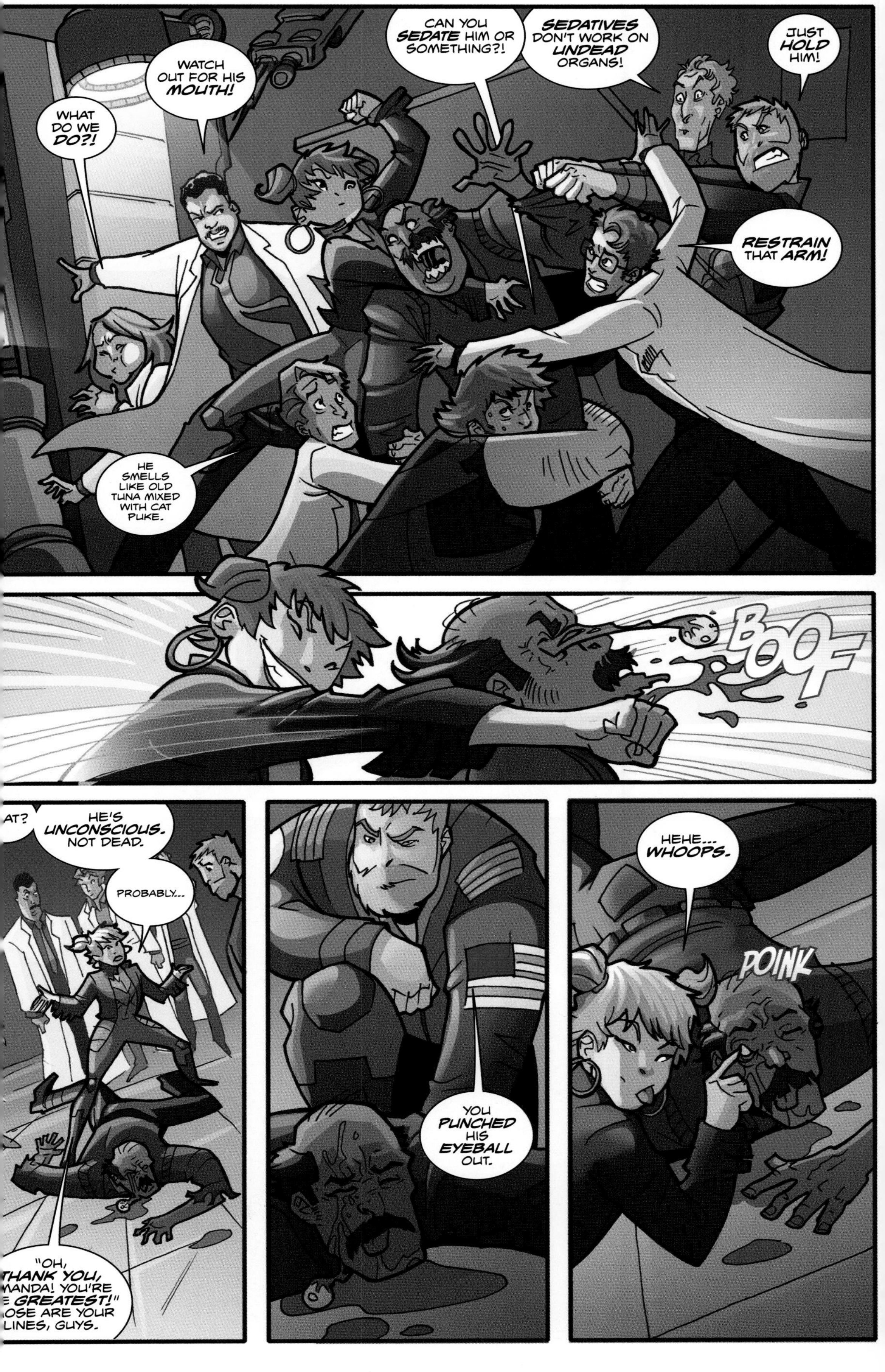

WHAT DO WE DO?!
WATCH OUT FOR HIS MOUTH!
CAN YOU SEDATE HIM OR SOMETHING?!
SEDATIVES DON'T WORK ON UNDEAD ORGANS!
JUST HOLD HIM!
RESTRAIN THAT ARM!
HE SMELLS LIKE OLD TUNA MIXED WITH CAT PUKE.
BOOF
AT?
HE'S UNCONSCIOUS. NOT DEAD.
PROBABLY...
"OH, THANK YOU, MANDA! YOU'RE E GREATEST!" OSE ARE YOUR LINES, GUYS.
YOU PUNCHED HIS EYEBALL OUT.
HEHE... WHOOPS.
POINK

UM, IS THERE A PLACE I COULD LIE DOWN? BEING IN SPACE FOR THE FIRST TIME IS *NOT SITTING WELL* WITH ME.

ARTIFICIAL GRAVITY WILL DO THAT TO YOU. AT THE END OF THE HALL, THERE IS A ROOM WITH *BEDS.*

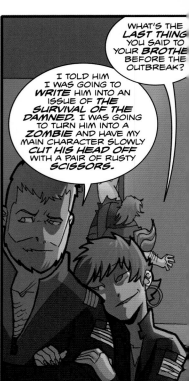

WHAT'S THE *LAST THING* YOU SAID TO YOUR *BROTHE* BEFORE THE OUTBREAK?

I TOLD HIM I WAS GOING TO *WRITE* HIM INTO AN ISSUE OF *THE SURVIVAL OF THE DAMNED.* I WAS GOING TO TURN HIM INTO A *ZOMBIE* AND HAVE MY MAIN CHARACTER SLOWLY *CUT HIS HEAD OFF* WITH A PAIR OF RUSTY *SCISSORS.*

BACK WHEN THAT WAS JUST *FICTION,* HE THOUGHT IT WAS SUCH AN *HONOR.*

WELL, IF THIS CURE *WORKS...*

...ZOMBIES MIGHT BECOME *FICTION* ONCE AGAIN.

...UHHH...

BALLS, MAN.

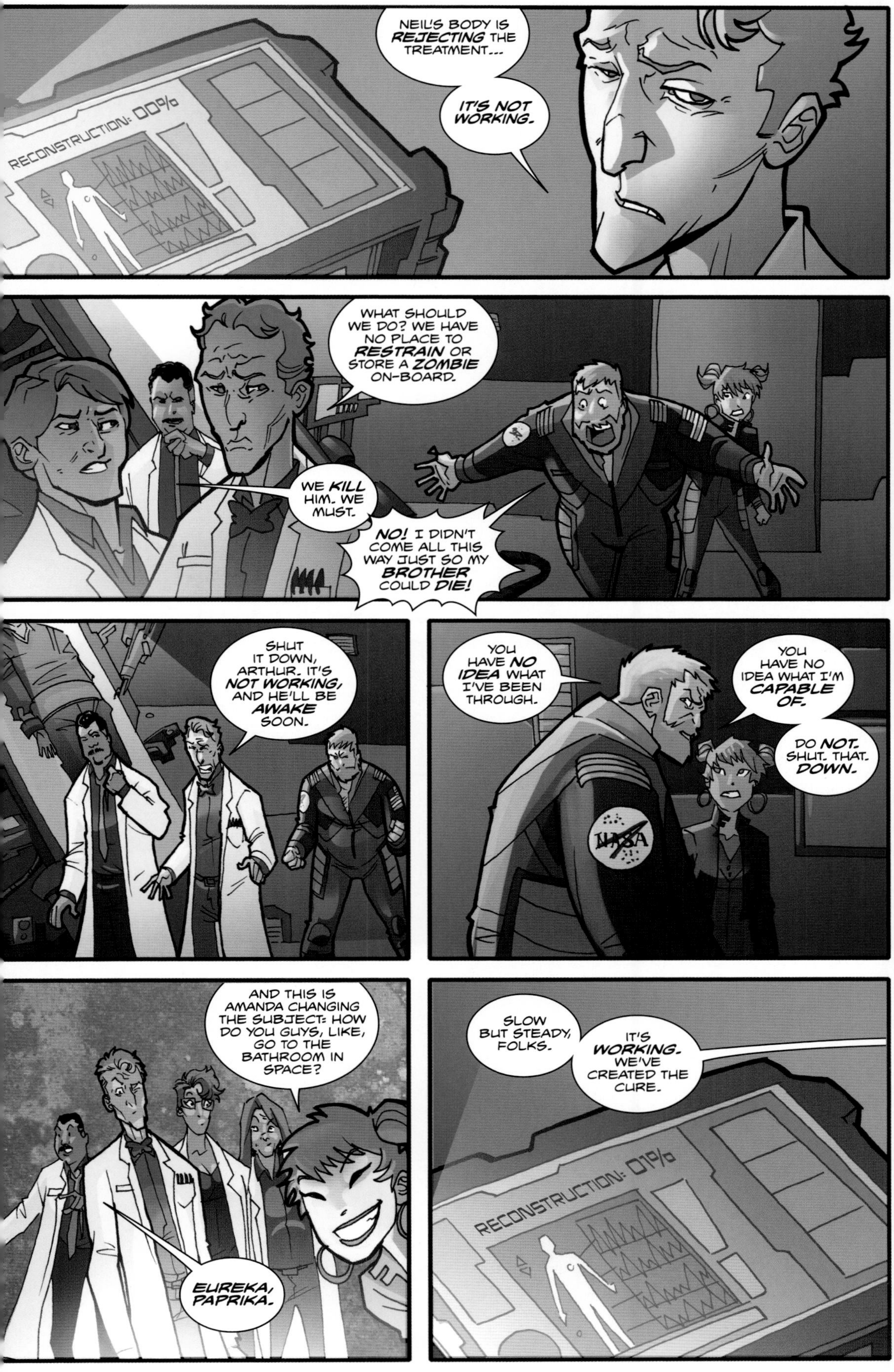
RECONSTRUCTION: 00%
NEIL'S BODY IS REJECTING THE TREATMENT...
IT'S NOT WORKING.
WHAT SHOULD WE DO? WE HAVE NO PLACE TO RESTRAIN OR STORE A ZOMBIE ON-BOARD.
WE KILL HIM. WE MUST.
NO! I DIDN'T COME ALL THIS WAY JUST SO MY BROTHER COULD DIE!
SHUT IT DOWN, ARTHUR. IT'S NOT WORKING, AND HE'LL BE AWAKE SOON.
YOU HAVE NO IDEA WHAT I'VE BEEN THROUGH.
YOU HAVE NO IDEA WHAT I'M CAPABLE OF.
DO NOT. SHUT. THAT. DOWN.
NASA
AND THIS IS AMANDA CHANGING THE SUBJECT: HOW DO YOU GUYS, LIKE, GO TO THE BATHROOM IN SPACE?
EUREKA, PAPRIKA.
SLOW BUT STEADY, FOLKS.
IT'S WORKING. WE'VE CREATED THE CURE.
RECONSTRUCTION: 01%

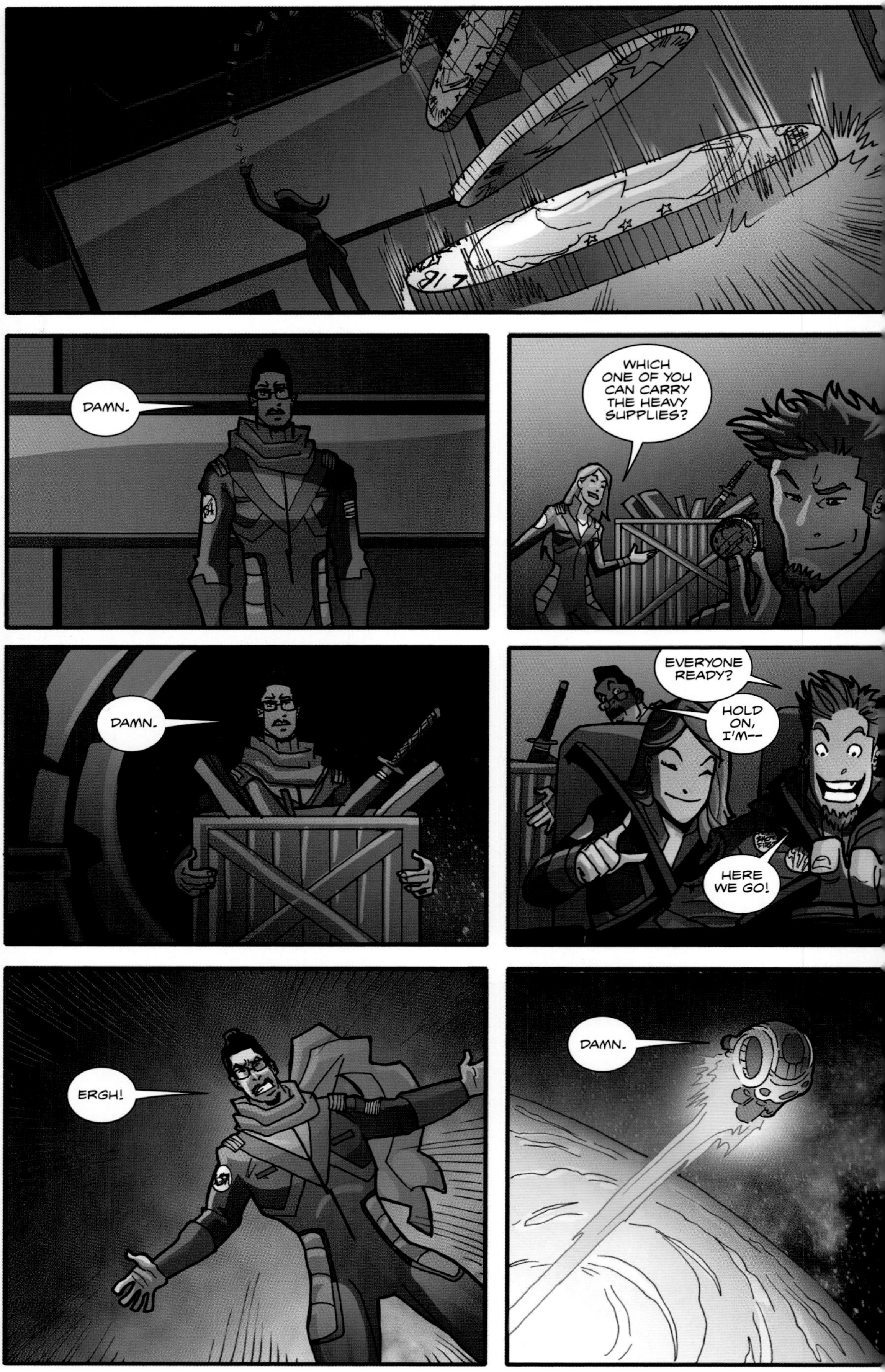
DAMN.
WHICH ONE OF YOU CAN CARRY THE HEAVY SUPPLIES?
DAMN.
EVERYONE READY?
HOLD ON, I'M--
HERE WE GO!
ERGH!
DAMN.

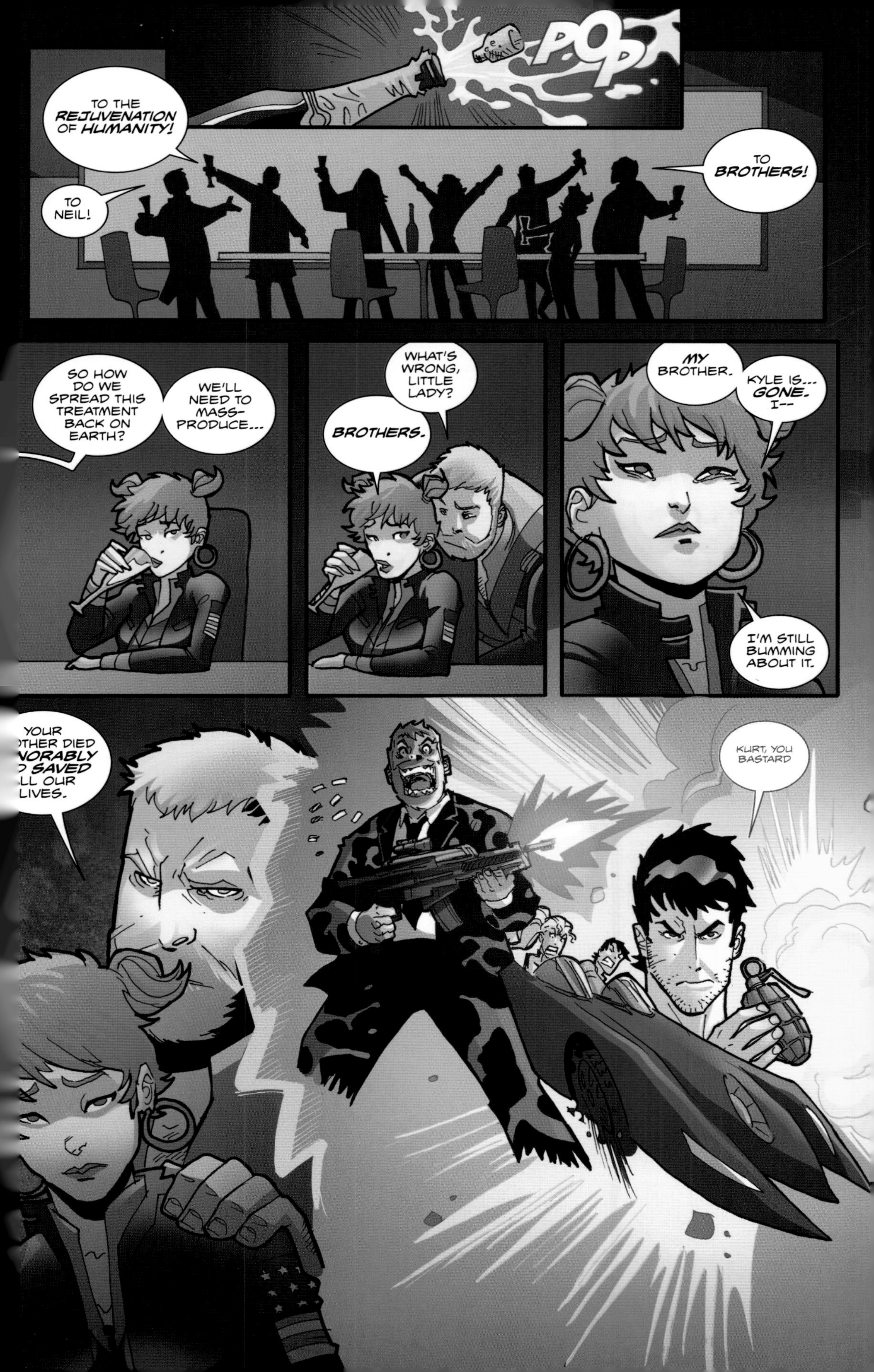
POP
TO THE REJUVENATION OF HUMANITY!
TO NEIL!
TO BROTHERS!
SO HOW DO WE SPREAD THIS TREATMENT BACK ON EARTH?
WE'LL NEED TO MASS-PRODUCE...
WHAT'S WRONG, LITTLE LADY?
BROTHERS.
MY BROTHER.
KYLE IS... GONE. I--
I'M STILL BUMMING ABOUT IT.
YOUR OTHER DIED NORABLY D SAVED LL OUR LIVES.
KURT, YOU BASTARD

I'M SICK OF *MONITORING* NEIL WHILE YOU ALL *PARTY* IT UP IN HERE. SOMEONE SWITCH ME OUT. FLO, HOW ABOUT YOU?

I'LL DO IT. DRINK UP, HYO!

YOU'RE MY *HERO*, BILL.

NEIL IS AT 47%. THANKS TO ARTHUR'S MACHINE, NEIL'S BODY IS *REGENERATING* TISSUE AND CELLS AT AN *INCREDIBLE RATE*. HIS BODY IS ABLE TO *NATURALLY* FIGHT OFF THE ZOMBIE VIRUS.

YOU'RE A *GENIUS*, ARTHUR!

IT'S NOTHING. I'M JUST GRATEFUL IT *WORKS*.

CAN YOU IMAGINE WHAT COULD HAVE HAPPENED IF OUR NEW FRIENDS HERE ARRIVED--

--AND ACCIDENTALLY LET A ZOMBIE LOOSE ABOARD A SMALL, ENCLOSED SPACECRAFT?

I JUST FINISHED *FINE-TUNING* THAT MACHINE.

IF YOU WOULD HAVE ARRIVED EVEN *ONE DAY EARLIER*, THAT MIGHT HAVE MEANT THE *DEATH* OF US ALL.

WE DIDN'T EXACTLY *PLAN* TO COME UP HERE. IT WAS SORT OF NEIL'S *FAULT*.

YEAH! WE EVEN LEFT BEHIND *THREE* OF OUR OTHER *FRIENDS*.

I WOND WHA THEY'RE TO RIG NOW.

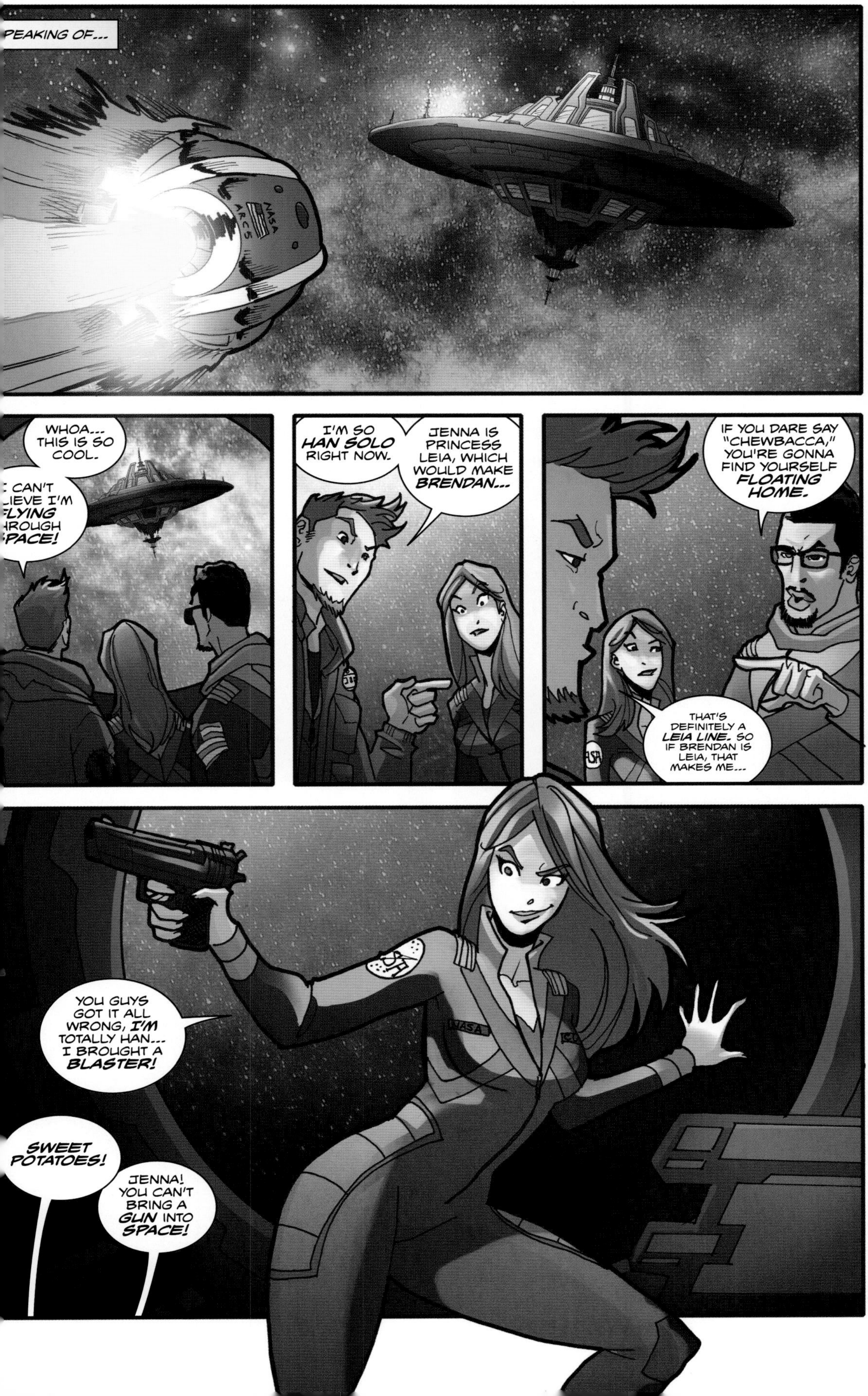
PEAKING OF...
NASA
ARC 5
WHOA... THIS IS SO COOL.
CAN'T LIEVE I'M FLYING THROUGH SPACE!
I'M SO HAN SOLO RIGHT NOW.
JENNA IS PRINCESS LEIA, WHICH WOULD MAKE BRENDAN...
IF YOU DARE SAY "CHEWBACCA," YOU'RE GONNA FIND YOURSELF FLOATING HOME.
THAT'S DEFINITELY A LEIA LINE. SO IF BRENDAN IS LEIA, THAT MAKES ME...
YOU GUYS GOT IT ALL WRONG, I'M TOTALLY HAN... I BROUGHT A BLASTER!
NASA
SWEET POTATOES!
JENNA! YOU CAN'T BRING A GUN INTO SPACE!

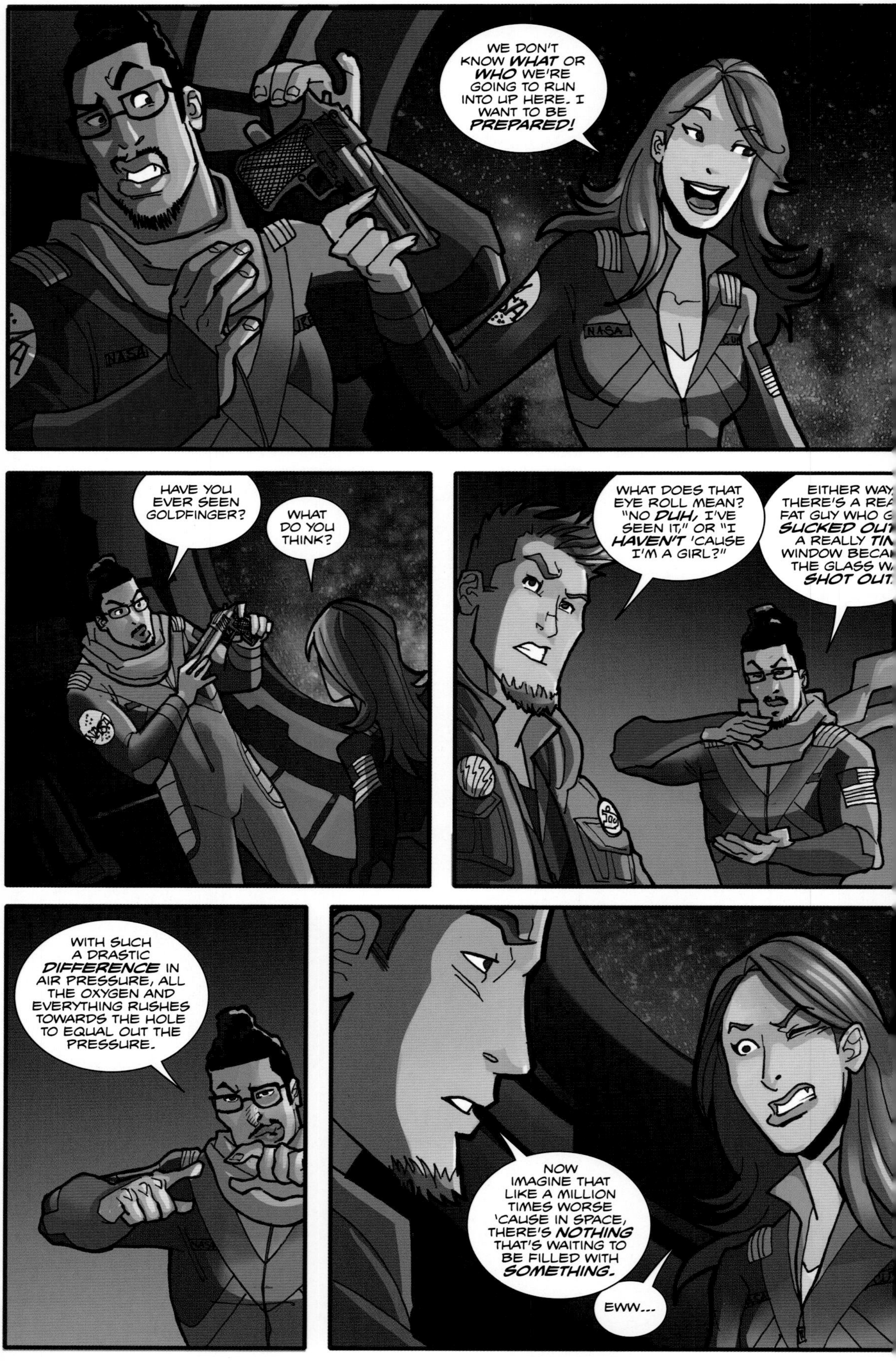
WE DON'T KNOW *WHAT* OR *WHO* WE'RE GOING TO RUN INTO UP HERE. I WANT TO BE *PREPARED!*
HAVE YOU EVER SEEN GOLDFINGER?
WHAT DO YOU THINK?
WHAT DOES THAT EYE ROLL MEAN? "NO *DUH,* I'VE SEEN IT," OR "I *HAVEN'T* 'CAUSE I'M A GIRL?"
EITHER WAY THERE'S A REA FAT GUY WHO G *SUCKED OUT* A REALLY *TIN* WINDOW BECA THE GLASS W *SHOT OUT*
WITH SUCH A DRASTIC *DIFFERENCE* IN AIR PRESSURE, ALL THE OXYGEN AND EVERYTHING RUSHES TOWARDS THE HOLE TO EQUAL OUT THE PRESSURE.
NOW IMAGINE THAT LIKE A MILLION TIMES WORSE 'CAUSE IN SPACE, THERE'S *NOTHING* THAT'S WAITING TO BE FILLED WITH *SOMETHING.*
EWW...

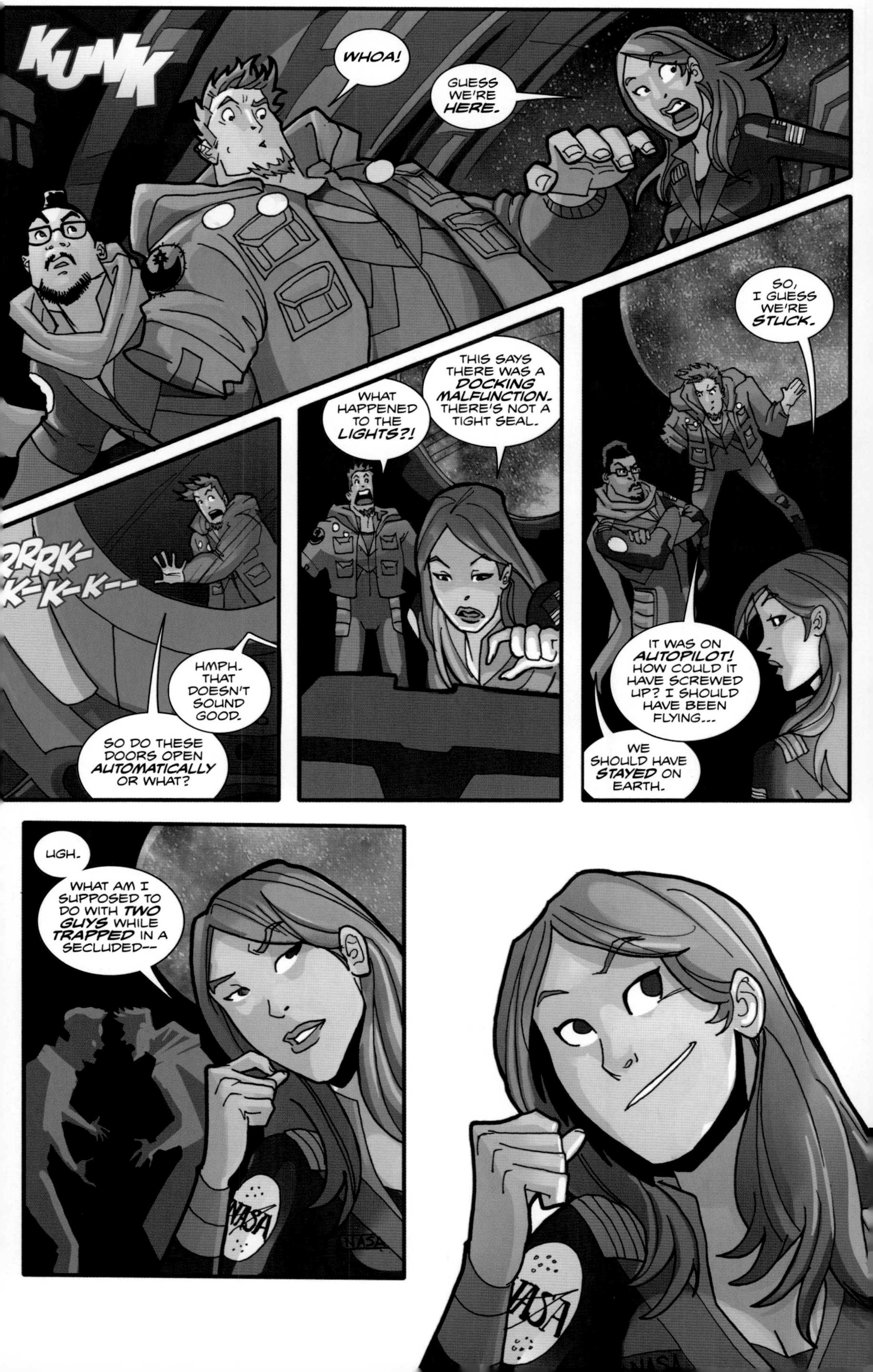
KUNK
WHOA!
GUESS WE'RE HERE.
RRRK-K-K-K--
HMPH. THAT DOESN'T SOUND GOOD.
SO DO THESE DOORS OPEN AUTOMATICALLY OR WHAT?
WHAT HAPPENED TO THE LIGHTS?!
THIS SAYS THERE WAS A DOCKING MALFUNCTION. THERE'S NOT A TIGHT SEAL.
SO, I GUESS WE'RE STUCK.
IT WAS ON AUTOPILOT! HOW COULD IT HAVE SCREWED UP? I SHOULD HAVE BEEN FLYING...
WE SHOULD HAVE STAYED ON EARTH.
UGH.
WHAT AM I SUPPOSED TO DO WITH TWO GUYS WHILE TRAPPED IN A SECLUDED--
NASA
NASA

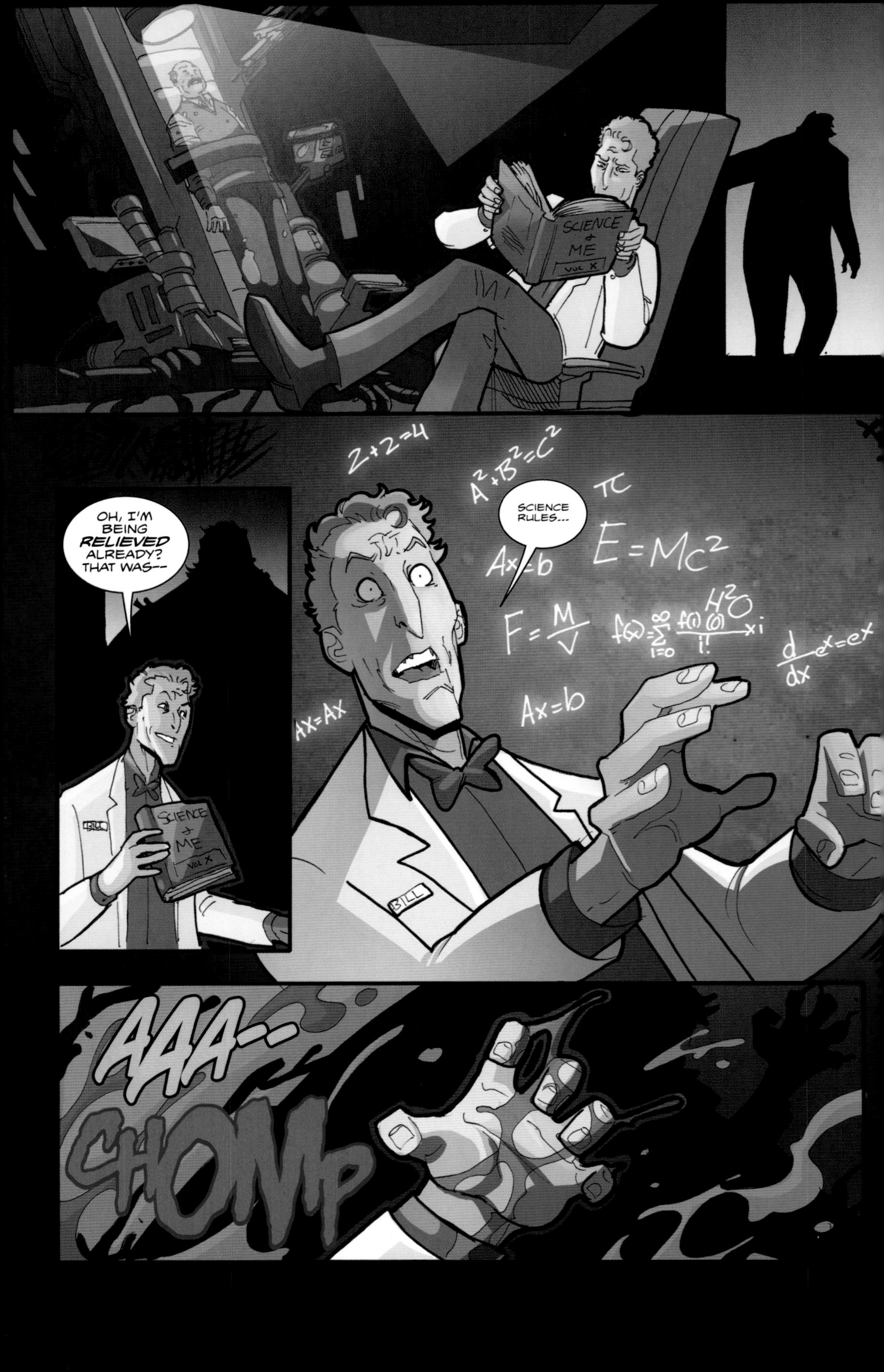
SCIENCE + ME VOL X
OH, I'M BEING RELIEVED ALREADY? THAT WAS--
SCIENCE RULES...
AAA--
CHOMP

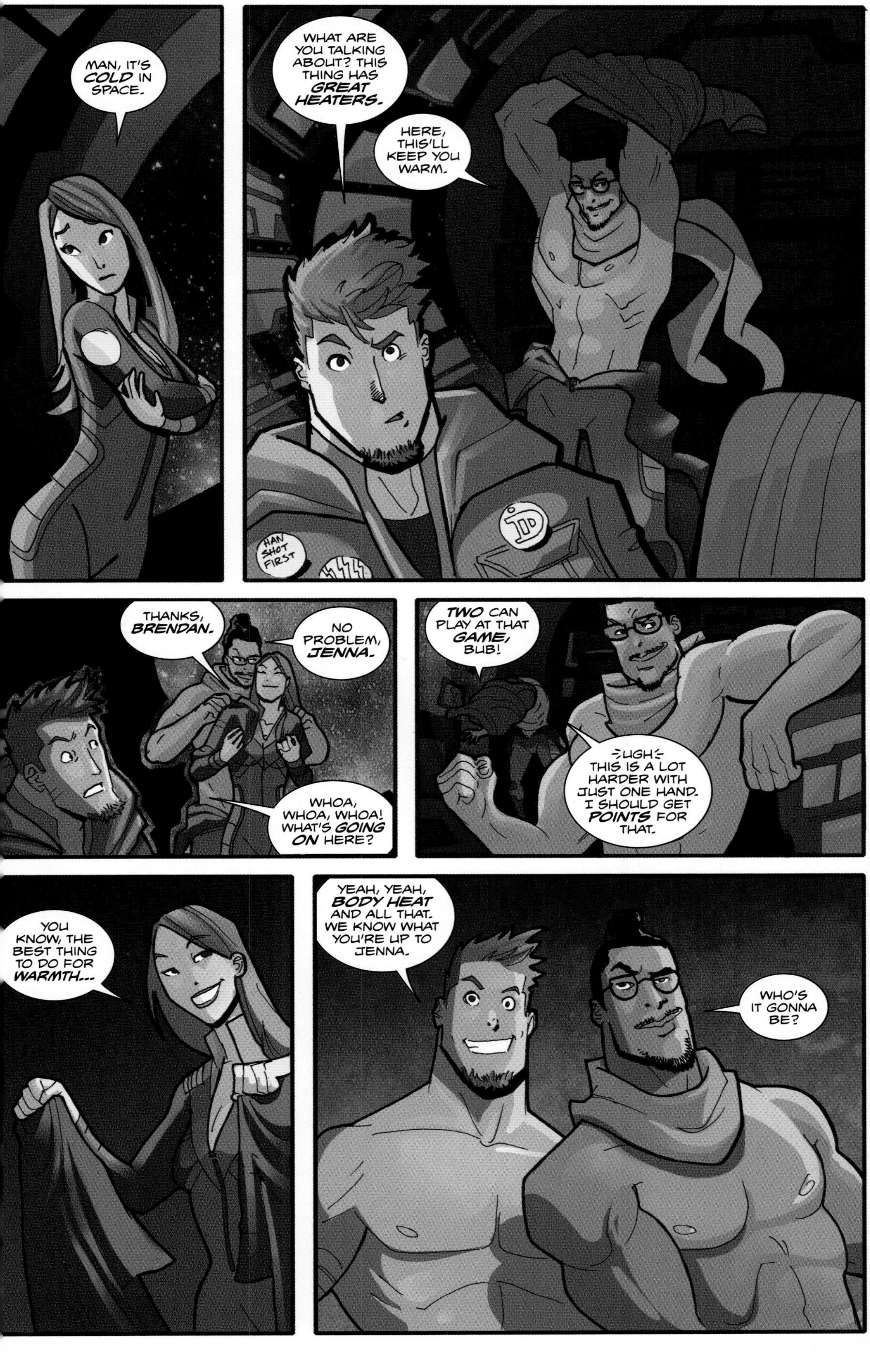
MAN, IT'S COLD IN SPACE.
WHAT ARE YOU TALKING ABOUT? THIS THING HAS GREAT HEATERS.
HERE, THIS'LL KEEP YOU WARM.
HAN SHOT FIRST
THANKS, BRENDAN.
NO PROBLEM, JENNA.
WHOA, WHOA, WHOA! WHAT'S GOING ON HERE?
TWO CAN PLAY AT THAT GAME, BUB!
UGH
THIS IS A LOT HARDER WITH JUST ONE HAND. I SHOULD GET POINTS FOR THAT.
YOU KNOW, THE BEST THING TO DO FOR WARMTH...
YEAH, YEAH, BODY HEAT AND ALL THAT. WE KNOW WHAT YOU'RE UP TO JENNA.
WHO'S IT GONNA BE?

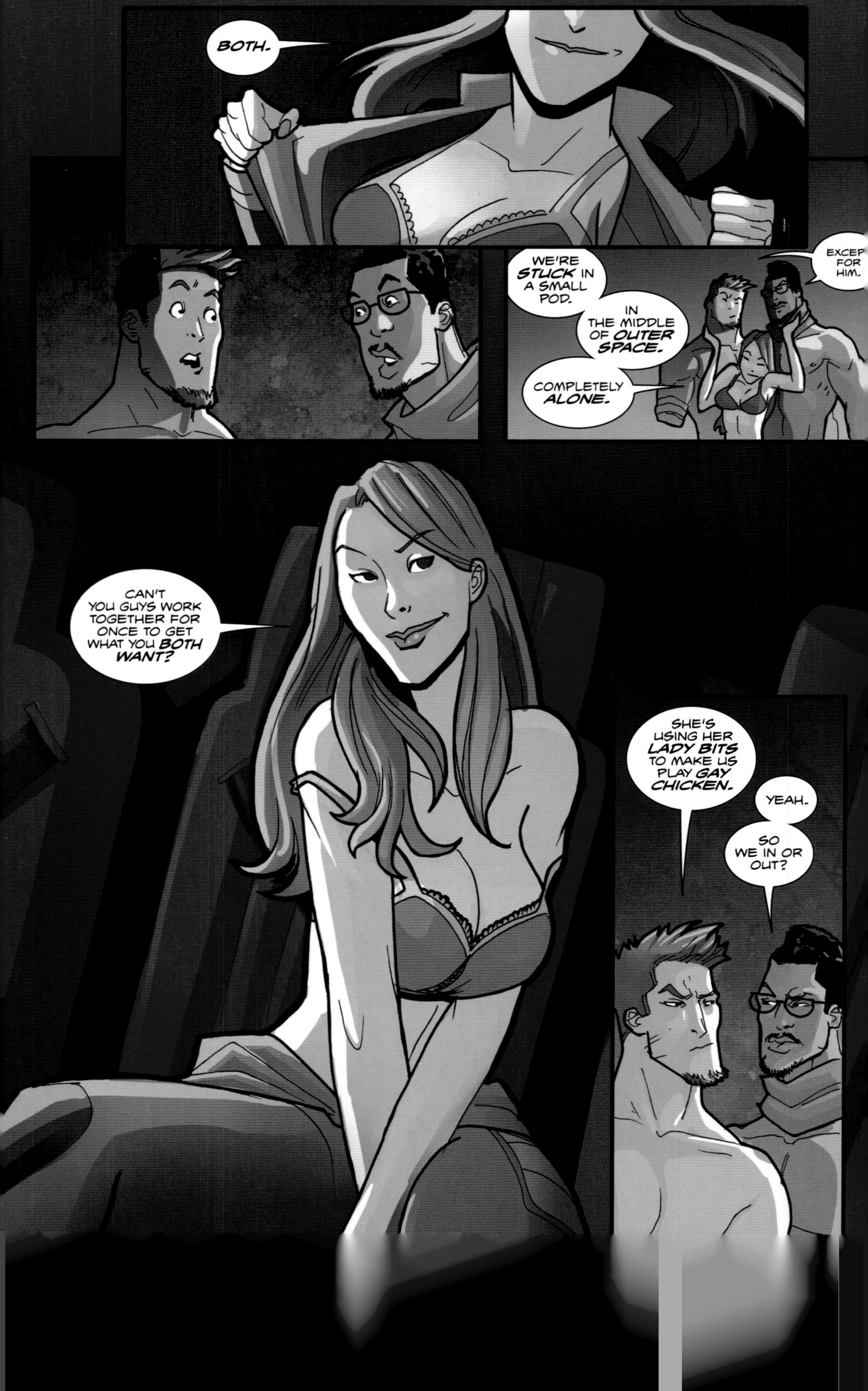

BOTH.
WE'RE STUCK IN A SMALL POD.
IN THE MIDDLE OF OUTER SPACE.
COMPLETELY ALONE.
EXCEP FOR HIM.
CAN'T YOU GUYS WORK TOGETHER FOR ONCE TO GET WHAT YOU BOTH WANT?
SHE'S USING HER LADY BITS TO MAKE US PLAY GAY CHICKEN.
YEAH.
SO WE IN OR OUT?

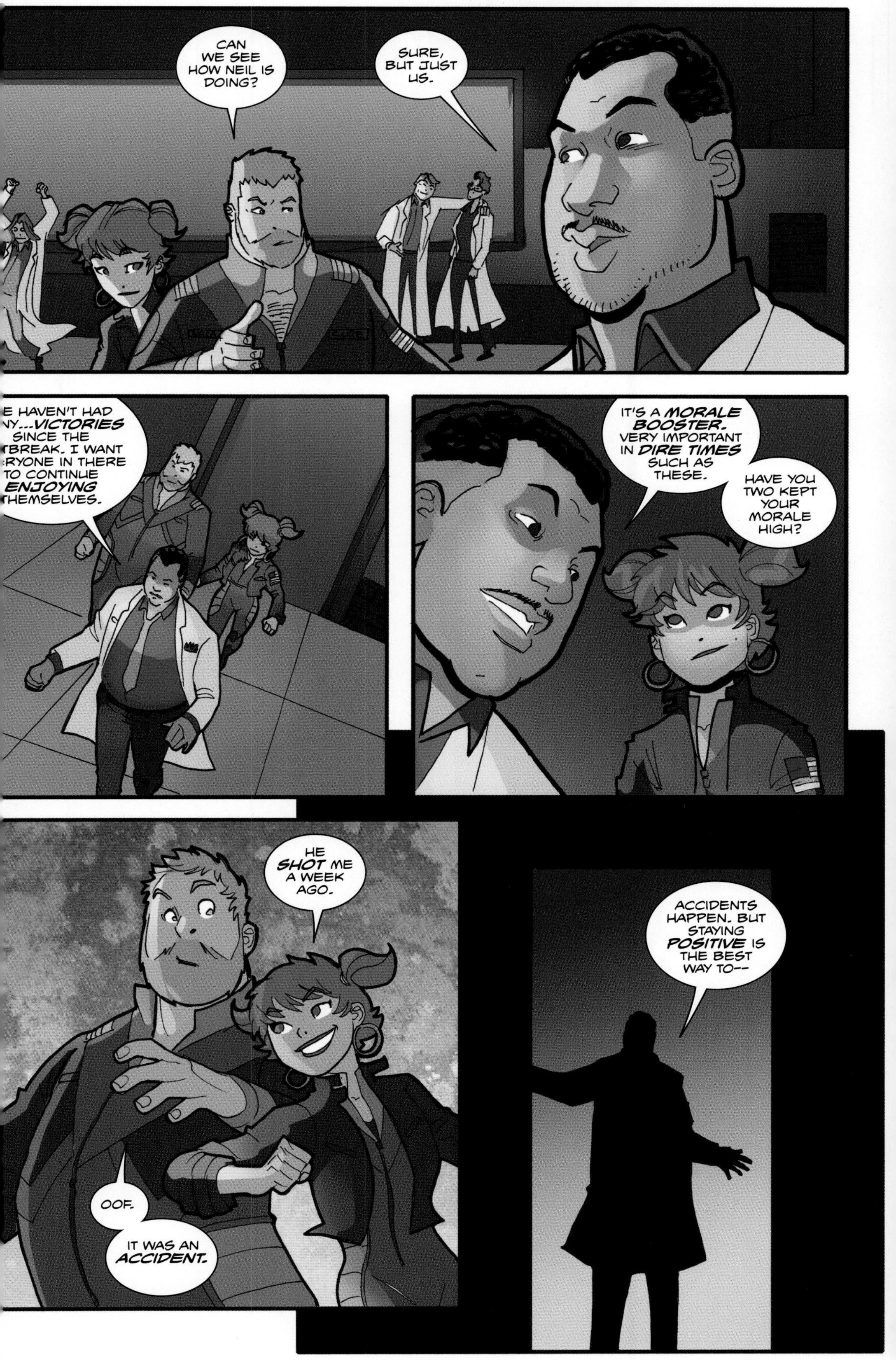
CAN WE SEE HOW NEIL IS DOING?
SURE, BUT JUST US.
E HAVEN'T HAD NY...VICTORIES SINCE THE TBREAK. I WANT RYONE IN THERE TO CONTINUE ENJOYING THEMSELVES.
IT'S A MORALE BOOSTER. VERY IMPORTANT IN DIRE TIMES SUCH AS THESE.
HAVE YOU TWO KEPT YOUR MORALE HIGH?
HE SHOT ME A WEEK AGO.
OOF.
IT WAS AN ACCIDENT.
ACCIDENTS HAPPEN. BUT STAYING POSITIVE IS THE BEST WAY TO--

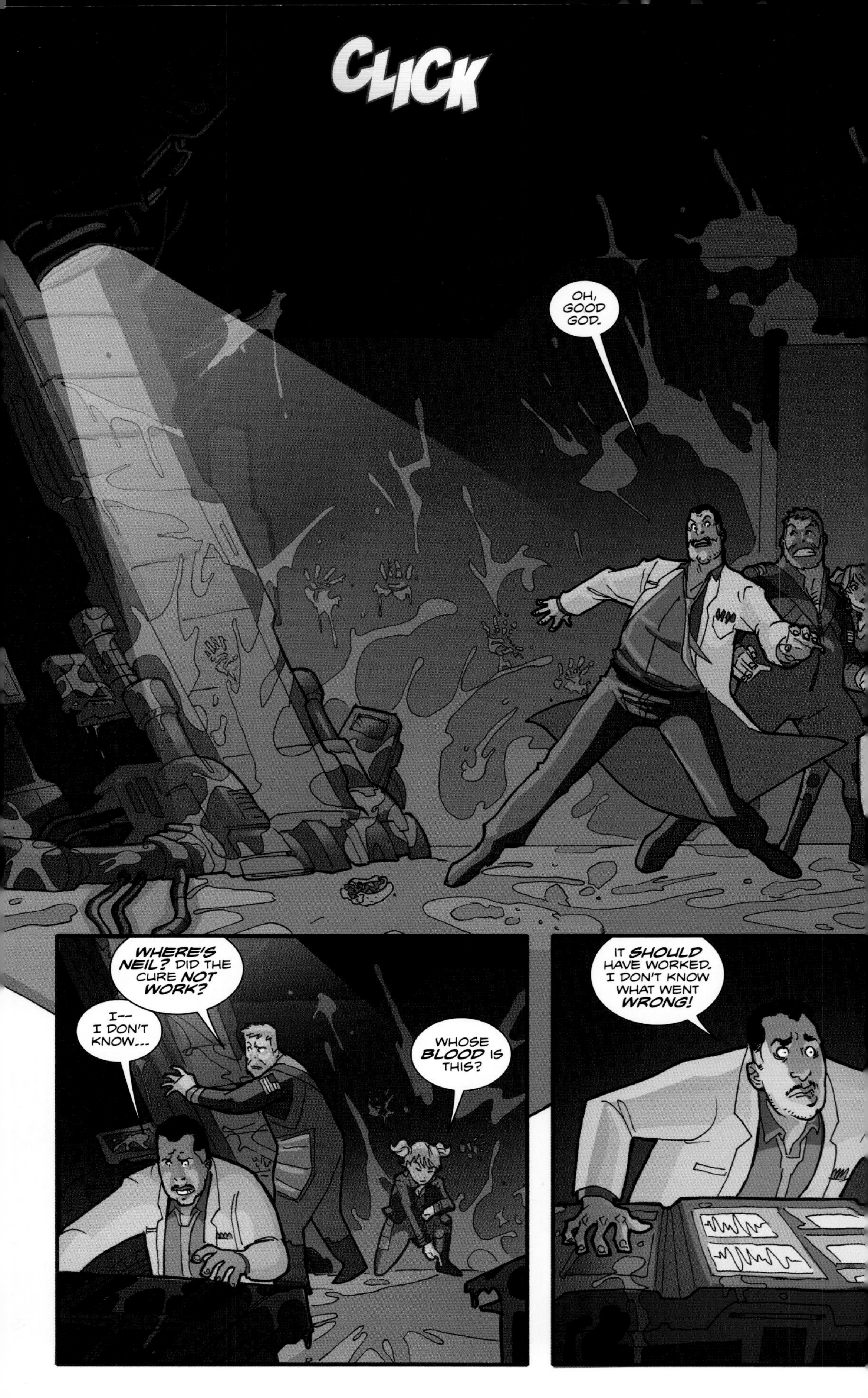
CLICK
OH, GOOD GOD.
WHERE'S NEIL? DID THE CURE NOT WORK?
I-- I DON'T KNOW...
WHOSE BLOOD IS THIS?
IT SHOULD HAVE WORKED. I DON'T KNOW WHAT WENT WRONG!

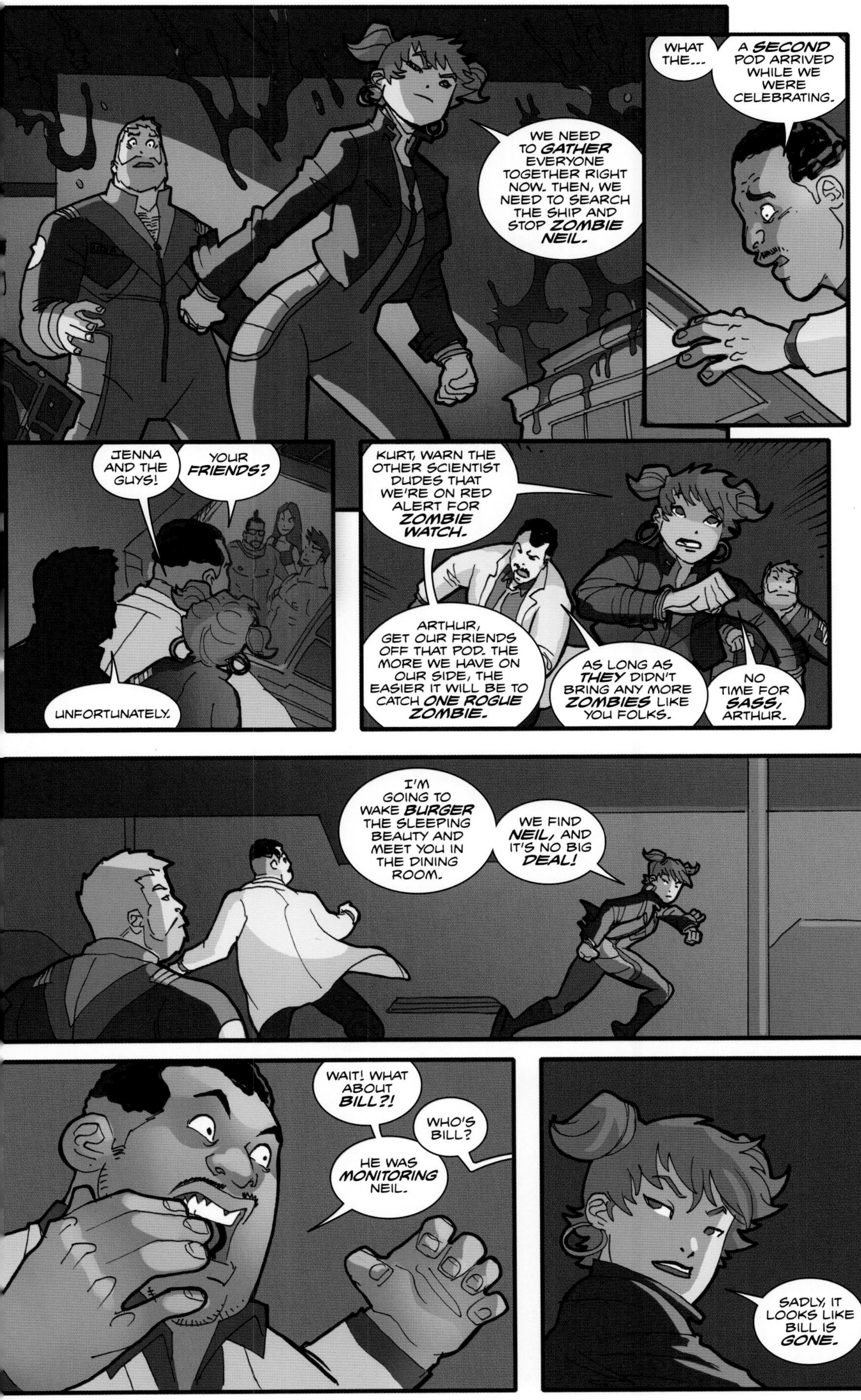
WE NEED TO GATHER EVERYONE TOGETHER RIGHT NOW. THEN, WE NEED TO SEARCH THE SHIP AND STOP ZOMBIE NEIL.
WHAT THE...
A SECOND POD ARRIVED WHILE WE WERE CELEBRATING.
JENNA AND THE GUYS!
YOUR FRIENDS?
UNFORTUNATELY.
KURT, WARN THE OTHER SCIENTIST DUDES THAT WE'RE ON RED ALERT FOR ZOMBIE WATCH.
ARTHUR, GET OUR FRIENDS OFF THAT POD. THE MORE WE HAVE ON OUR SIDE, THE EASIER IT WILL BE TO CATCH ONE ROGUE ZOMBIE.
AS LONG AS THEY DIDN'T BRING ANY MORE ZOMBIES LIKE YOU FOLKS.
NO TIME FOR SASS, ARTHUR.
I'M GOING TO WAKE BURGER THE SLEEPING BEAUTY AND MEET YOU IN THE DINING ROOM.
WE FIND NEIL, AND IT'S NO BIG DEAL!
WAIT! WHAT ABOUT BILL?!
WHO'S BILL?
HE WAS MONITORING NEIL.
SADLY, IT LOOKS LIKE BILL IS GONE.

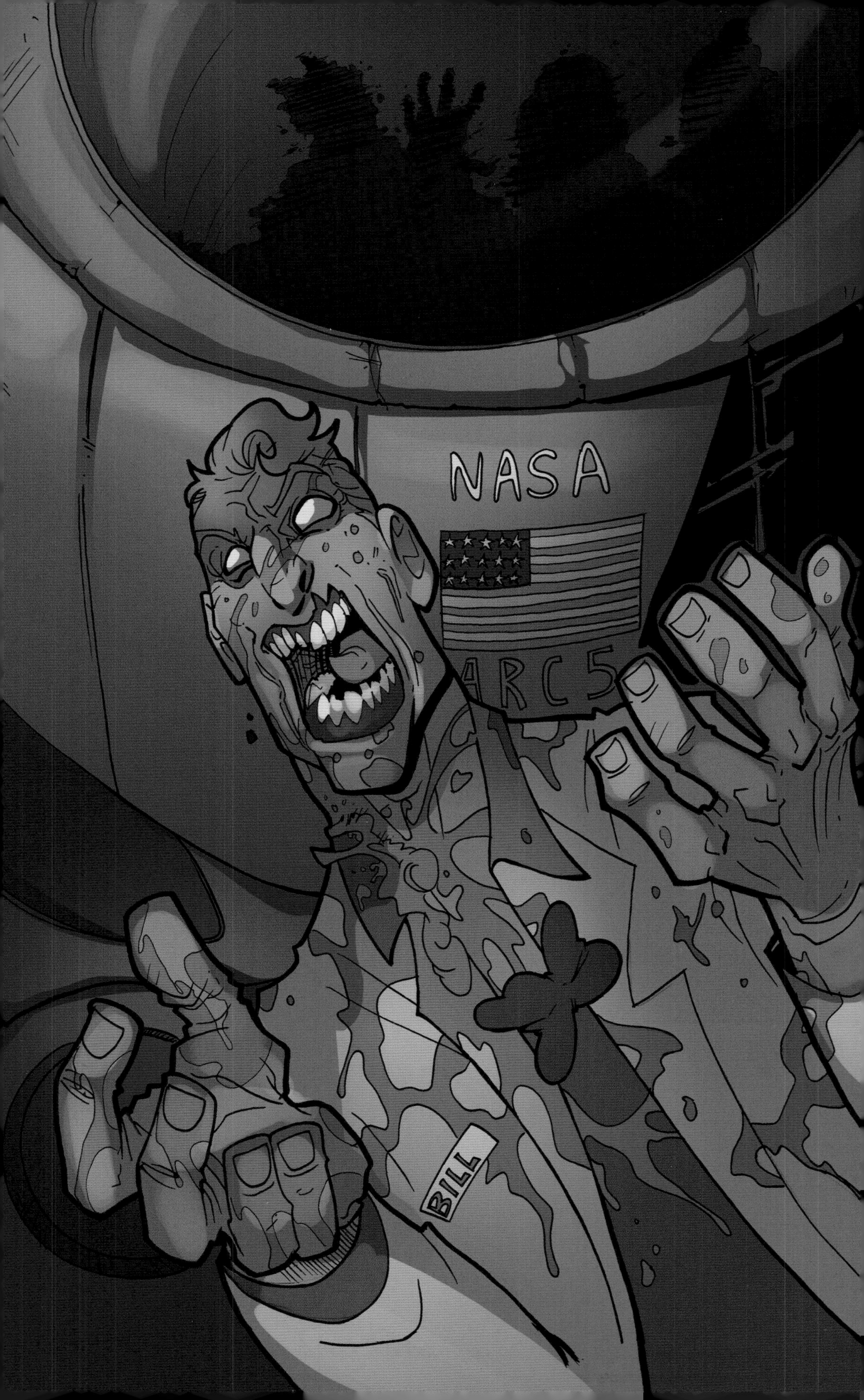
NASA
ARC5
BILL

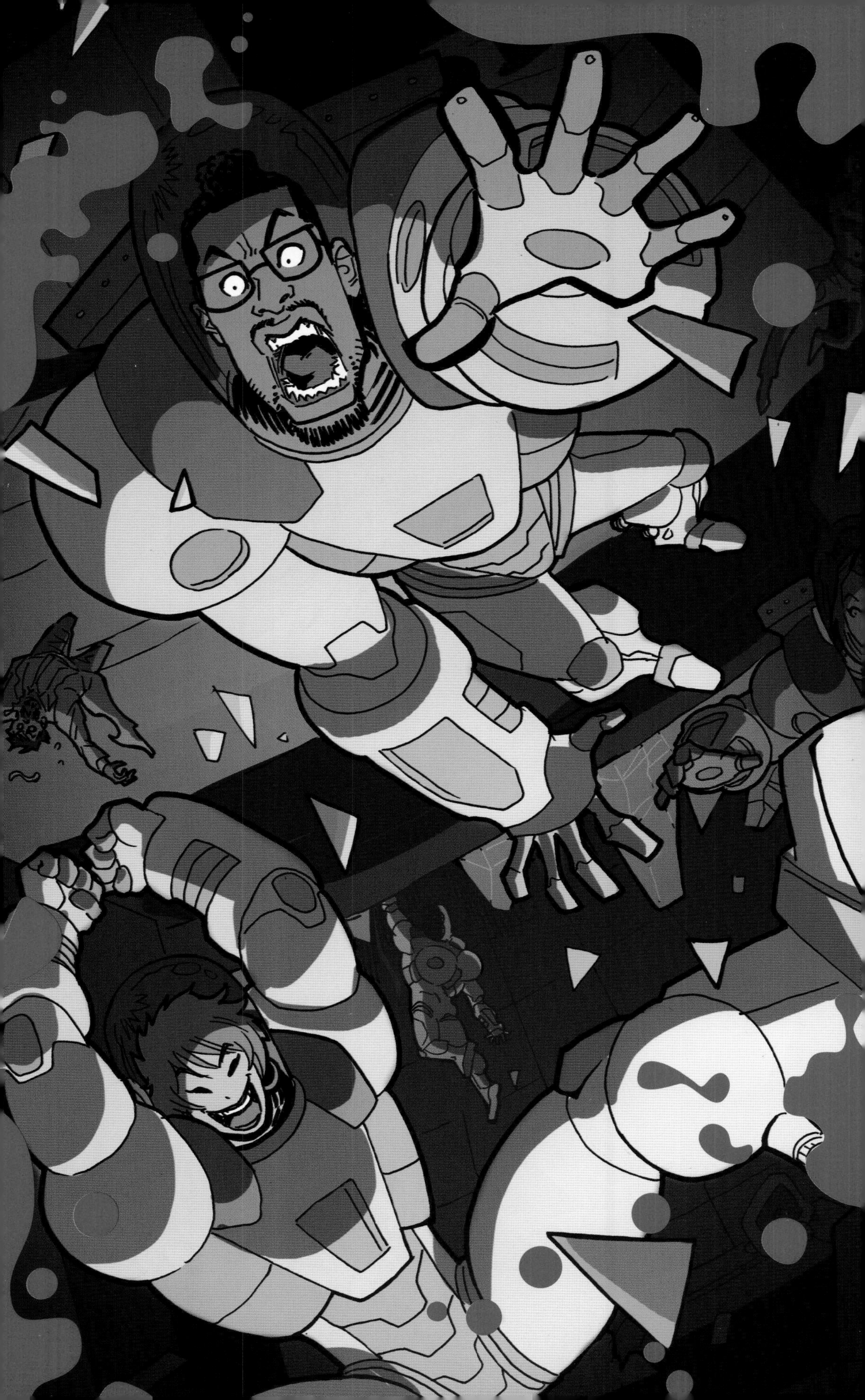

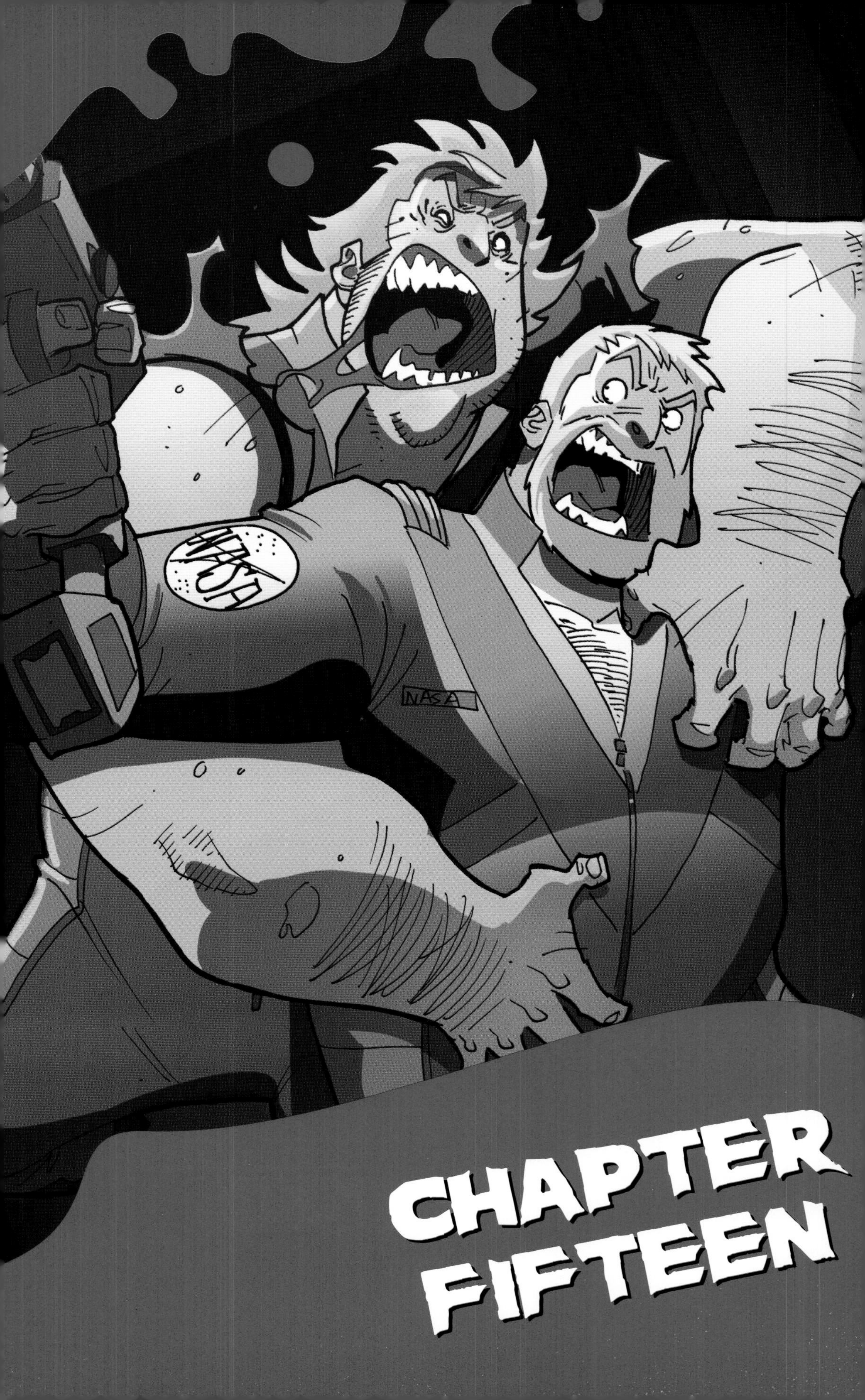
NASA
NASA

CHAPTER FIFTEEN

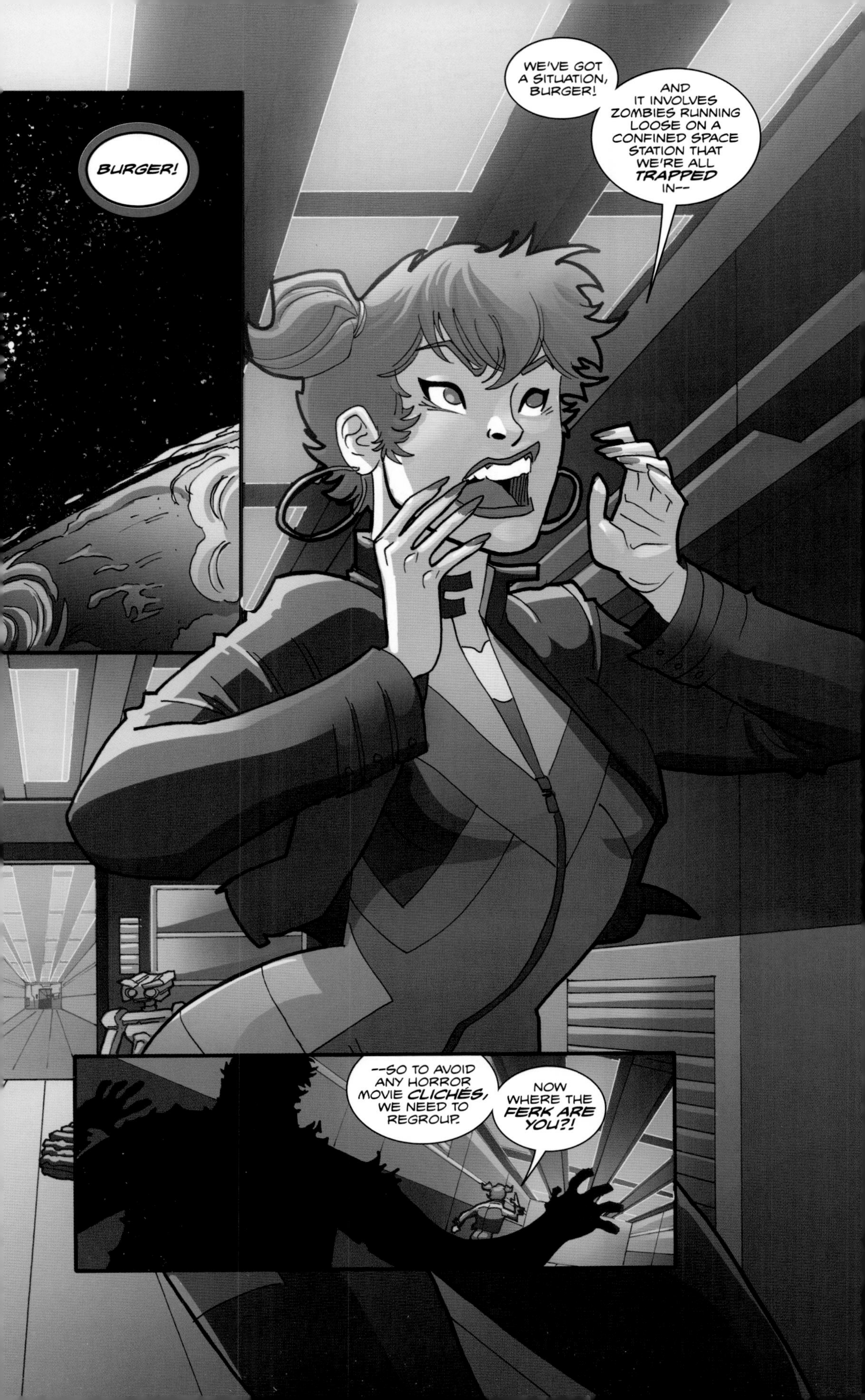
BURGER!
WE'VE GOT A SITUATION, BURGER!
AND IT INVOLVES ZOMBIES RUNNING LOOSE ON A CONFINED SPACE STATION THAT WE'RE ALL TRAPPED IN--
--SO TO AVOID ANY HORROR MOVIE CLICHÉS, WE NEED TO REGROUP.
NOW WHERE THE FERK ARE YOU?!

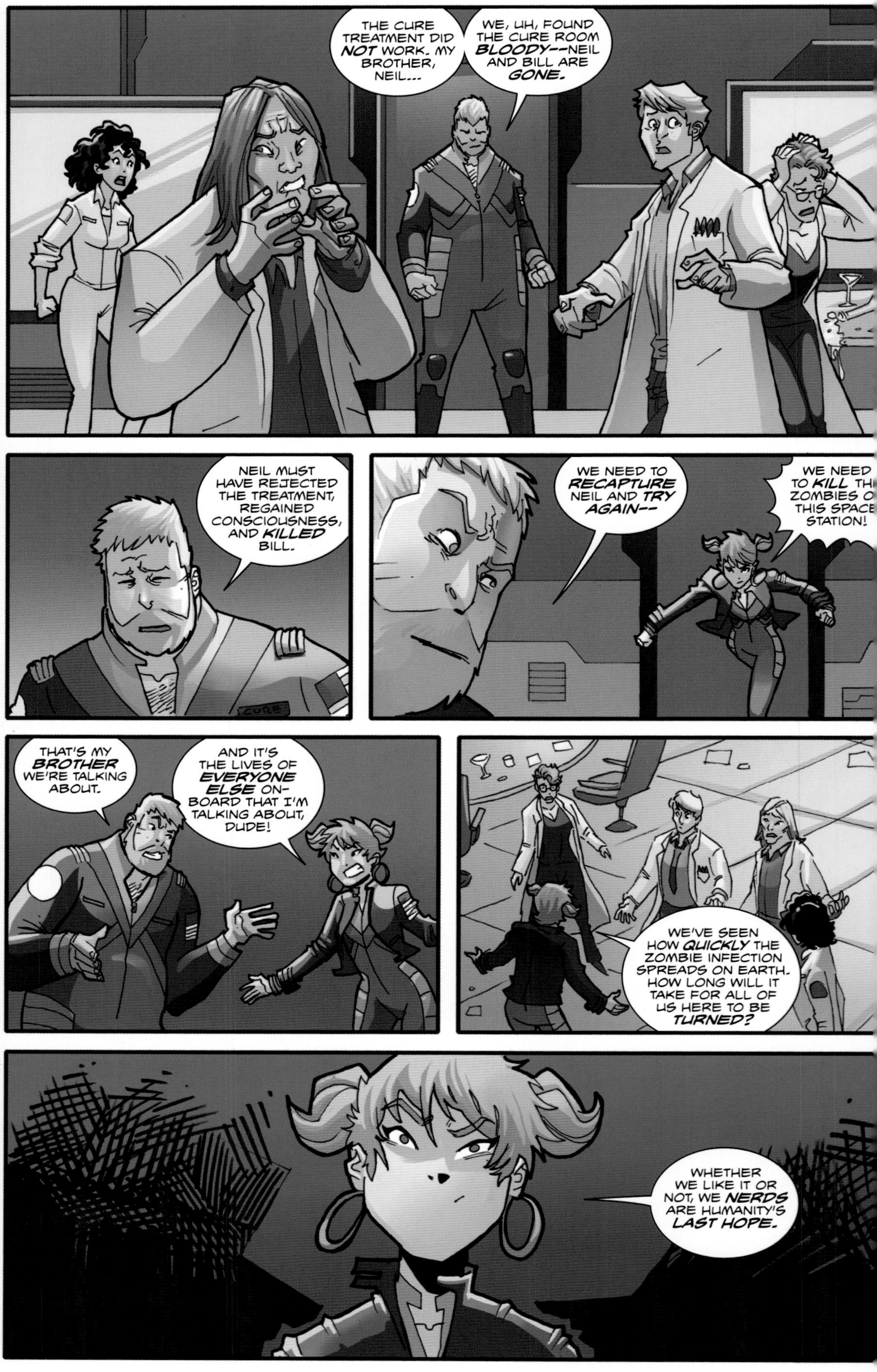
THE CURE TREATMENT DID NOT WORK. MY BROTHER, NEIL...
WE, UH, FOUND THE CURE ROOM BLOODY--NEIL AND BILL ARE GONE.
NEIL MUST HAVE REJECTED THE TREATMENT, REGAINED CONSCIOUSNESS, AND KILLED BILL.
WE NEED TO RECAPTURE NEIL AND TRY AGAIN--
WE NEED TO KILL TH ZOMBIES O THIS SPACE STATION!
CURE
THAT'S MY BROTHER WE'RE TALKING ABOUT.
AND IT'S THE LIVES OF EVERYONE ELSE ON-BOARD THAT I'M TALKING ABOUT, DUDE!
WE'VE SEEN HOW QUICKLY THE ZOMBIE INFECTION SPREADS ON EARTH. HOW LONG WILL IT TAKE FOR ALL OF US HERE TO BE TURNED?
WHETHER WE LIKE IT OR NOT, WE NERDS ARE HUMANITY'S LAST HOPE.

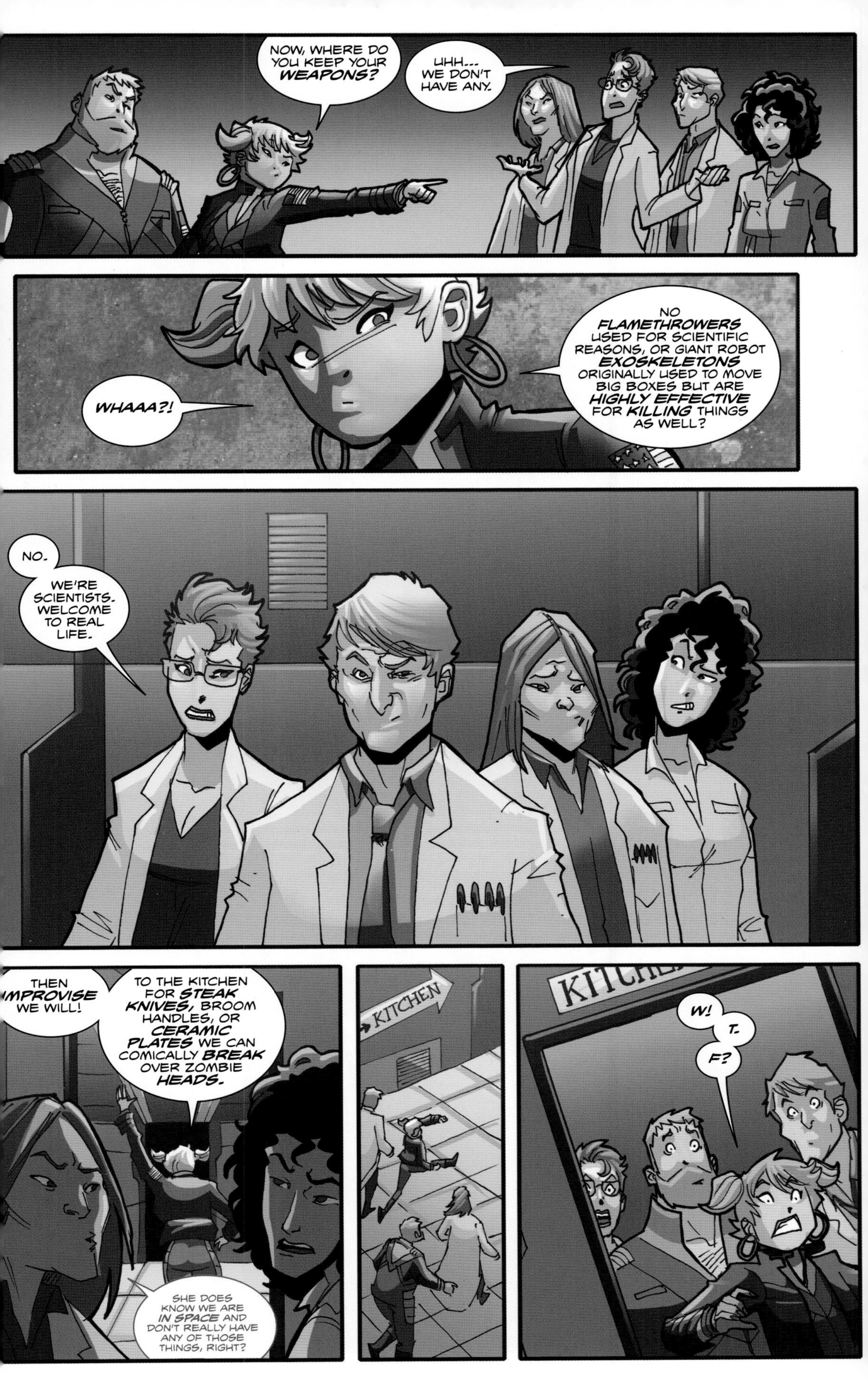
NOW, WHERE DO YOU KEEP YOUR WEAPONS?
UHH... WE DON'T HAVE ANY.
NO FLAMETHROWERS USED FOR SCIENTIFIC REASONS, OR GIANT ROBOT EXOSKELETONS ORIGINALLY USED TO MOVE BIG BOXES BUT ARE HIGHLY EFFECTIVE FOR KILLING THINGS AS WELL?
WHAAA?!
NO.
WE'RE SCIENTISTS. WELCOME TO REAL LIFE.
THEN IMPROVISE WE WILL!
TO THE KITCHEN FOR STEAK KNIVES, BROOM HANDLES, OR CERAMIC PLATES WE CAN COMICALLY BREAK OVER ZOMBIE HEADS.
SHE DOES KNOW WE ARE IN SPACE AND DON'T REALLY HAVE ANY OF THOSE THINGS, RIGHT?
KITCHEN
W!
T.
F?

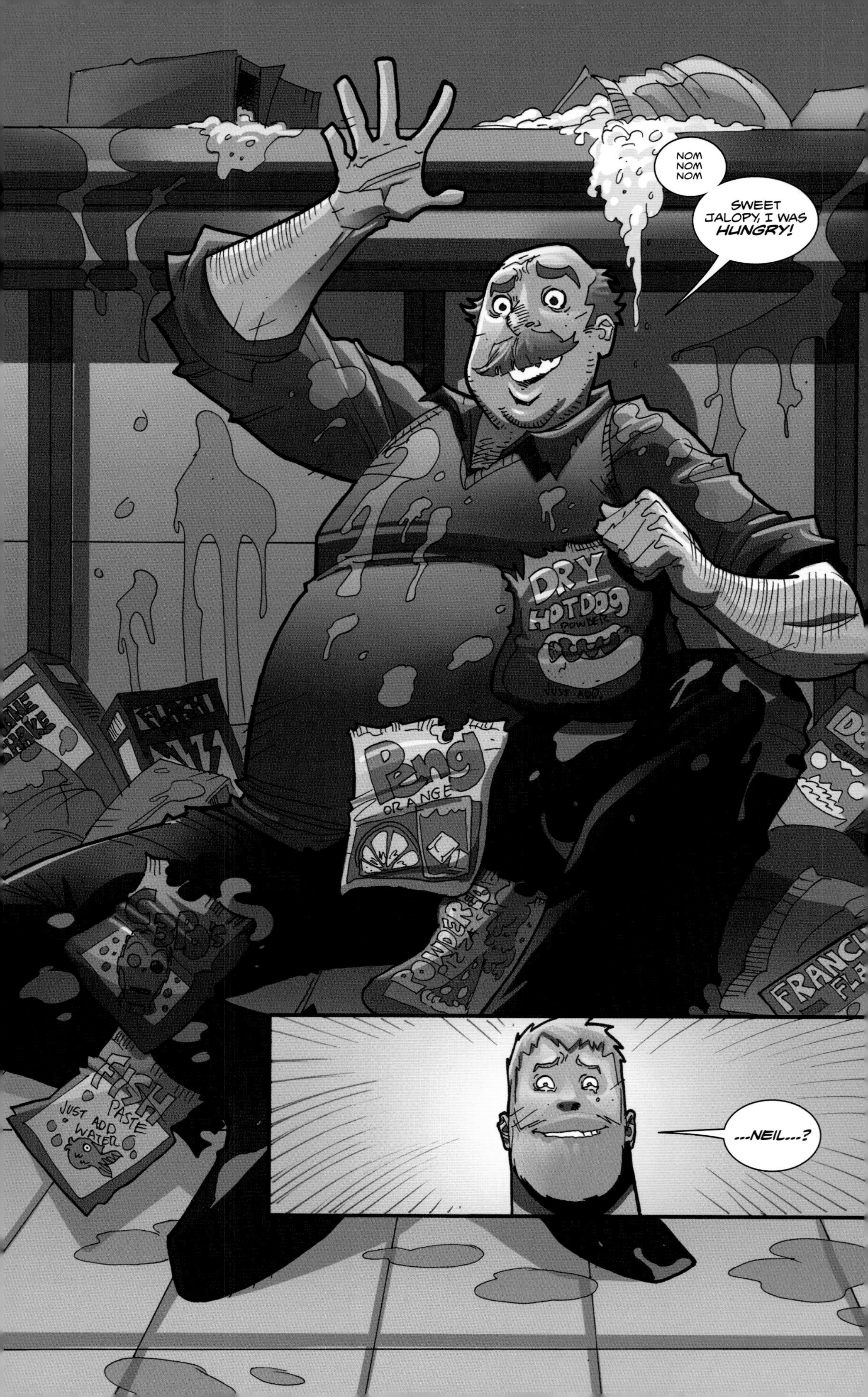
NOM NOM NOM
SWEET JALOPY, I WAS *HUNGRY!*
DRY HOT DOG POWDER
JUST ADD
Peng ORANGE
POWDERED
FISH PASTE JUST ADD WATER
...NEIL...?

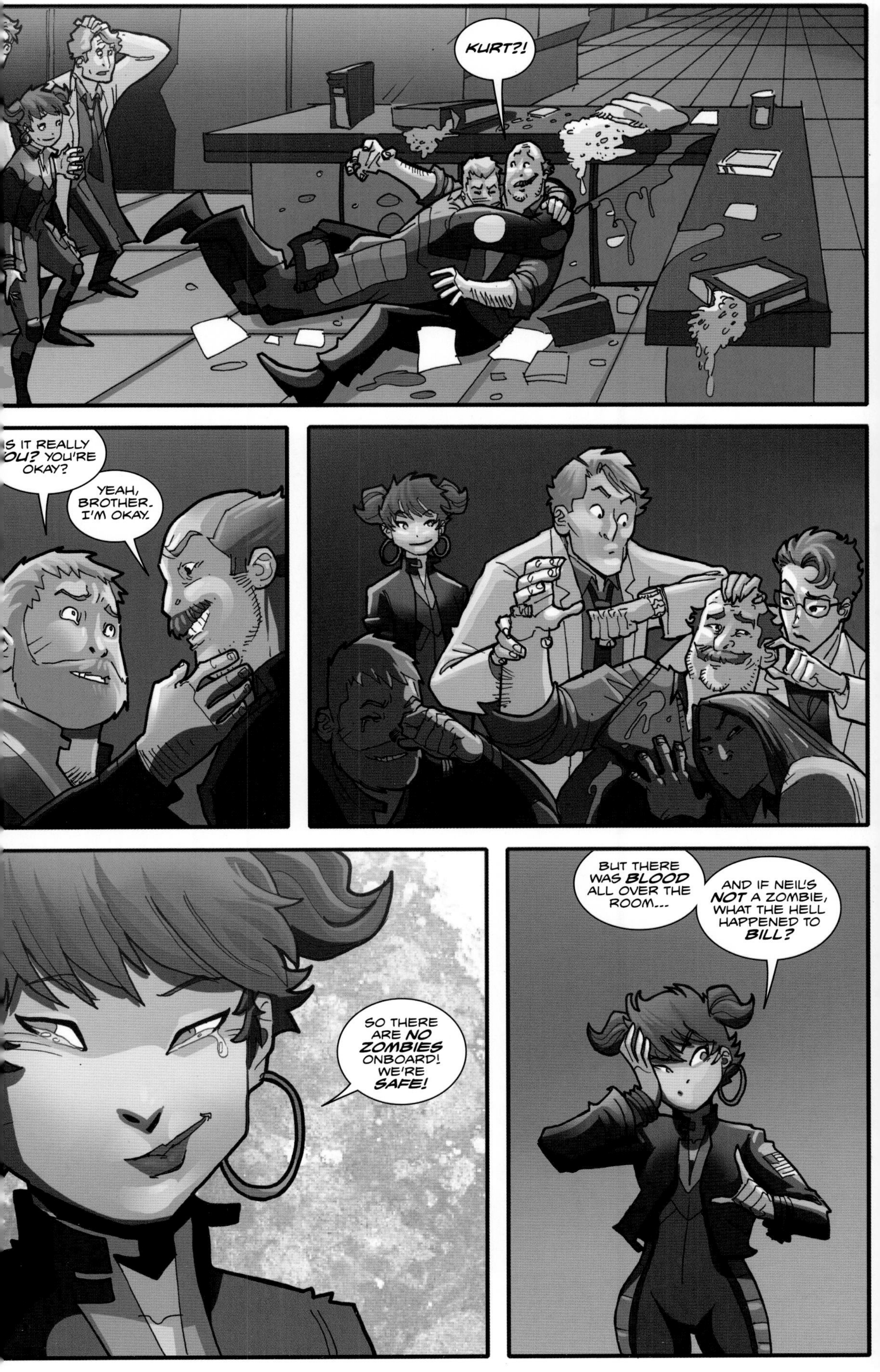
KURT?!
IS IT REALLY YOU? YOU'RE OKAY?
YEAH, BROTHER. I'M OKAY.
SO THERE ARE NO ZOMBIES ONBOARD! WE'RE SAFE!
BUT THERE WAS BLOOD ALL OVER THE ROOM...
AND IF NEIL'S NOT A ZOMBIE, WHAT THE HELL HAPPENED TO BILL?

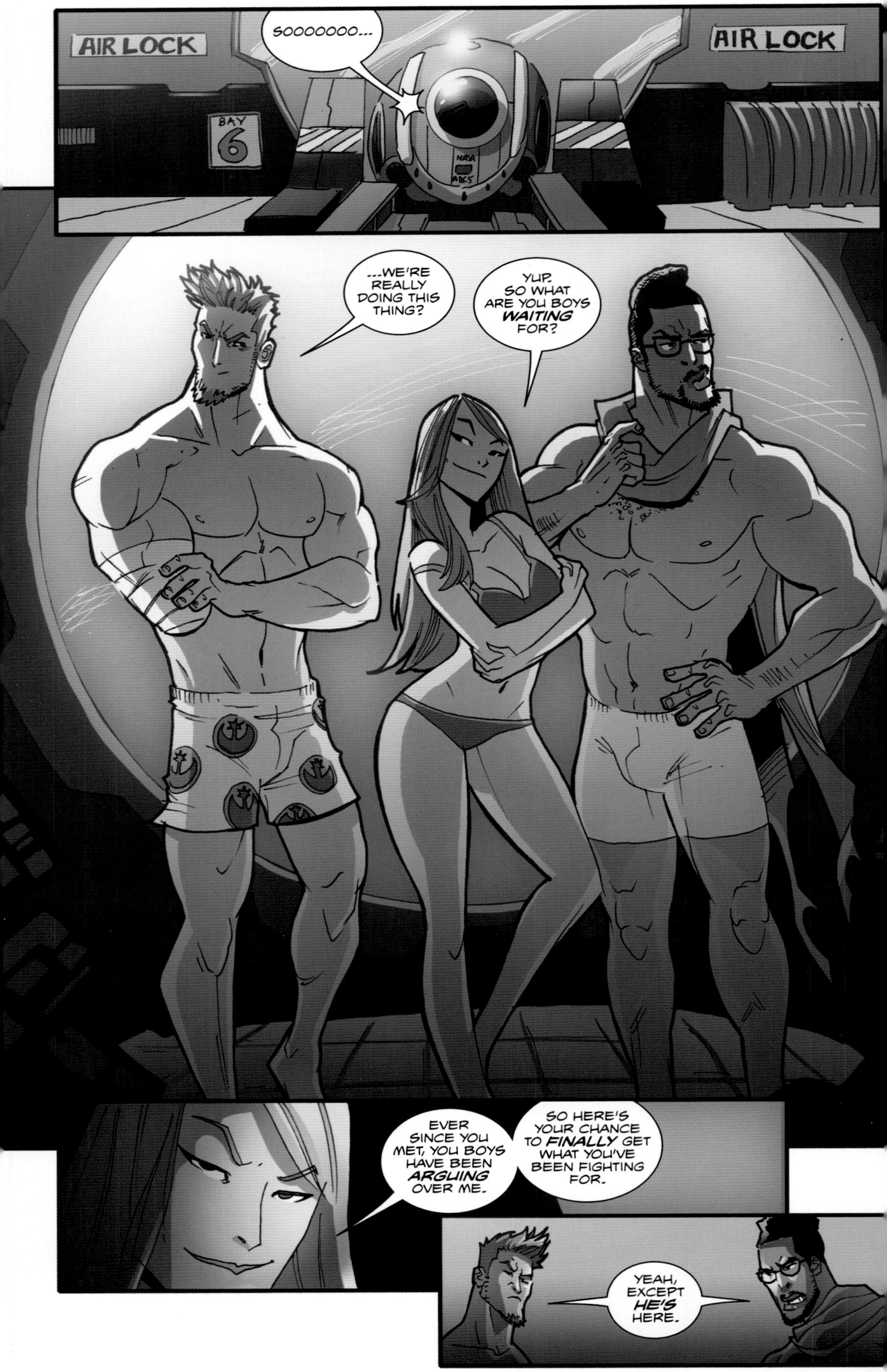
AIR LOCK
SOOOOOOO...
AIR LOCK
BAY 6
NASA
ABC5
...WE'RE REALLY DOING THIS THING?
YUP. SO WHAT ARE YOU BOYS *WAITING* FOR?
EVER SINCE YOU MET, YOU BOYS HAVE BEEN *ARGUING* OVER ME.
SO HERE'S YOUR CHANCE TO *FINALLY* GET WHAT YOU'VE BEEN FIGHTING FOR.
YEAH, EXCEPT *HE'S* HERE.

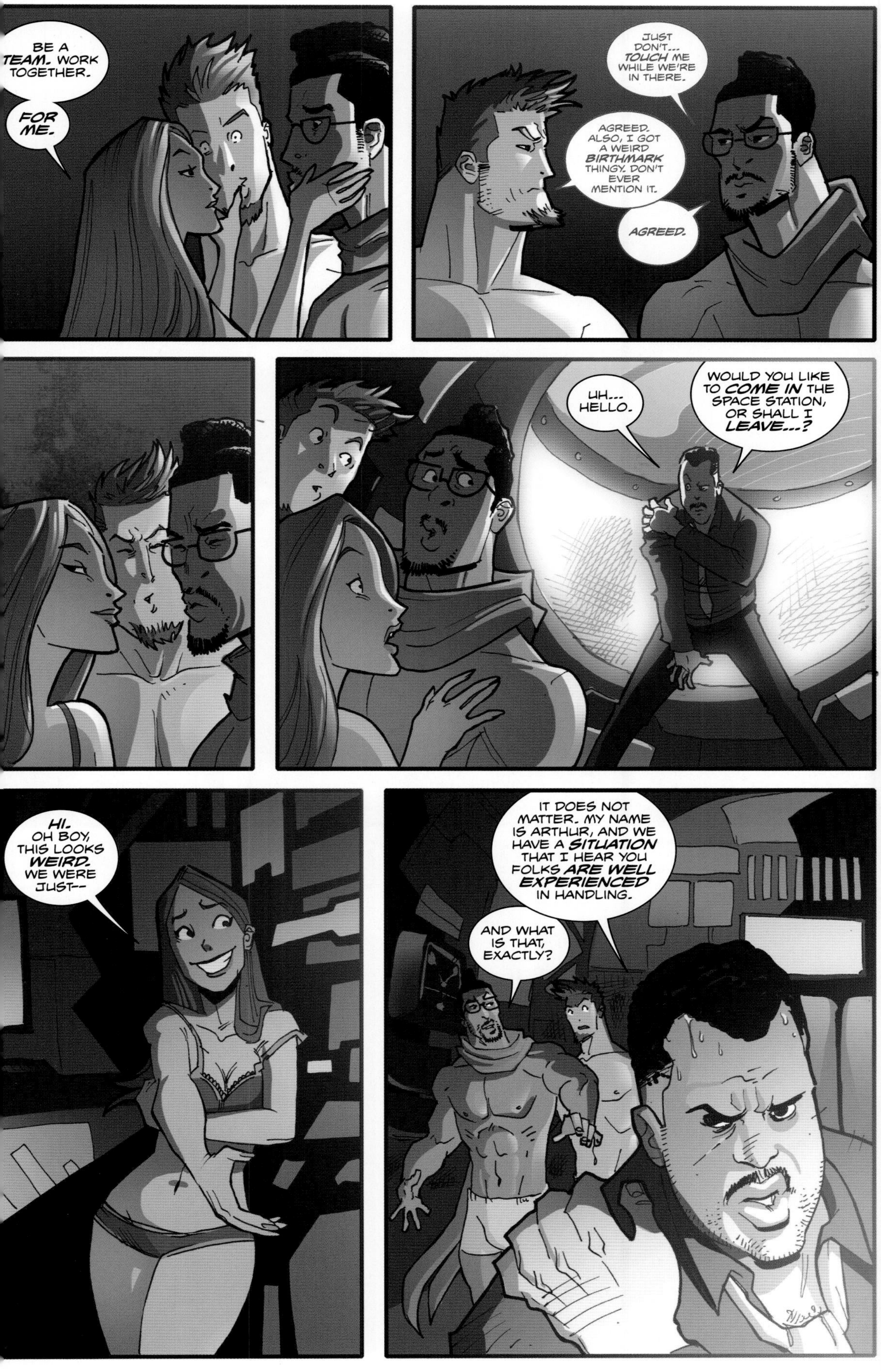
BE A TEAM. WORK TOGETHER.
FOR ME.
JUST DON'T... TOUCH ME WHILE WE'RE IN THERE.
AGREED. ALSO, I GOT A WEIRD BIRTHMARK THINGY. DON'T EVER MENTION IT.
AGREED.
UH... HELLO.
WOULD YOU LIKE TO COME IN THE SPACE STATION, OR SHALL I LEAVE...?
HI. OH BOY, THIS LOOKS WEIRD. WE WERE JUST--
IT DOES NOT MATTER. MY NAME IS ARTHUR, AND WE HAVE A SITUATION THAT I HEAR YOU FOLKS ARE WELL EXPERIENCED IN HANDLING.
AND WHAT IS THAT, EXACTLY?

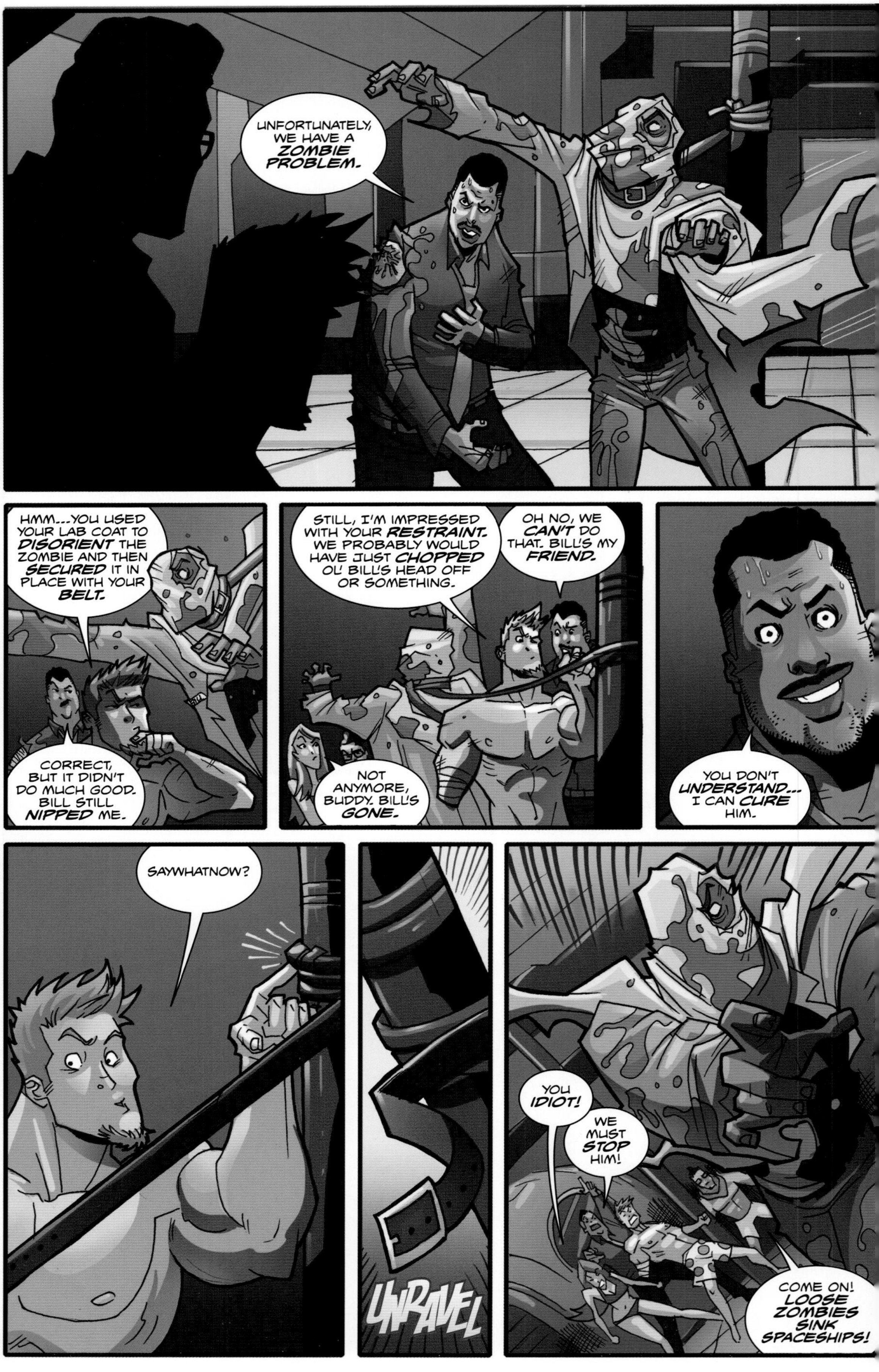
UNFORTUNATELY, WE HAVE A ZOMBIE PROBLEM.
HMM...YOU USED YOUR LAB COAT TO DISORIENT THE ZOMBIE AND THEN SECURED IT IN PLACE WITH YOUR BELT.
CORRECT, BUT IT DIDN'T DO MUCH GOOD. BILL STILL NIPPED ME.
STILL, I'M IMPRESSED WITH YOUR RESTRAINT. WE PROBABLY WOULD HAVE JUST CHOPPED OL' BILL'S HEAD OFF OR SOMETHING.
OH NO, WE CAN'T DO THAT. BILL'S MY FRIEND.
NOT ANYMORE, BUDDY. BILL'S GONE.
YOU DON'T UNDERSTAND... I CAN CURE HIM.
SAYWHATNOW?
UNRAVEL
YOU IDIOT!
WE MUST STOP HIM!
COME ON! LOOSE ZOMBIES SINK SPACESHIPS!

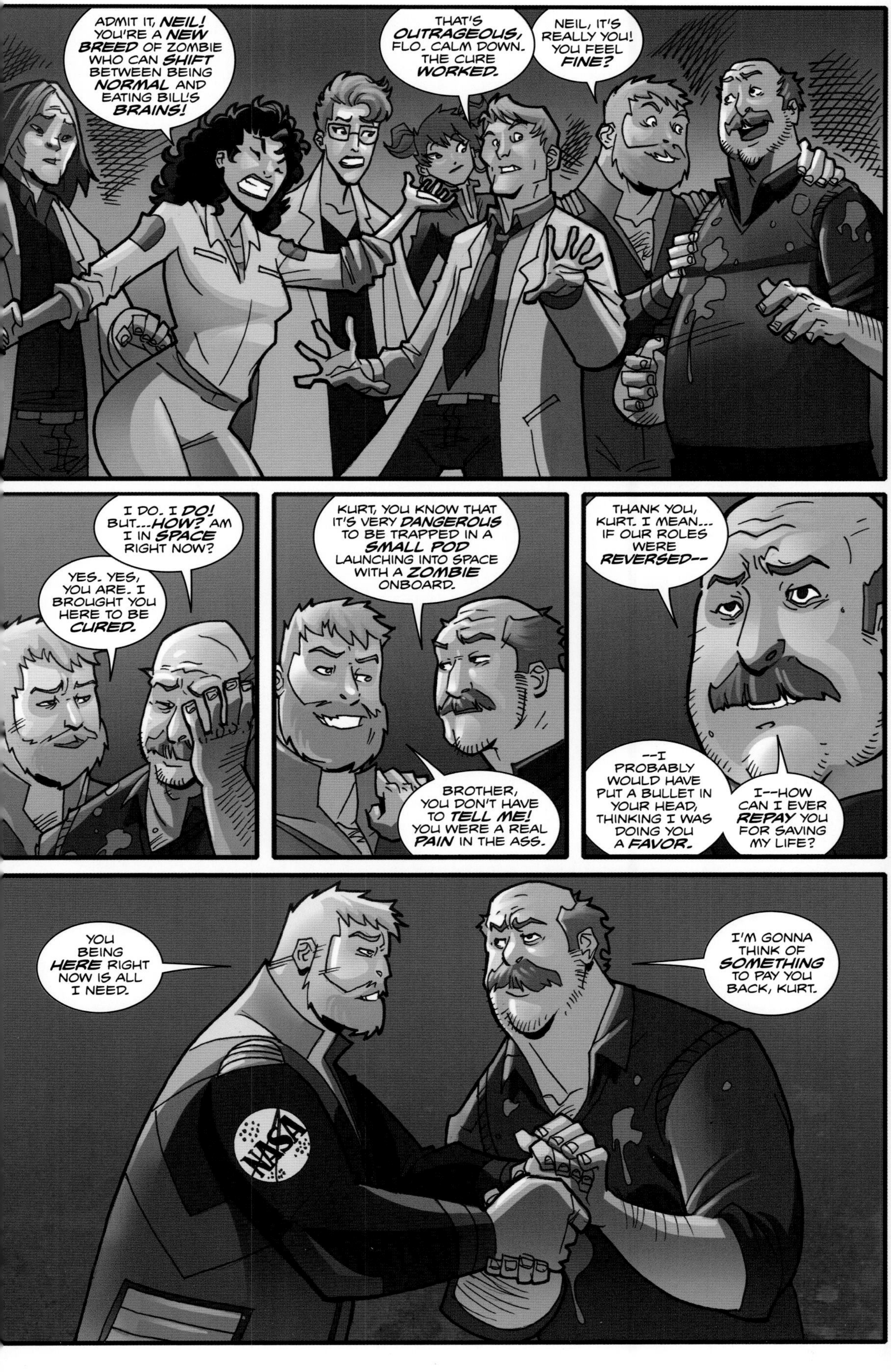

ADMIT IT, NEIL! YOU'RE A NEW BREED OF ZOMBIE WHO CAN SHIFT BETWEEN BEING NORMAL AND EATING BILL'S BRAINS!
THAT'S OUTRAGEOUS, FLO. CALM DOWN. THE CURE WORKED.
NEIL, IT'S REALLY YOU! YOU FEEL FINE?
I DO. I DO! BUT...HOW? AM I IN SPACE RIGHT NOW?
YES. YES, YOU ARE. I BROUGHT YOU HERE TO BE CURED.
KURT, YOU KNOW THAT IT'S VERY DANGEROUS TO BE TRAPPED IN A SMALL POD LAUNCHING INTO SPACE WITH A ZOMBIE ONBOARD.
BROTHER, YOU DON'T HAVE TO TELL ME! YOU WERE A REAL PAIN IN THE ASS.
THANK YOU, KURT. I MEAN... IF OUR ROLES WERE REVERSED--
--I PROBABLY WOULD HAVE PUT A BULLET IN YOUR HEAD, THINKING I WAS DOING YOU A FAVOR.
I--HOW CAN I EVER REPAY YOU FOR SAVING MY LIFE?
YOU BEING HERE RIGHT NOW IS ALL I NEED.
I'M GONNA THINK OF SOMETHING TO PAY YOU BACK, KURT.
NASA

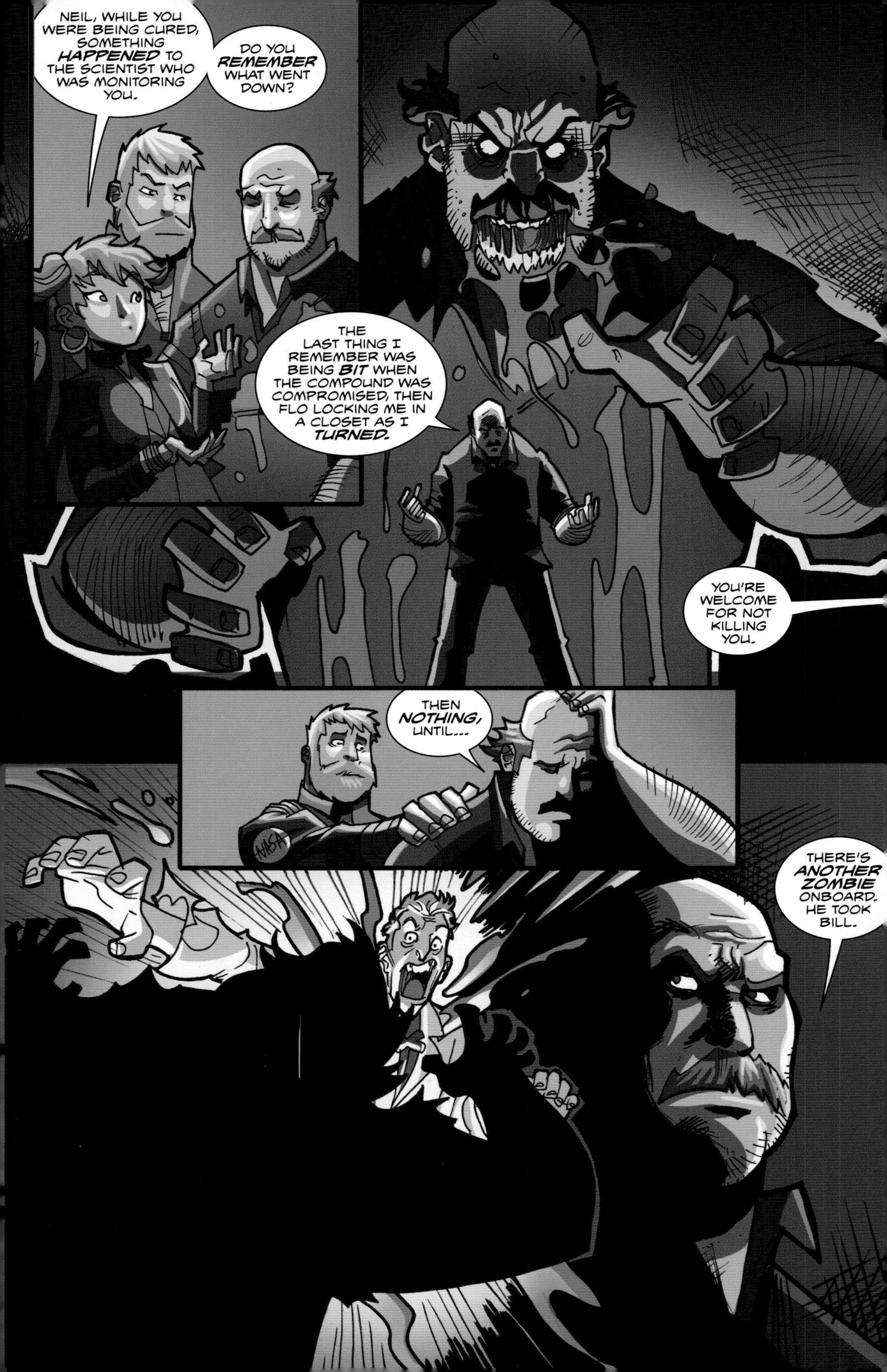
NEIL, WHILE YOU WERE BEING CURED, SOMETHING HAPPENED TO THE SCIENTIST WHO WAS MONITORING YOU.
DO YOU REMEMBER WHAT WENT DOWN?
THE LAST THING I REMEMBER WAS BEING BIT WHEN THE COMPOUND WAS COMPROMISED, THEN FLO LOCKING ME IN A CLOSET AS I TURNED.
YOU'RE WELCOME FOR NOT KILLING YOU.
THEN NOTHING, UNTIL...
NASA
THERE'S ANOTHER ZOMBIE ONBOARD. HE TOOK BILL.

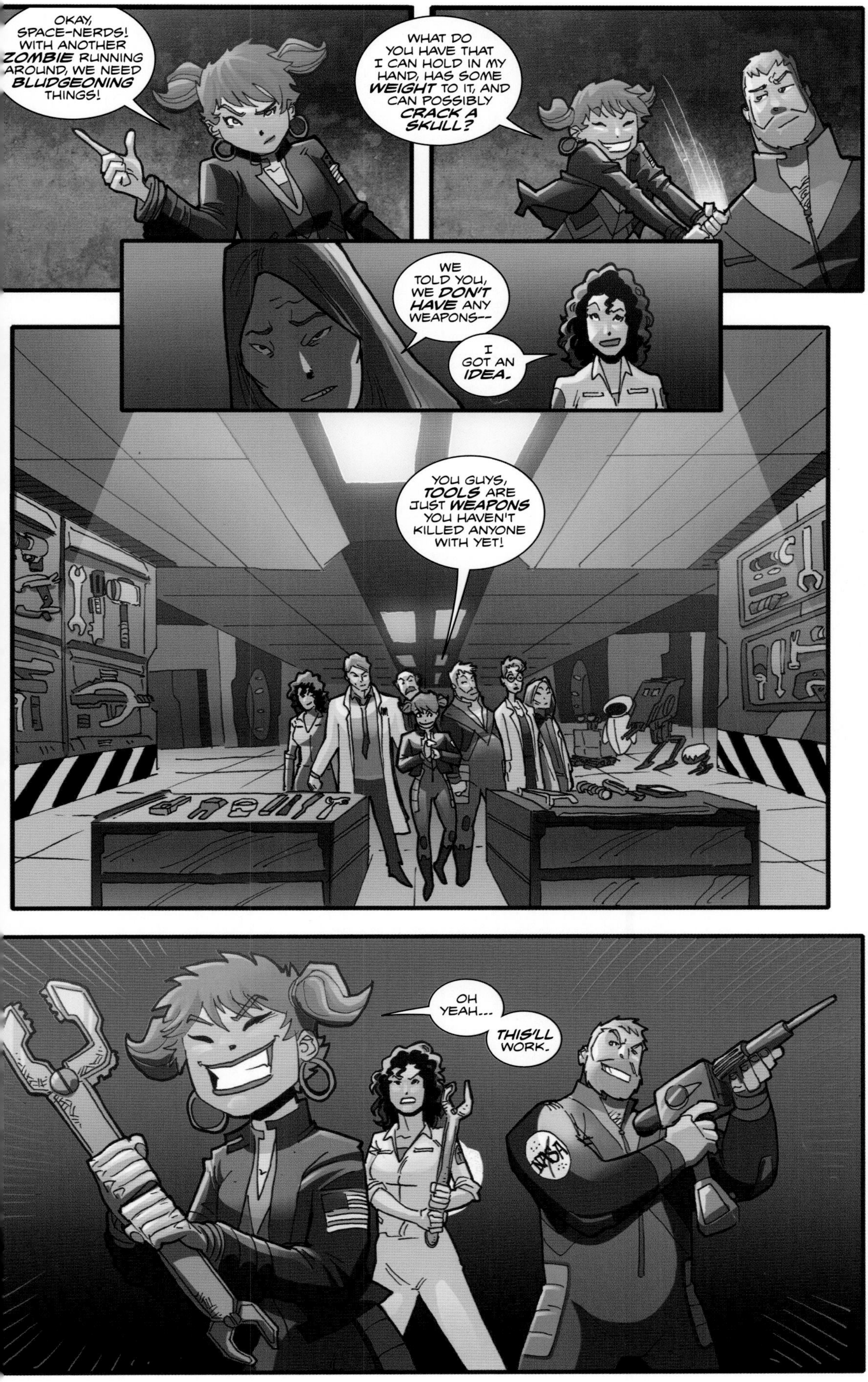
OKAY, SPACE-NERDS! WITH ANOTHER ZOMBIE RUNNING AROUND, WE NEED BLUDGEONING THINGS!
WHAT DO YOU HAVE THAT I CAN HOLD IN MY HAND, HAS SOME WEIGHT TO IT, AND CAN POSSIBLY CRACK A SKULL?
WE TOLD YOU, WE DON'T HAVE ANY WEAPONS--
I GOT AN IDEA.
YOU GUYS, TOOLS ARE JUST WEAPONS YOU HAVEN'T KILLED ANYONE WITH YET!
OH YEAH... THIS'LL WORK.

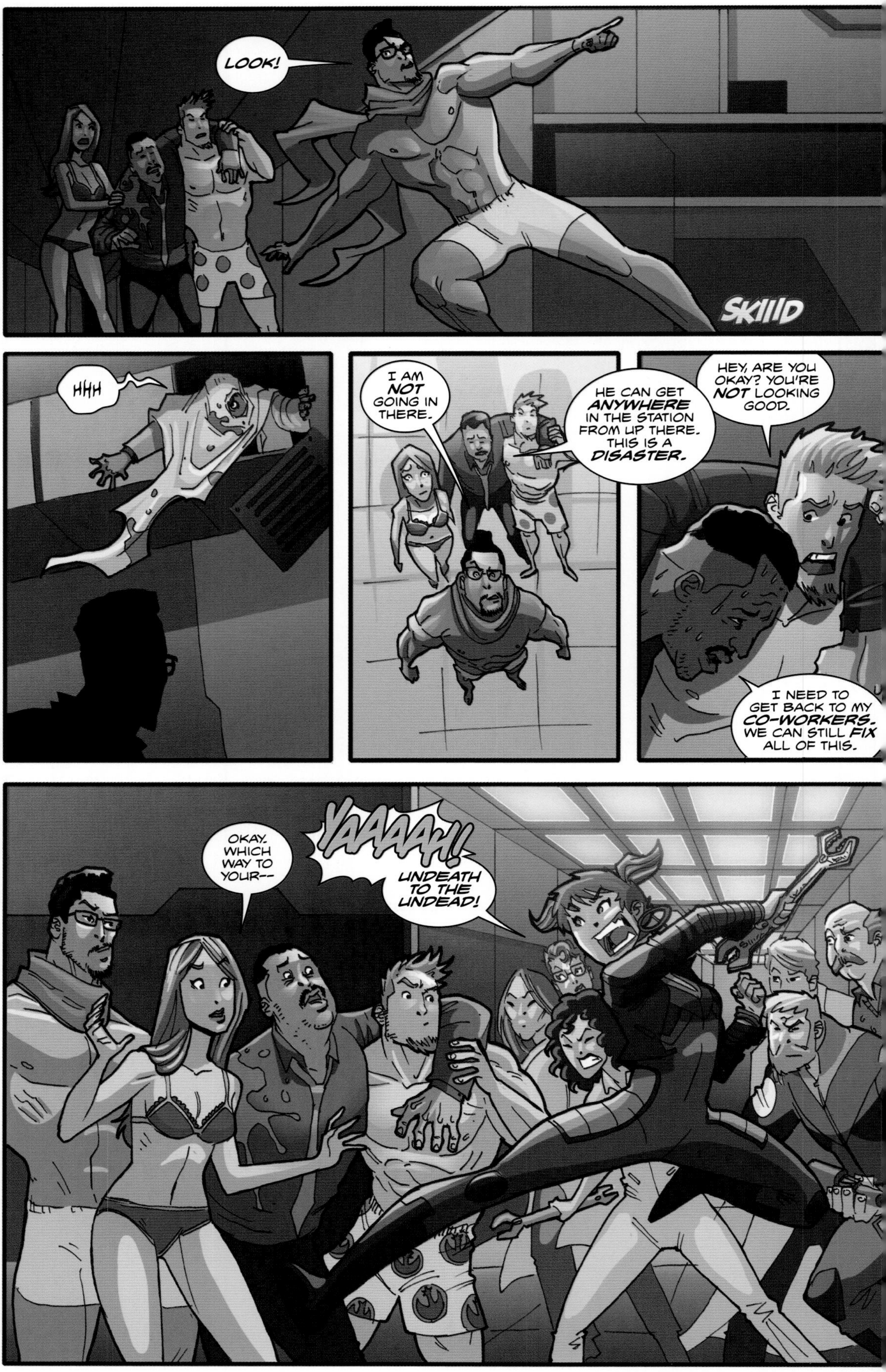
LOOK!
SKIIID
HHH
I AM NOT GOING IN THERE.
HE CAN GET ANYWHERE IN THE STATION FROM UP THERE. THIS IS A DISASTER.
HEY, ARE YOU OKAY? YOU'RE NOT LOOKING GOOD.
I NEED TO GET BACK TO MY CO-WORKERS. WE CAN STILL FIX ALL OF THIS.
OKAY. WHICH WAY TO YOUR--
YAAAAAH!
UNDEATH TO THE UNDEAD!

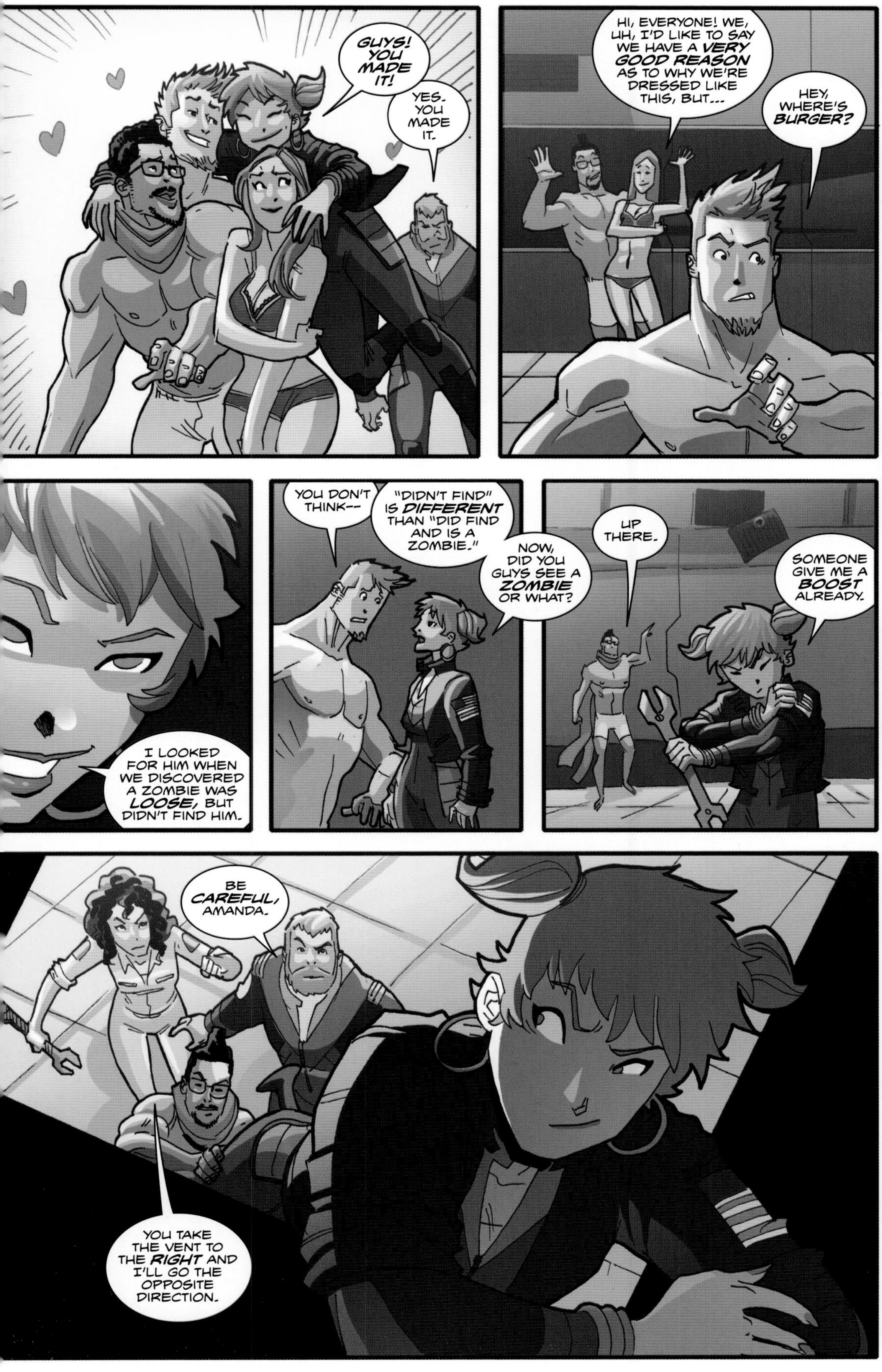
GUYS! YOU MADE IT!
YES. YOU MADE IT.
HI, EVERYONE! WE, UH, I'D LIKE TO SAY WE HAVE A VERY GOOD REASON AS TO WHY WE'RE DRESSED LIKE THIS, BUT...
HEY, WHERE'S BURGER?
I LOOKED FOR HIM WHEN WE DISCOVERED A ZOMBIE WAS LOOSE, BUT DIDN'T FIND HIM.
YOU DON'T THINK--
"DIDN'T FIND" IS DIFFERENT THAN "DID FIND AND IS A ZOMBIE."
NOW, DID YOU GUYS SEE A ZOMBIE OR WHAT?
UP THERE.
SOMEONE GIVE ME A BOOST ALREADY.
BE CAREFUL, AMANDA.
YOU TAKE THE VENT TO THE RIGHT AND I'LL GO THE OPPOSITE DIRECTION.

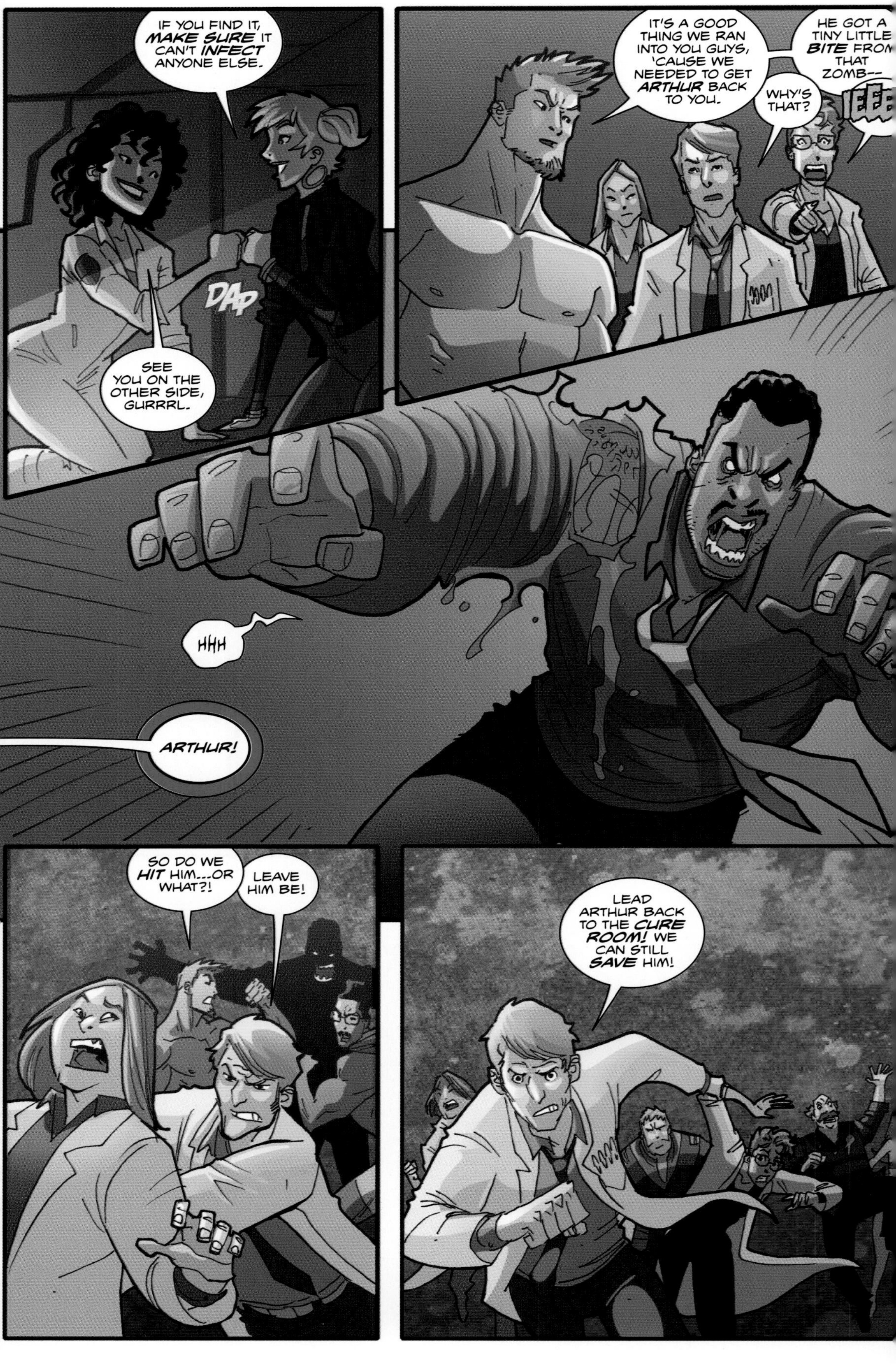
IF YOU FIND IT, MAKE SURE IT CAN'T INFECT ANYONE ELSE.
DAP
SEE YOU ON THE OTHER SIDE, GURRRL.
IT'S A GOOD THING WE RAN INTO YOU GUYS, 'CAUSE WE NEEDED TO GET ARTHUR BACK TO YOU.
WHY'S THAT?
HE GOT A TINY LITTLE BITE FROM THAT ZOMB--
IEEE
HHH
ARTHUR!
SO DO WE HIT HIM...OR WHAT?!
LEAVE HIM BE!
LEAD ARTHUR BACK TO THE CURE ROOM! WE CAN STILL SAVE HIM!

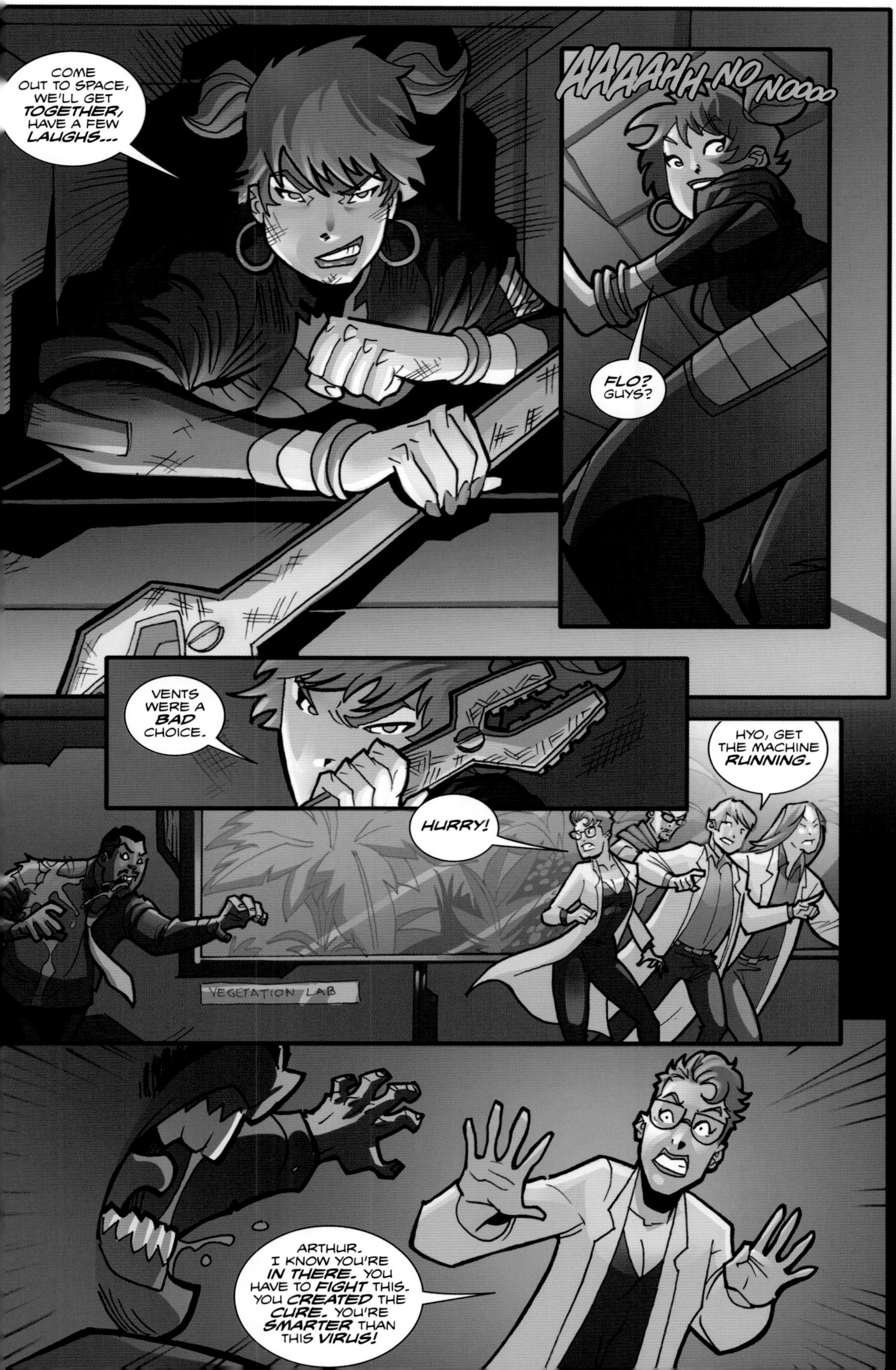

COME OUT TO SPACE, WE'LL GET TOGETHER, HAVE A FEW LAUGHS...
AAAAHH NO NOooo
FLO? GUYS?
VENTS WERE A BAD CHOICE.
HYO, GET THE MACHINE RUNNING.
HURRY!
VEGETATION LAB
ARTHUR. I KNOW YOU'RE IN THERE. YOU HAVE TO FIGHT THIS. YOU CREATED THE CURE. YOU'RE SMARTER THAN THIS VIRUS!

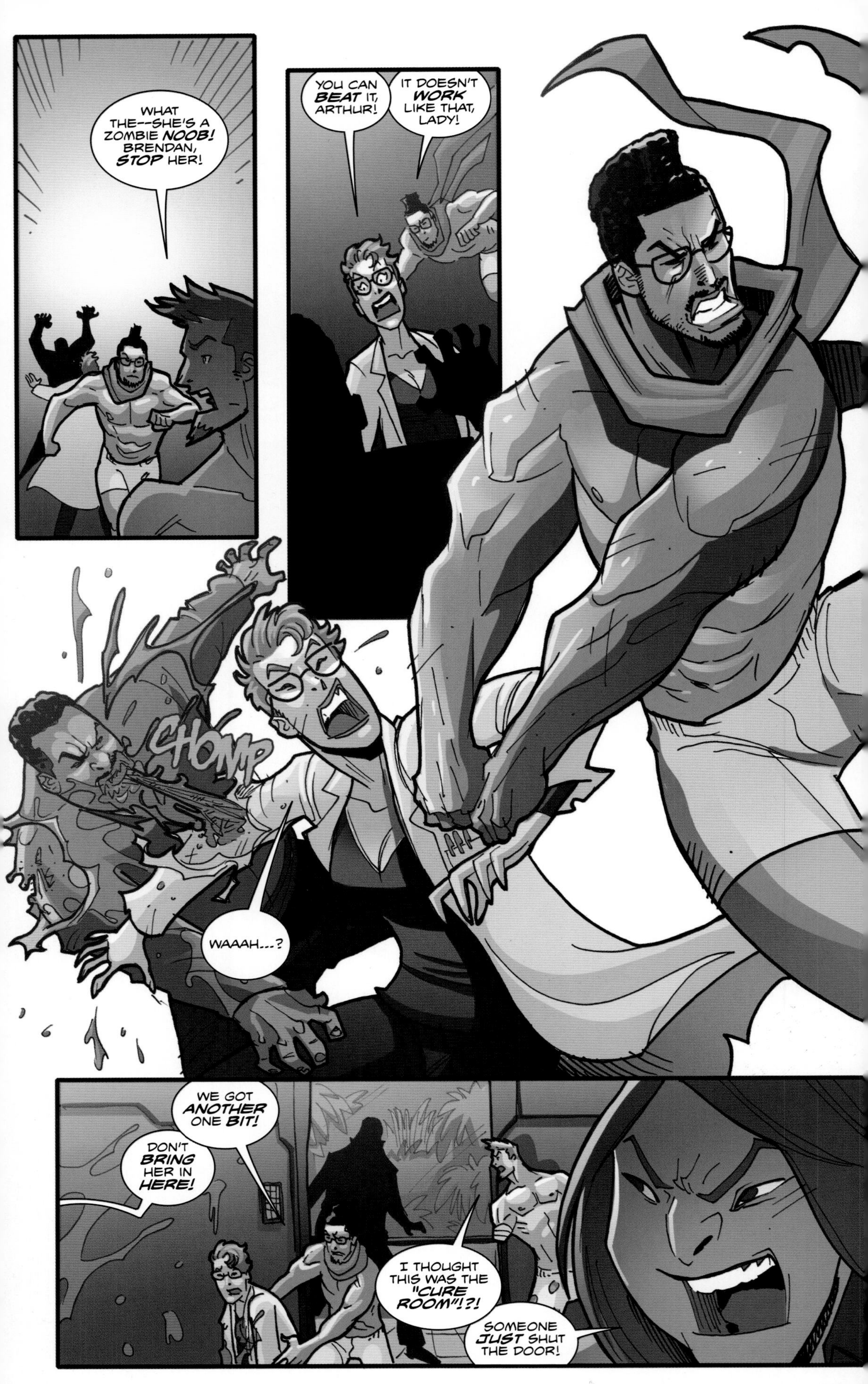
WHAT THE--SHE'S A ZOMBIE NOOB! BRENDAN, STOP HER!
YOU CAN BEAT IT, ARTHUR!
IT DOESN'T WORK LIKE THAT, LADY!
CHOMP
WAAAH...?
WE GOT ANOTHER ONE BIT!
DON'T BRING HER IN HERE!
I THOUGHT THIS WAS THE "CURE ROOM"!?!
SOMEONE JUST SHUT THE DOOR!

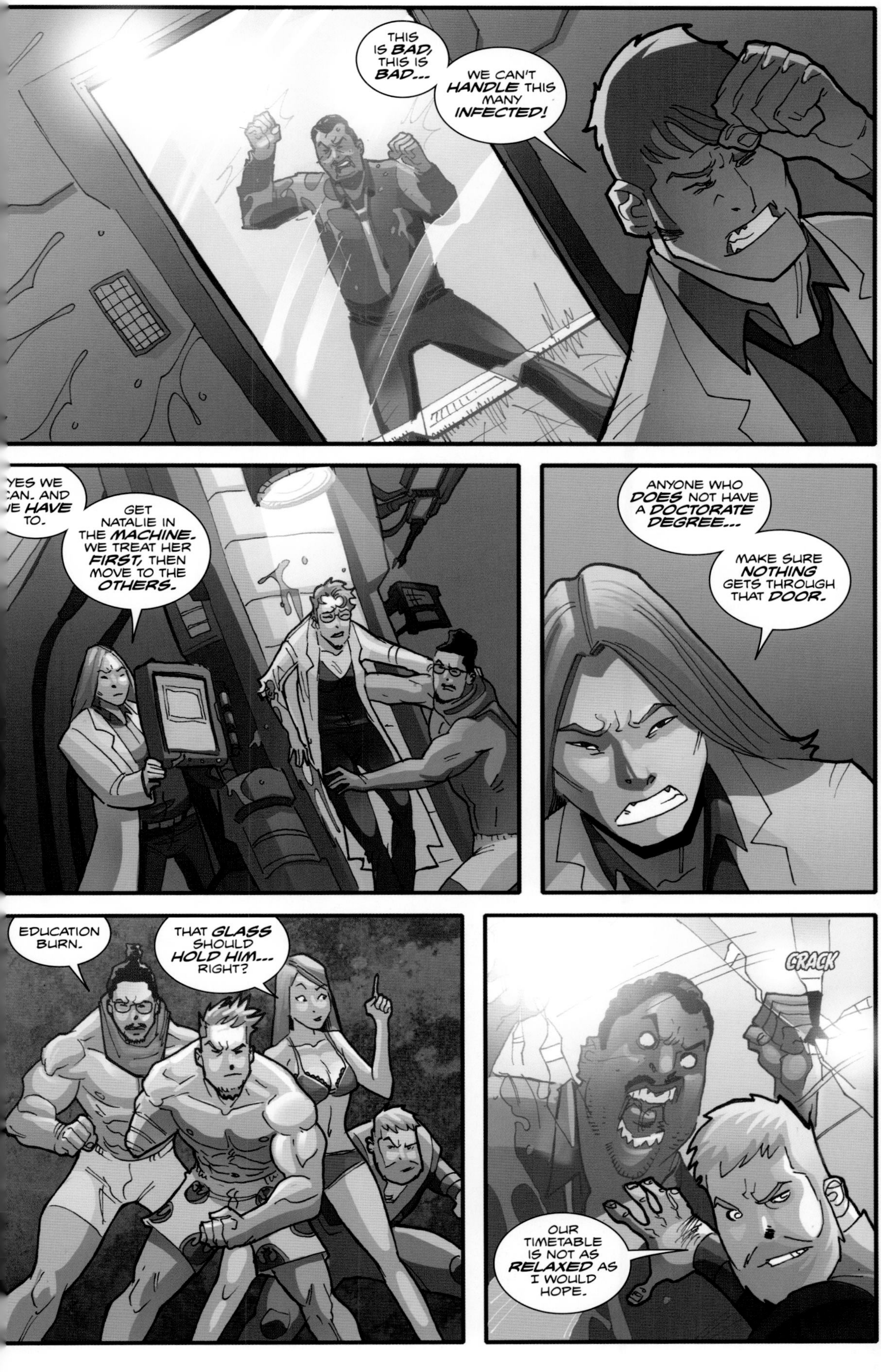
THIS IS BAD, THIS IS BAD...
WE CAN'T HANDLE THIS MANY INFECTED!
YES WE CAN. AND WE HAVE TO.
GET NATALIE IN THE MACHINE. WE TREAT HER FIRST, THEN MOVE TO THE OTHERS.
ANYONE WHO DOES NOT HAVE A DOCTORATE DEGREE...
MAKE SURE NOTHING GETS THROUGH THAT DOOR.
EDUCATION BURN.
THAT GLASS SHOULD HOLD HIM... RIGHT?
CRACK
OUR TIMETABLE IS NOT AS RELAXED AS I WOULD HOPE.

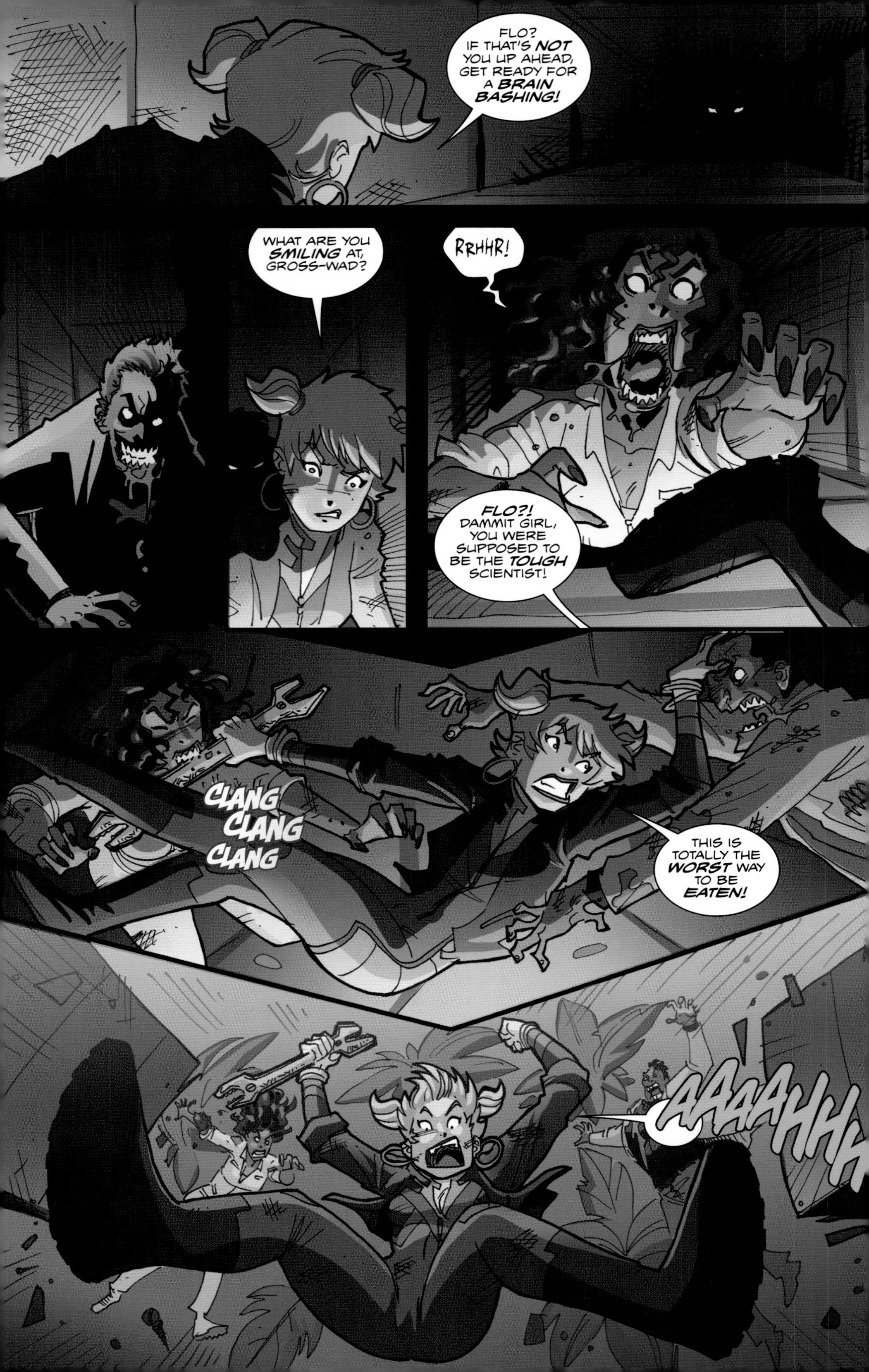
FLO? IF THAT'S NOT YOU UP AHEAD, GET READY FOR A BRAIN BASHING!
WHAT ARE YOU SMILING AT, GROSS-WAD?
RRHHR!
FLO?! DAMMIT GIRL, YOU WERE SUPPOSED TO BE THE TOUGH SCIENTIST!
CLANG
CLANG
CLANG
THIS IS TOTALLY THE WORST WAY TO BE EATEN!
AAAAHHH

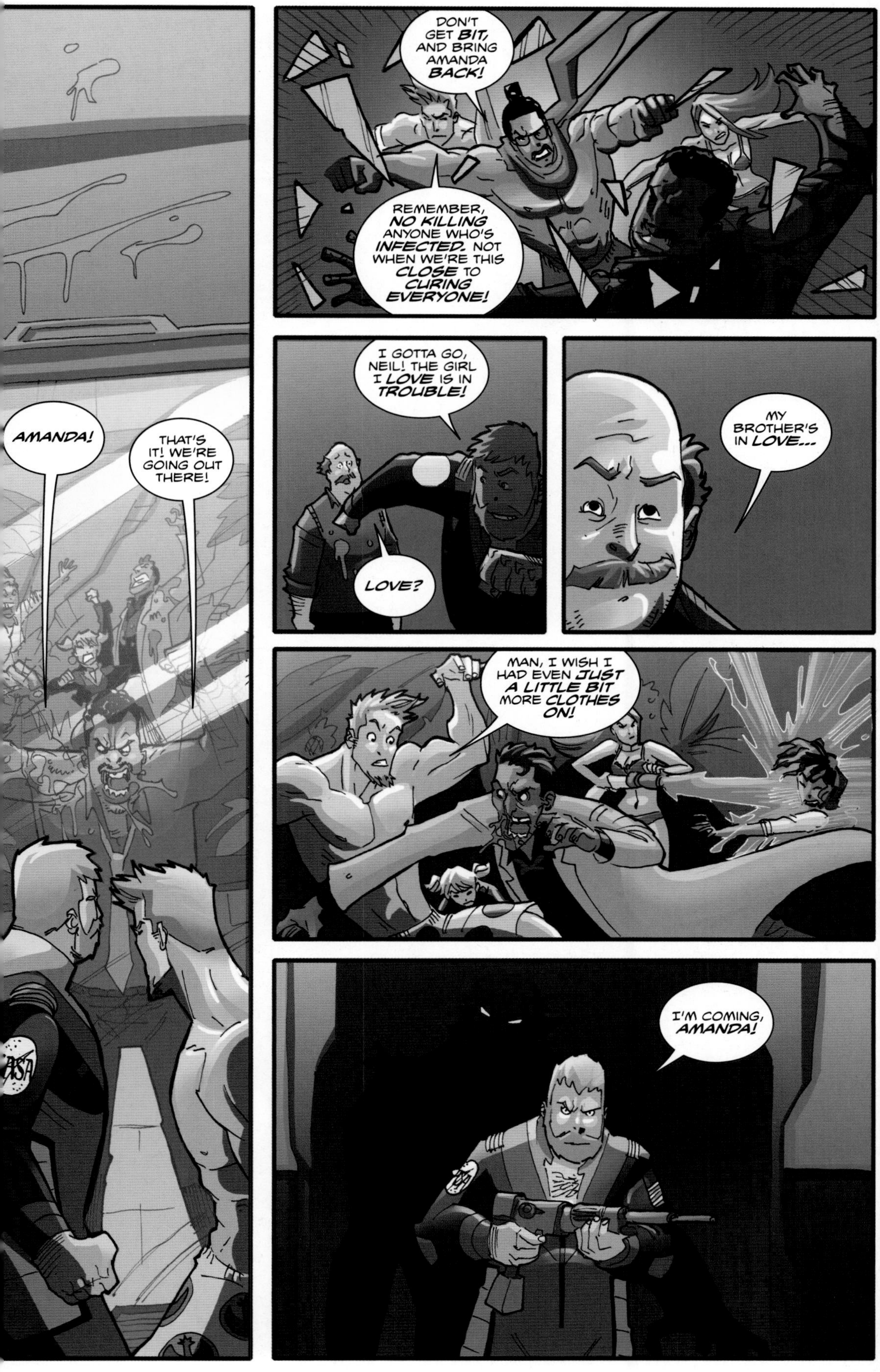
AMANDA!
THAT'S IT! WE'RE GOING OUT THERE!
DON'T GET BIT, AND BRING AMANDA BACK!
REMEMBER, NO KILLING ANYONE WHO'S INFECTED. NOT WHEN WE'RE THIS CLOSE TO CURING EVERYONE!
I GOTTA GO, NEIL! THE GIRL I LOVE IS IN TROUBLE!
LOVE?
MY BROTHER'S IN LOVE...
MAN, I WISH I HAD EVEN JUST A LITTLE BIT MORE CLOTHES ON!
I'M COMING, AMANDA!

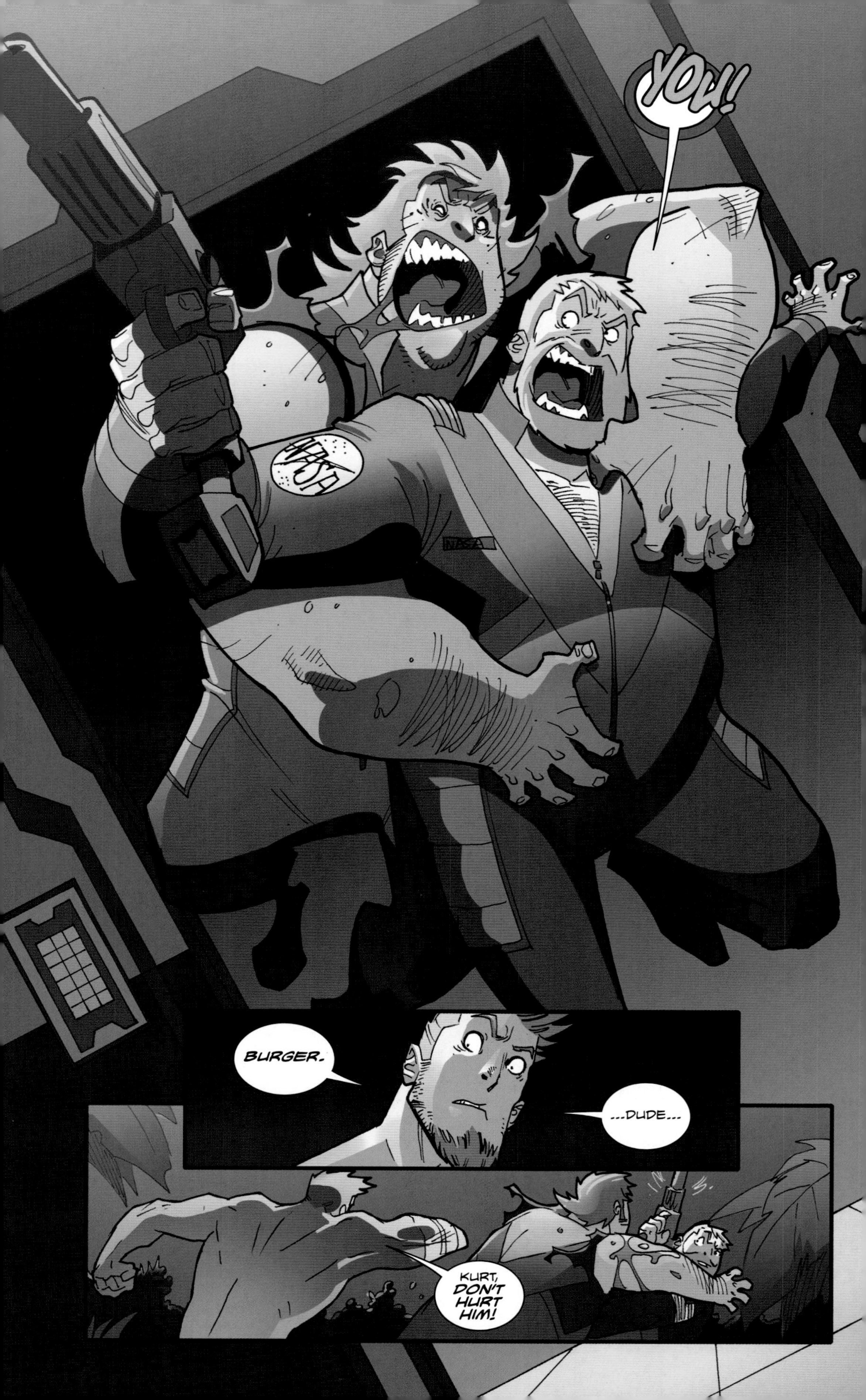

YOW!
NASA
NASA
BURGER.
...DUDE...
KURT, DON'T HURT HIM!

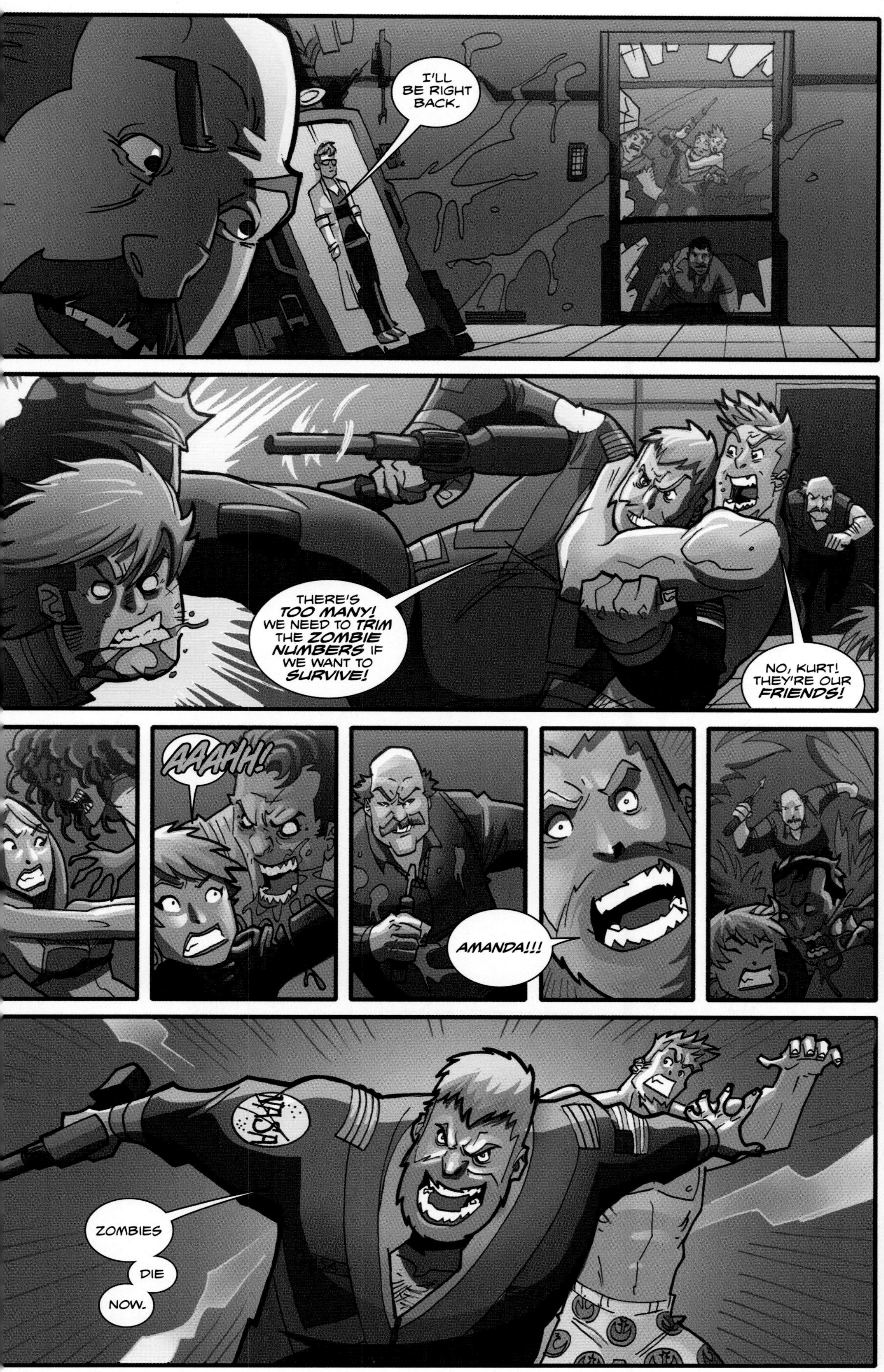
I'LL BE RIGHT BACK.
THERE'S TOO MANY! WE NEED TO TRIM THE ZOMBIE NUMBERS IF WE WANT TO SURVIVE!
NO, KURT! THEY'RE OUR FRIENDS!
AAAHH!
AMANDA!!!
ZOMBIES
DIE
NOW.

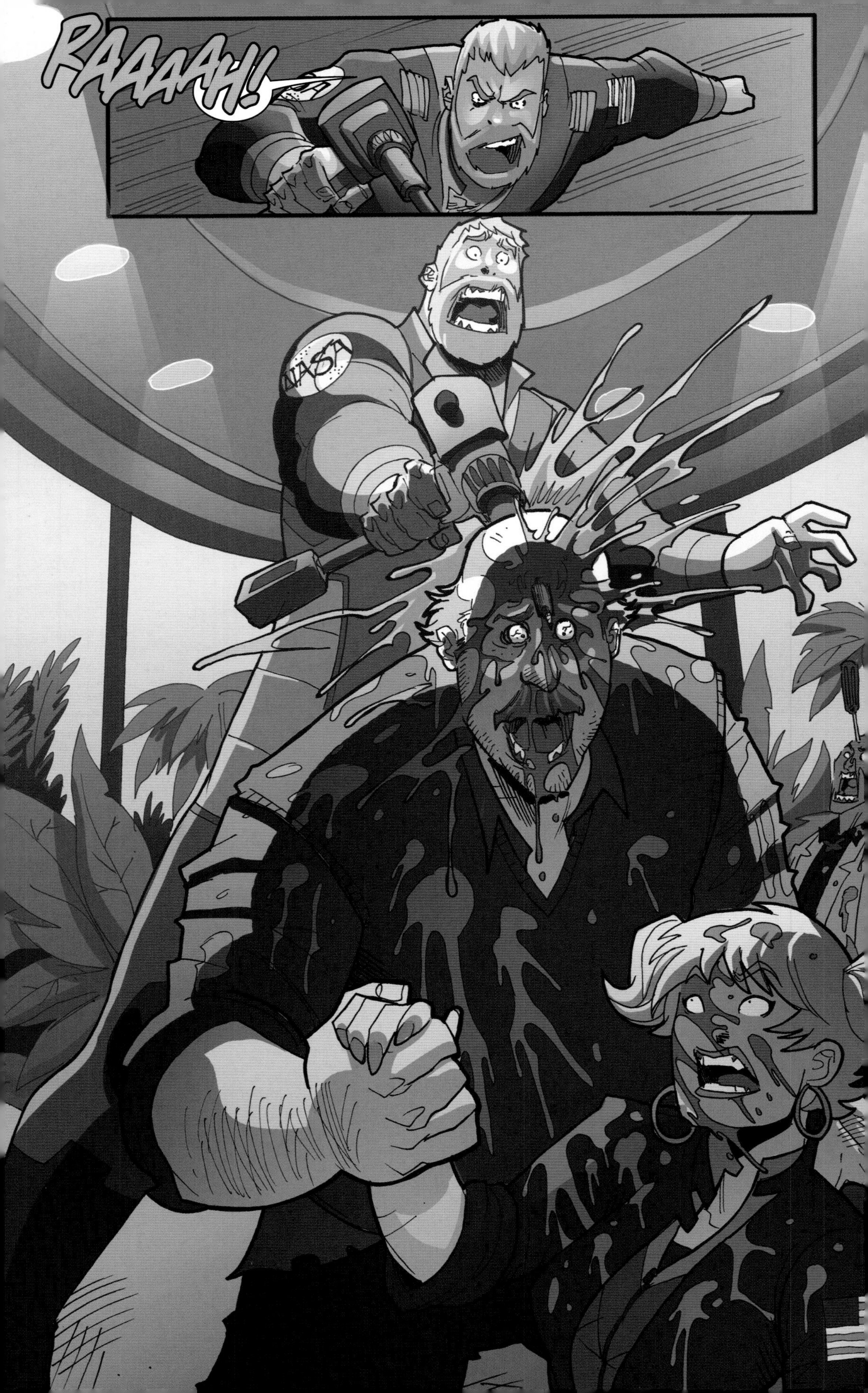
RAAAAH!

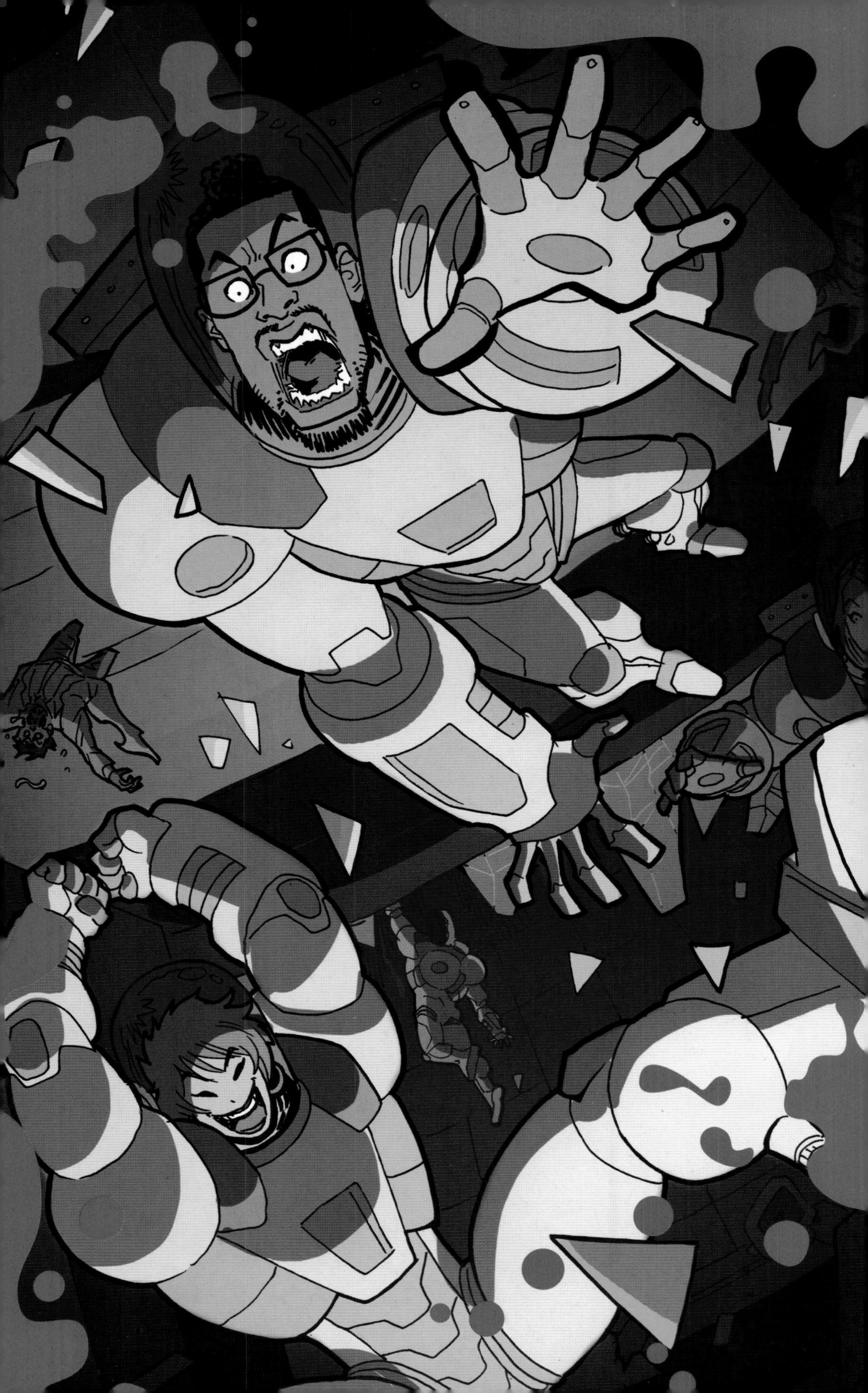

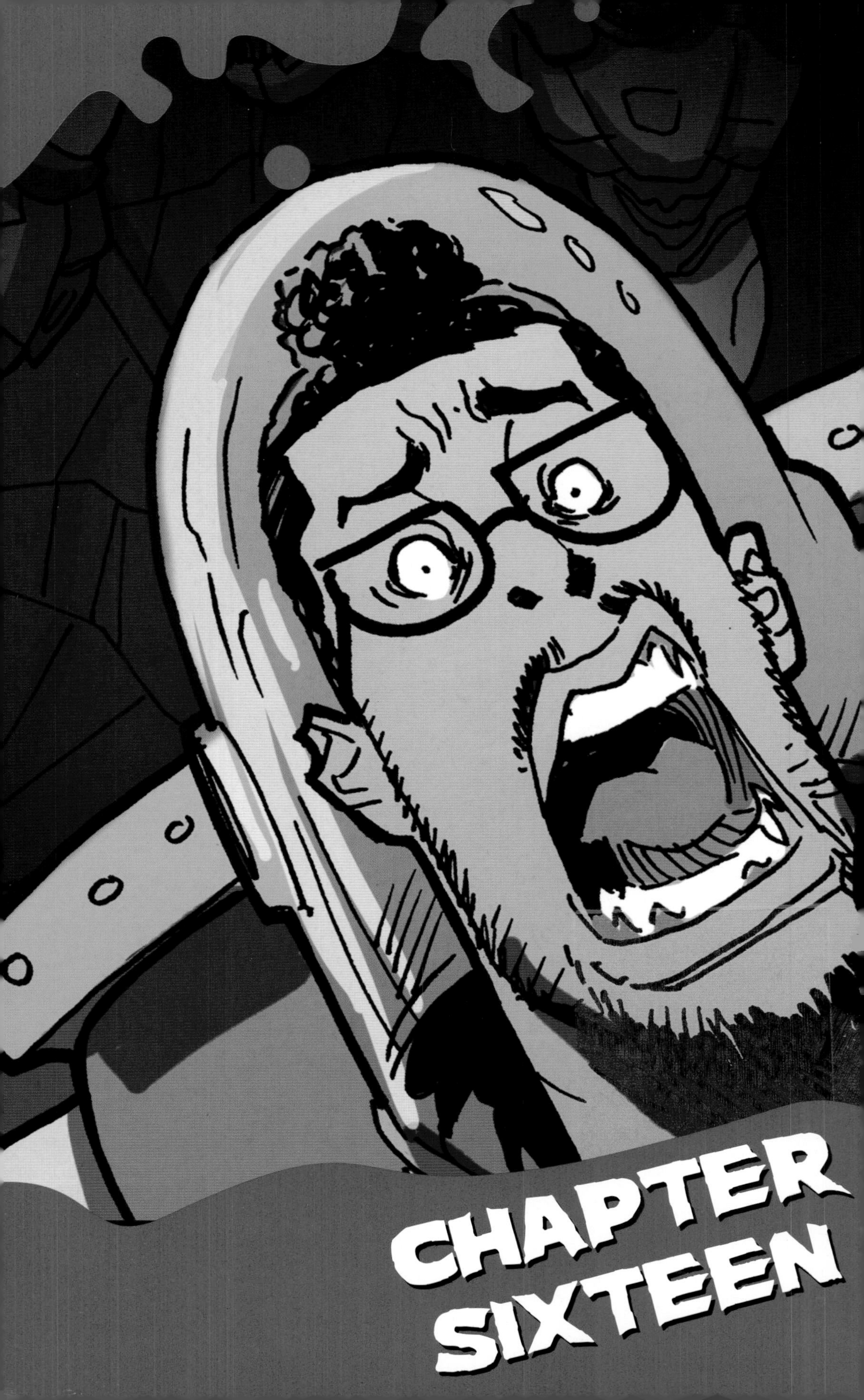

CHAPTER SIXTEEN

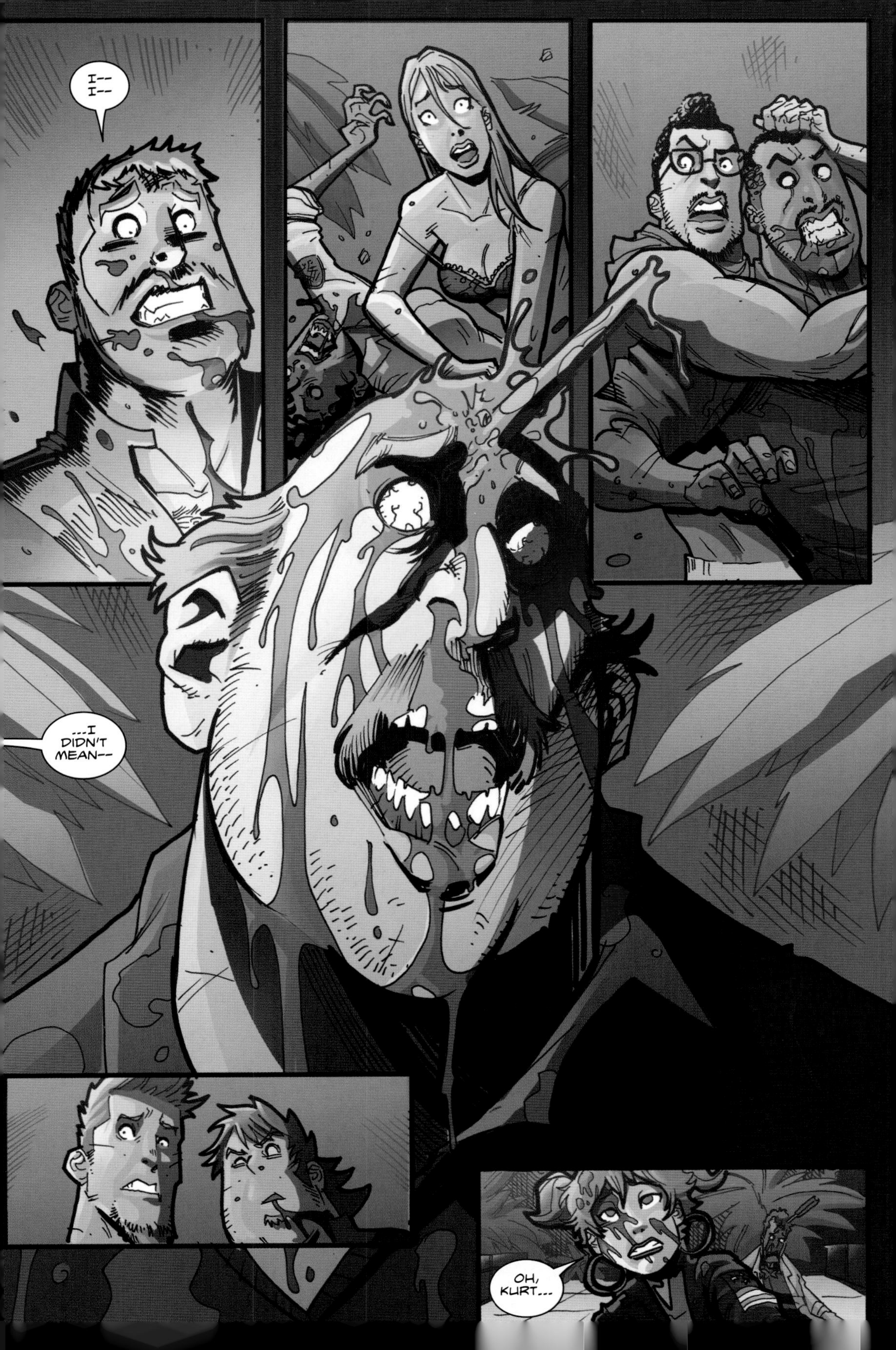
I--
I--
...I DIDN'T MEAN--
OH, KURT...

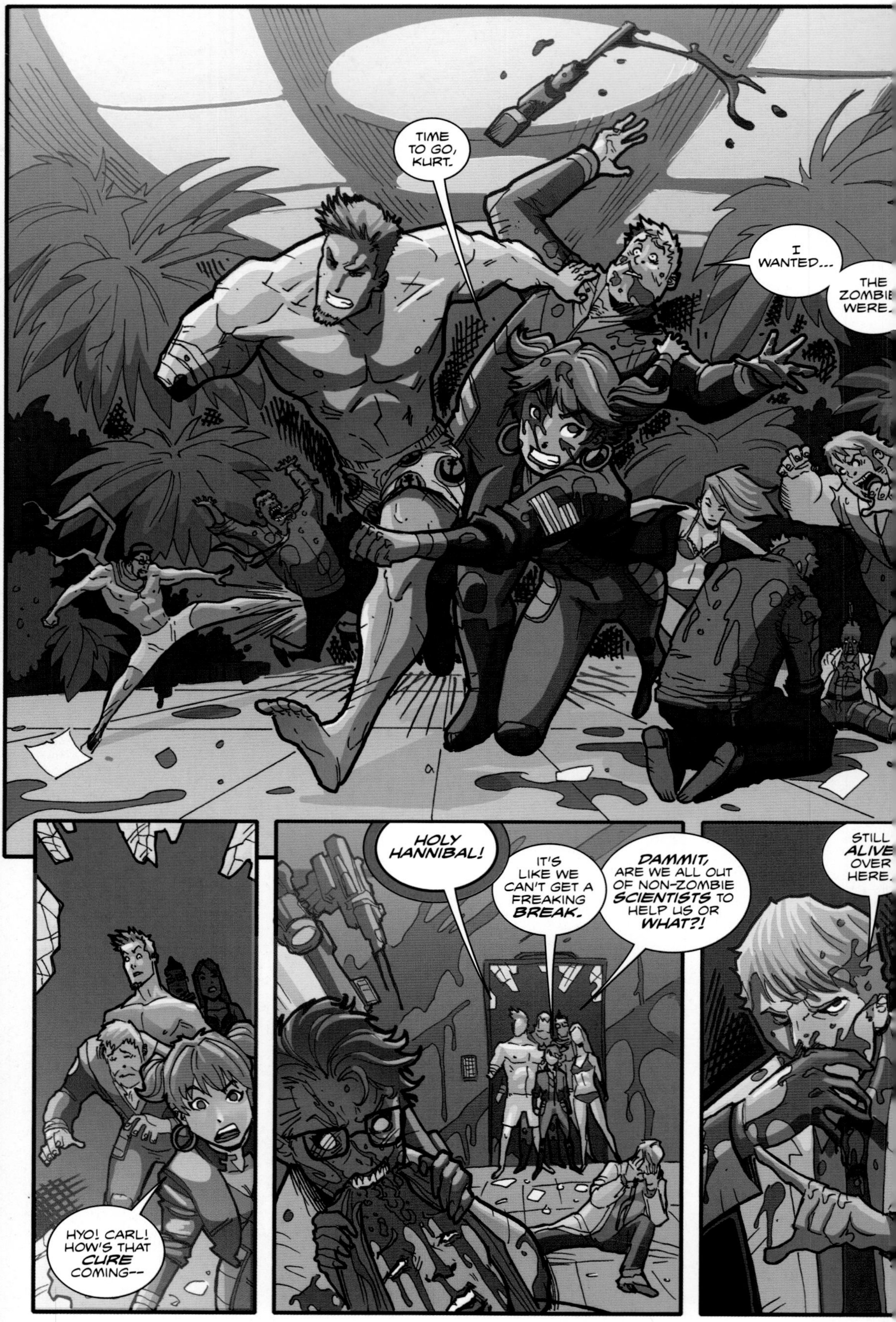
TIME TO GO, KURT.
I WANTED...
THE ZOMBIE WERE.
HYO! CARL! HOW'S THAT CURE COMING--
HOLY HANNIBAL!
IT'S LIKE WE CAN'T GET A FREAKING BREAK.
DAMMIT, ARE WE ALL OUT OF NON-ZOMBIE SCIENTISTS TO HELP US OR WHAT?!
STILL ALIVE OVER HERE.

THIS IS A *MESS!* SPACE IS NOT AT *ALL* WHAT I THOUGHT IT WOULD BE LIKE.

CARL, WHERE CAN WE GO TO BE *SAFE?*

IN HERE. THE STATION'S *CENTRAL COMMAND* ROOM.

CARL, ARE YOU *OKAY?* WHAT *HAPPENED?*

WHILE HYO AND I WERE PREPPING THE MACHINE, NATALIE *TURNED* AND ATTACKED US.

NATALIE *BIT* ME IN THE *FACE* AND THEN CRACKED OPEN HYO'S HEAD.

I DON'T HAVE MUCH TIME.

DUDE, HOW MUCH DOES THAT *HURT* RIGHT NOW? YOU'RE A *TROOPER.*

CARL, IF WE *LOSE* YOU...HOW CAN WE RUN THE *CURE MACHINE* AND FIX EVERYONE?

OKAY... *PAY* ATTENTION NOW...

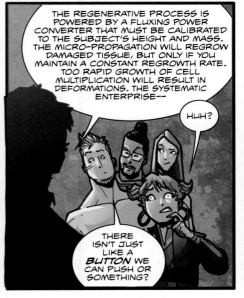

THE REGENERATIVE PROCESS IS POWERED BY A FLUXING POWER CONVERTER THAT MUST BE CALIBRATED TO THE SUBJECT'S HEIGHT AND MASS. THE MICRO-PROPAGATION WILL REGROW DAMAGED TISSUE, BUT ONLY IF YOU MAINTAIN A CONSTANT REGROWTH RATE. TOO RAPID GROWTH OF CELL MULTIPLICATION WILL RESULT IN DEFORMATIONS. THE SYSTEMATIC ENTERPRISE--

HUH?

THERE ISN'T JUST LIKE A *BUTTON* WE CAN PUSH OR SOMETHING?

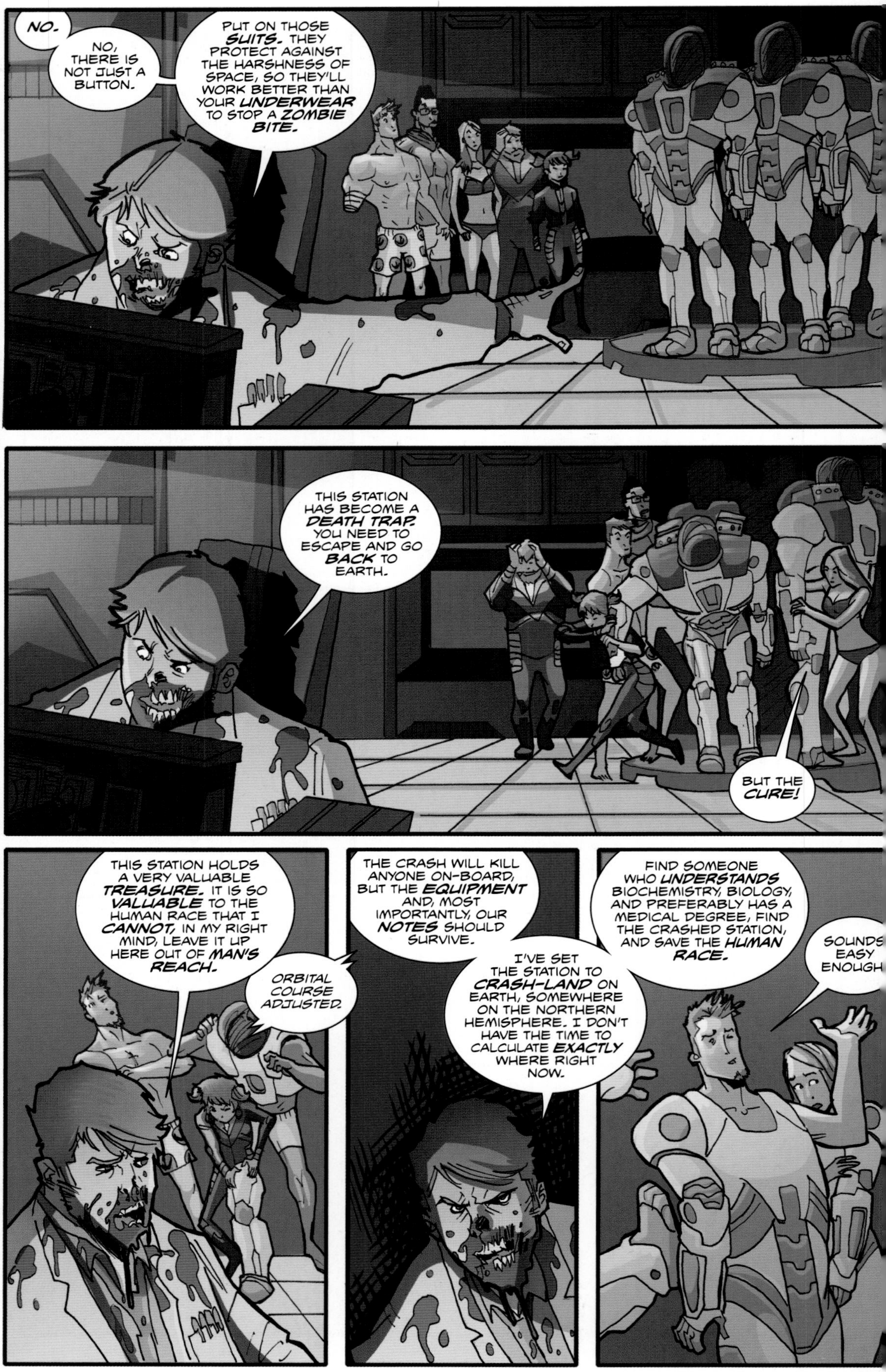

NO.
NO, THERE IS NOT JUST A BUTTON.
PUT ON THOSE SUITS. THEY PROTECT AGAINST THE HARSHNESS OF SPACE, SO THEY'LL WORK BETTER THAN YOUR UNDERWEAR TO STOP A ZOMBIE BITE.
THIS STATION HAS BECOME A DEATH TRAP. YOU NEED TO ESCAPE AND GO BACK TO EARTH.
BUT THE CURE!
THIS STATION HOLDS A VERY VALUABLE TREASURE. IT IS SO VALUABLE TO THE HUMAN RACE THAT I CANNOT, IN MY RIGHT MIND, LEAVE IT UP HERE OUT OF MAN'S REACH.
ORBITAL COURSE ADJUSTED.
THE CRASH WILL KILL ANYONE ON-BOARD, BUT THE EQUIPMENT AND, MOST IMPORTANTLY, OUR NOTES SHOULD SURVIVE.
I'VE SET THE STATION TO CRASH-LAND ON EARTH, SOMEWHERE ON THE NORTHERN HEMISPHERE. I DON'T HAVE THE TIME TO CALCULATE EXACTLY WHERE RIGHT NOW.
FIND SOMEONE WHO UNDERSTANDS BIOCHEMISTRY, BIOLOGY, AND PREFERABLY HAS A MEDICAL DEGREE, FIND THE CRASHED STATION, AND SAVE THE HUMAN RACE.
SOUNDS EASY ENOUGH

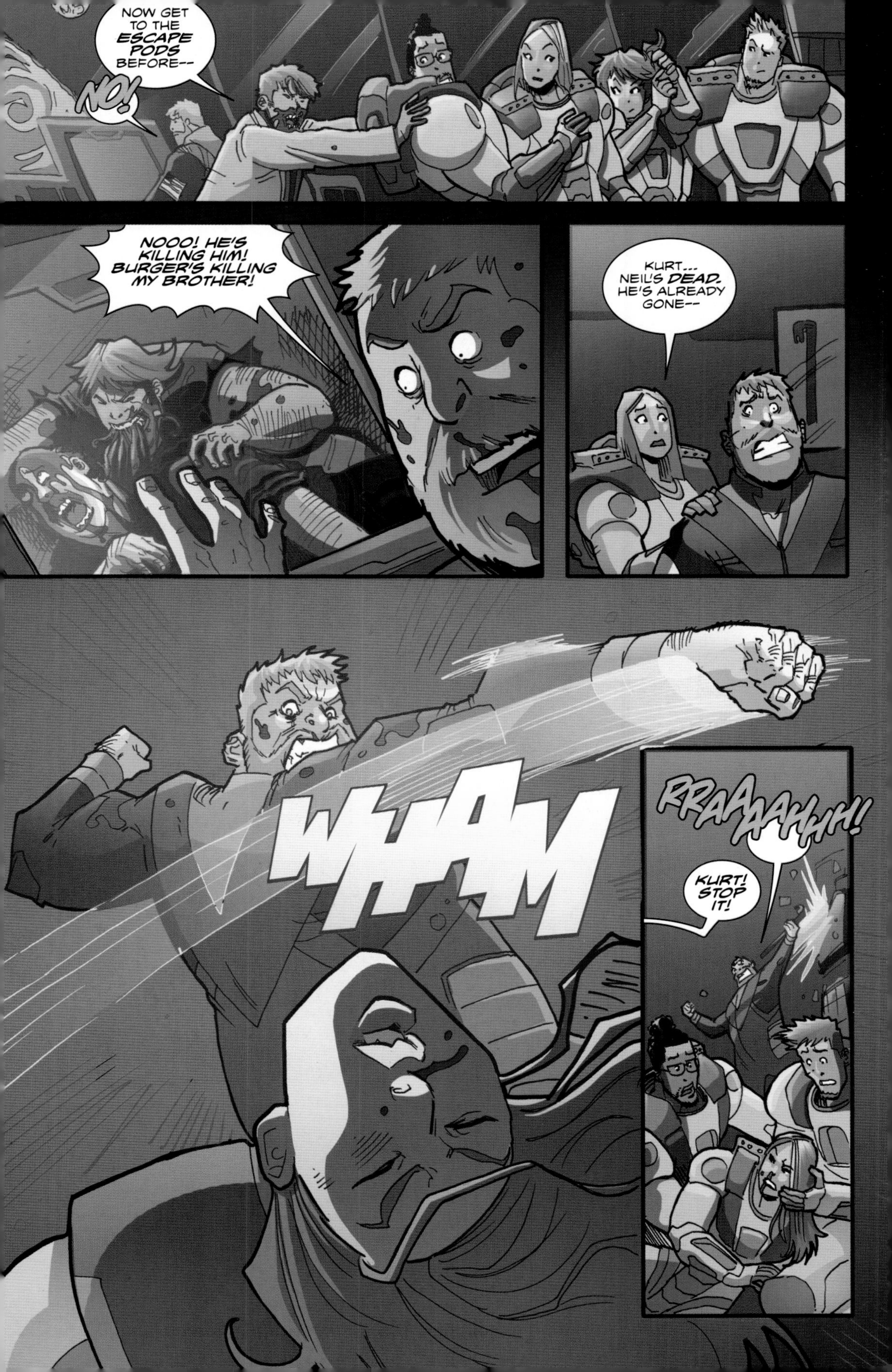
NOW GET TO THE ESCAPE PODS BEFORE--
NO!
NOOO! HE'S KILLING HIM! BURGER'S KILLING MY BROTHER!
KURT... NEIL'S DEAD. HE'S ALREADY GONE--
WHAM
RRAAAAAHHH!
KURT! STOP IT!

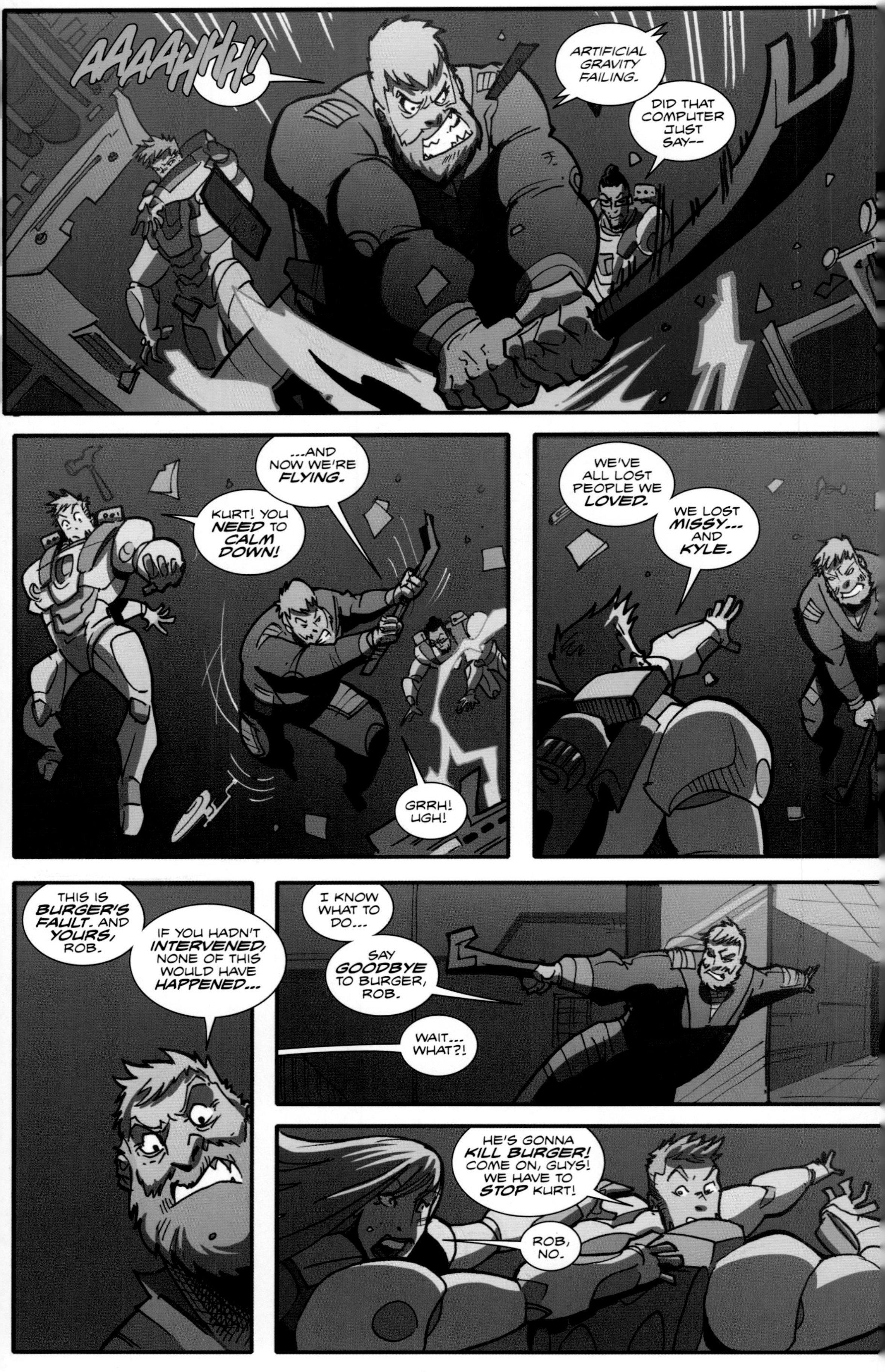
AAAAHHH!
ARTIFICIAL GRAVITY FAILING.
DID THAT COMPUTER JUST SAY--
...AND NOW WE'RE FLYING.
KURT! YOU NEED TO CALM DOWN!
GRRH! UGH!
WE'VE ALL LOST PEOPLE WE LOVED.
WE LOST MISSY... AND KYLE.
THIS IS BURGER'S FAULT. AND YOURS, ROB.
IF YOU HADN'T INTERVENED, NONE OF THIS WOULD HAVE HAPPENED...
I KNOW WHAT TO DO...
SAY GOODBYE TO BURGER, ROB.
WAIT... WHAT?!
HE'S GONNA KILL BURGER! COME ON, GUYS! WE HAVE TO STOP KURT!
ROB, NO.

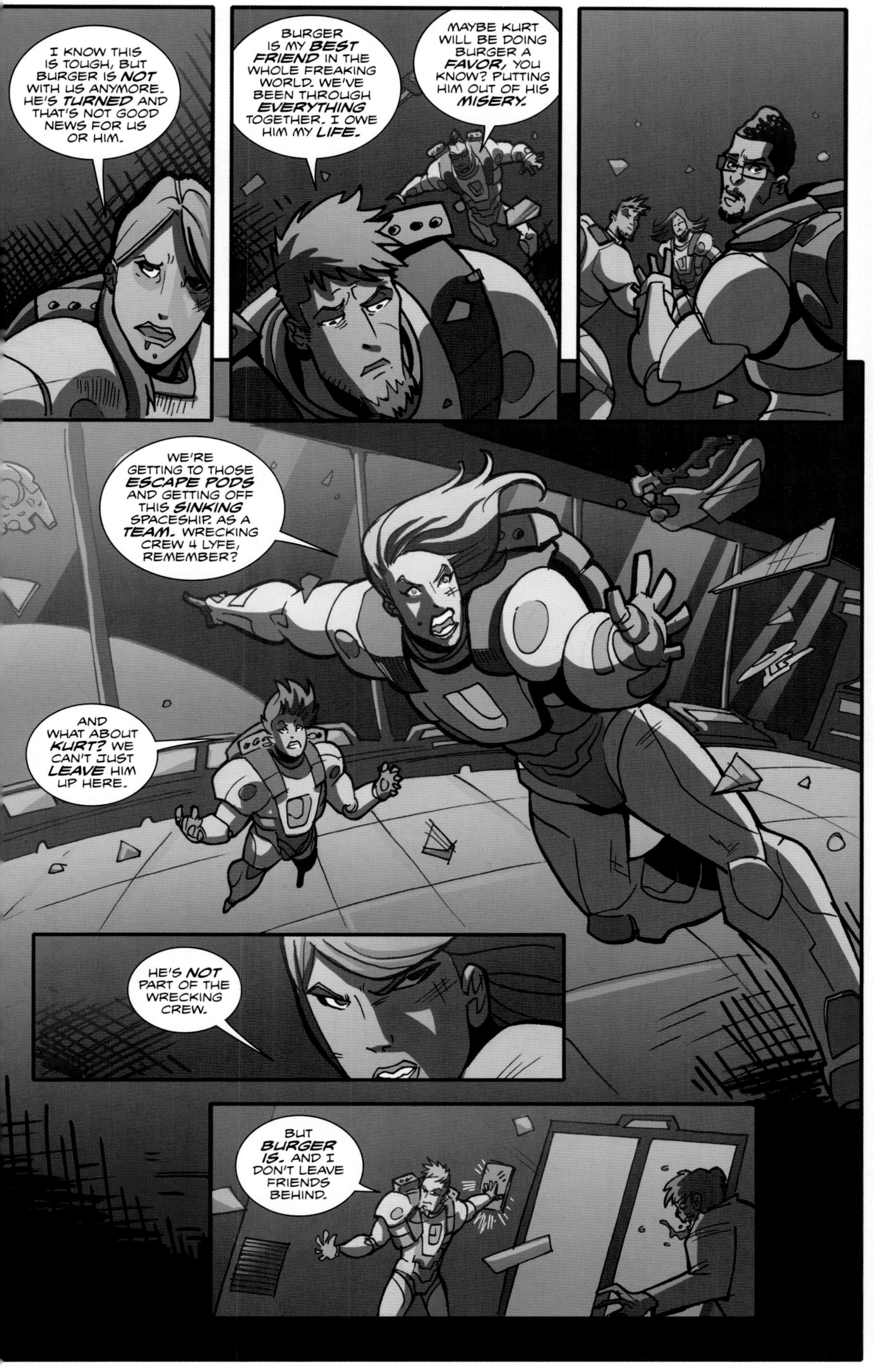
I KNOW THIS IS TOUGH, BUT BURGER IS NOT WITH US ANYMORE. HE'S TURNED AND THAT'S NOT GOOD NEWS FOR US OR HIM.
BURGER IS MY BEST FRIEND IN THE WHOLE FREAKING WORLD. WE'VE BEEN THROUGH EVERYTHING TOGETHER. I OWE HIM MY LIFE.
MAYBE KURT WILL BE DOING BURGER A FAVOR, YOU KNOW? PUTTING HIM OUT OF HIS MISERY.
WE'RE GETTING TO THOSE ESCAPE PODS AND GETTING OFF THIS SINKING SPACESHIP. AS A TEAM. WRECKING CREW 4 LYFE, REMEMBER?
AND WHAT ABOUT KURT? WE CAN'T JUST LEAVE HIM UP HERE.
HE'S NOT PART OF THE WRECKING CREW.
BUT BURGER IS. AND I DON'T LEAVE FRIENDS BEHIND.

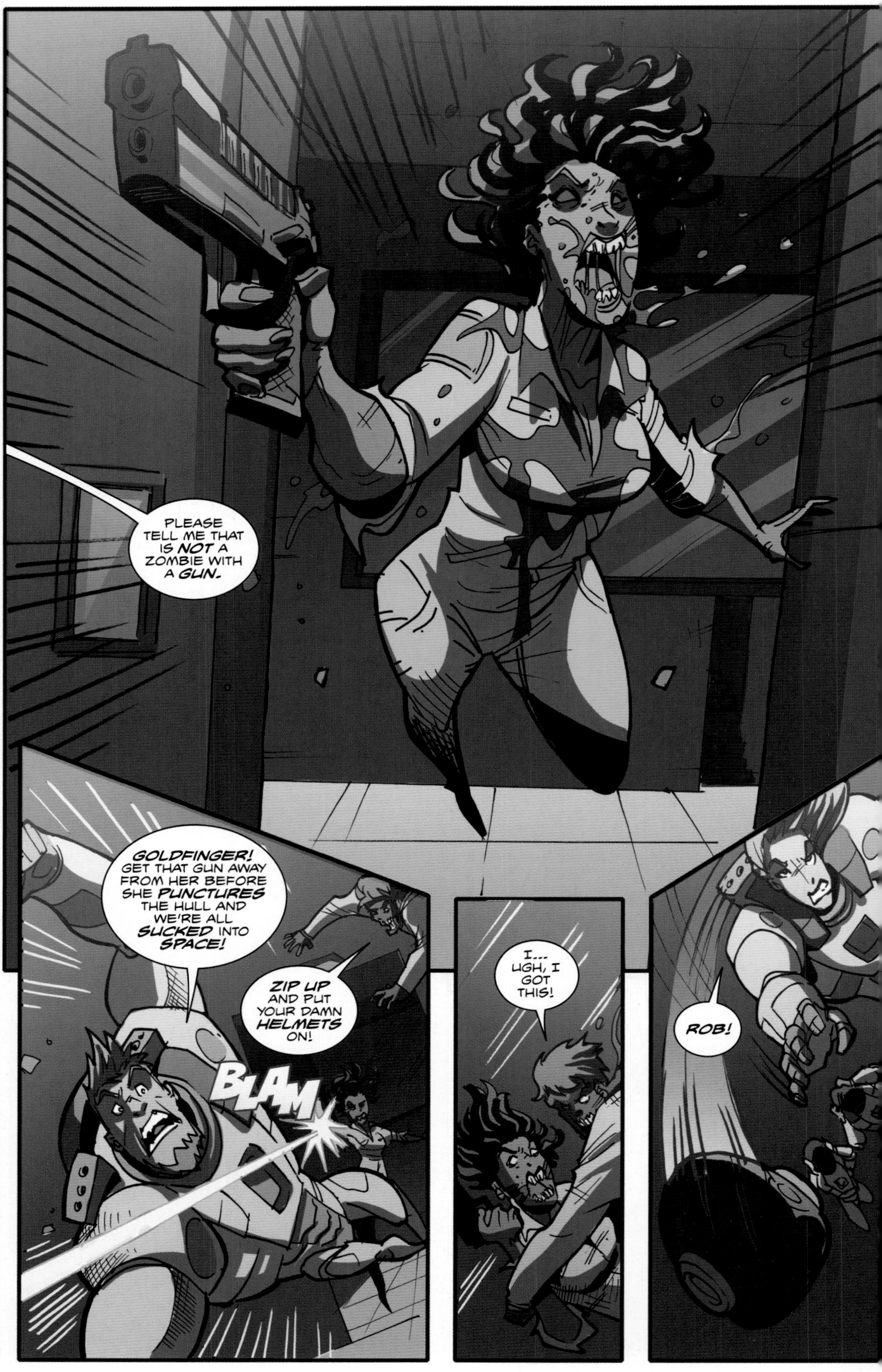
PLEASE TELL ME THAT IS NOT A ZOMBIE WITH A GUN.
GOLDFINGER! GET THAT GUN AWAY FROM HER BEFORE SHE PUNCTURES THE HULL AND WE'RE ALL SUCKED INTO SPACE!
ZIP UP AND PUT YOUR DAMN HELMETS ON!
BLAM
I... UGH, I GOT THIS!
ROB!

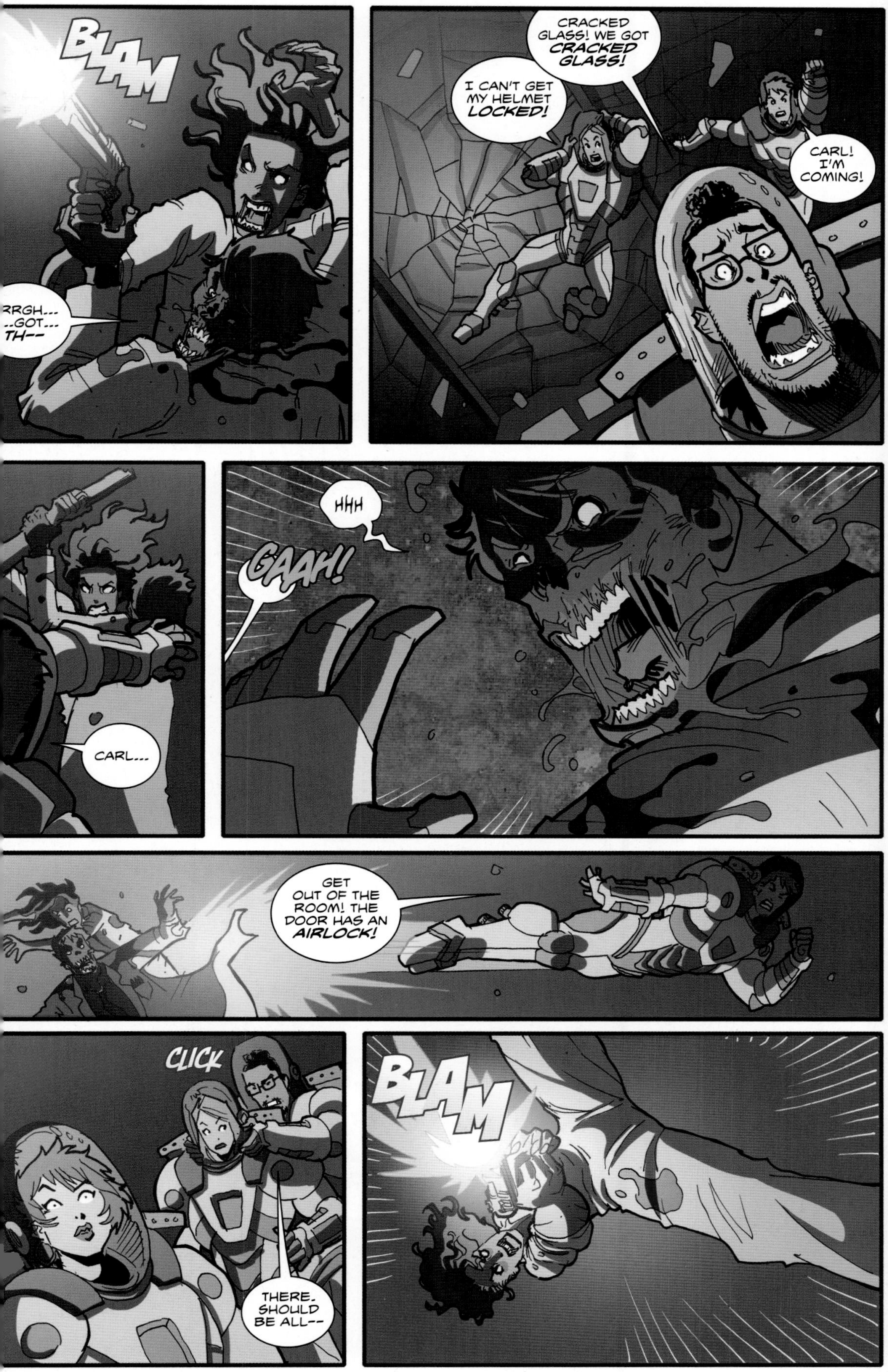
BLAM
RRGH... ...GOT... TH--
CRACKED GLASS! WE GOT CRACKED GLASS!
I CAN'T GET MY HELMET LOCKED!
CARL! I'M COMING!
HHH
GAAH!
CARL...
GET OUT OF THE ROOM! THE DOOR HAS AN AIRLOCK!
CLICK
THERE. SHOULD BE ALL--
BLAM

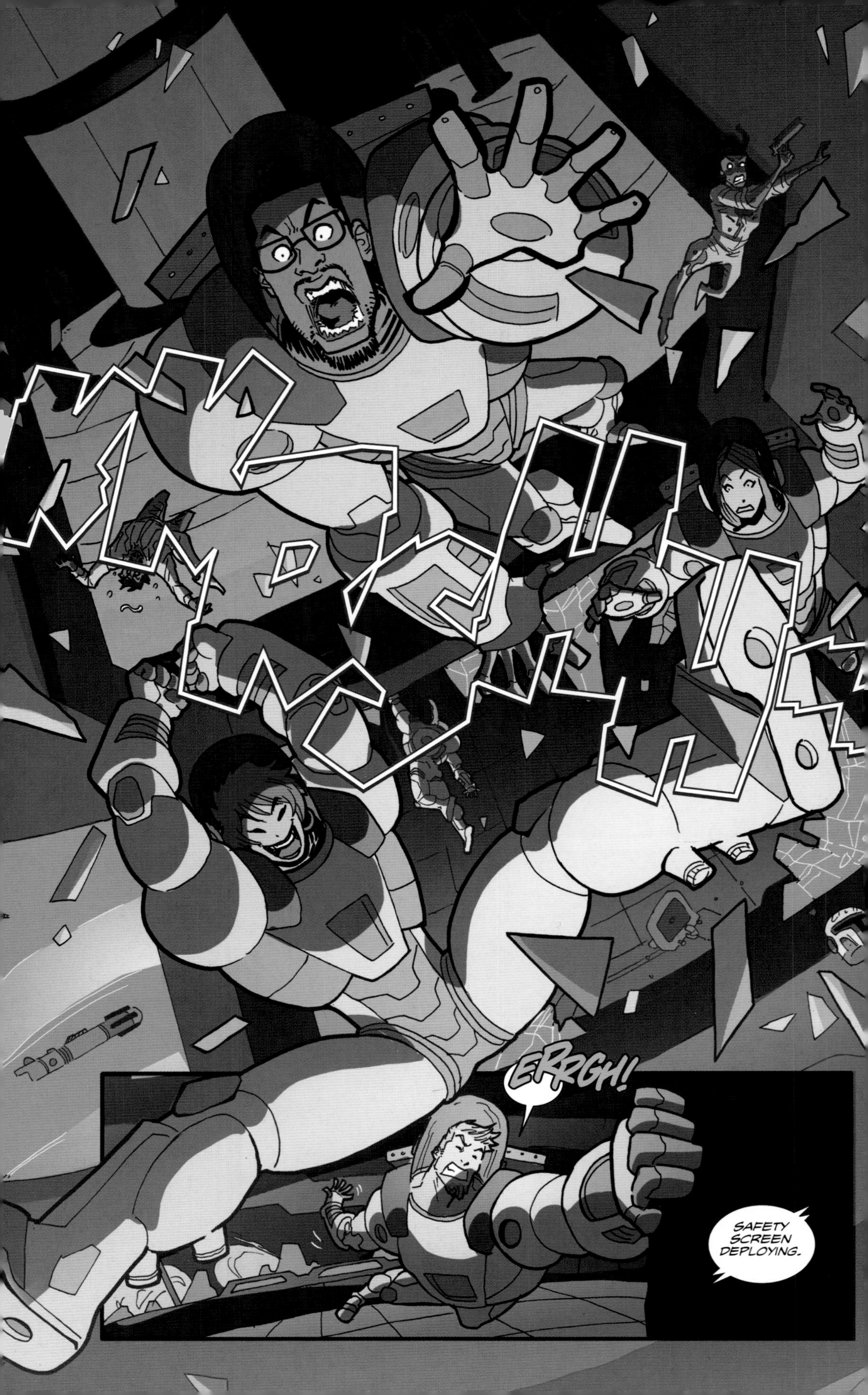
ERRGH!
SAFETY SCREEN DEPLOYING.

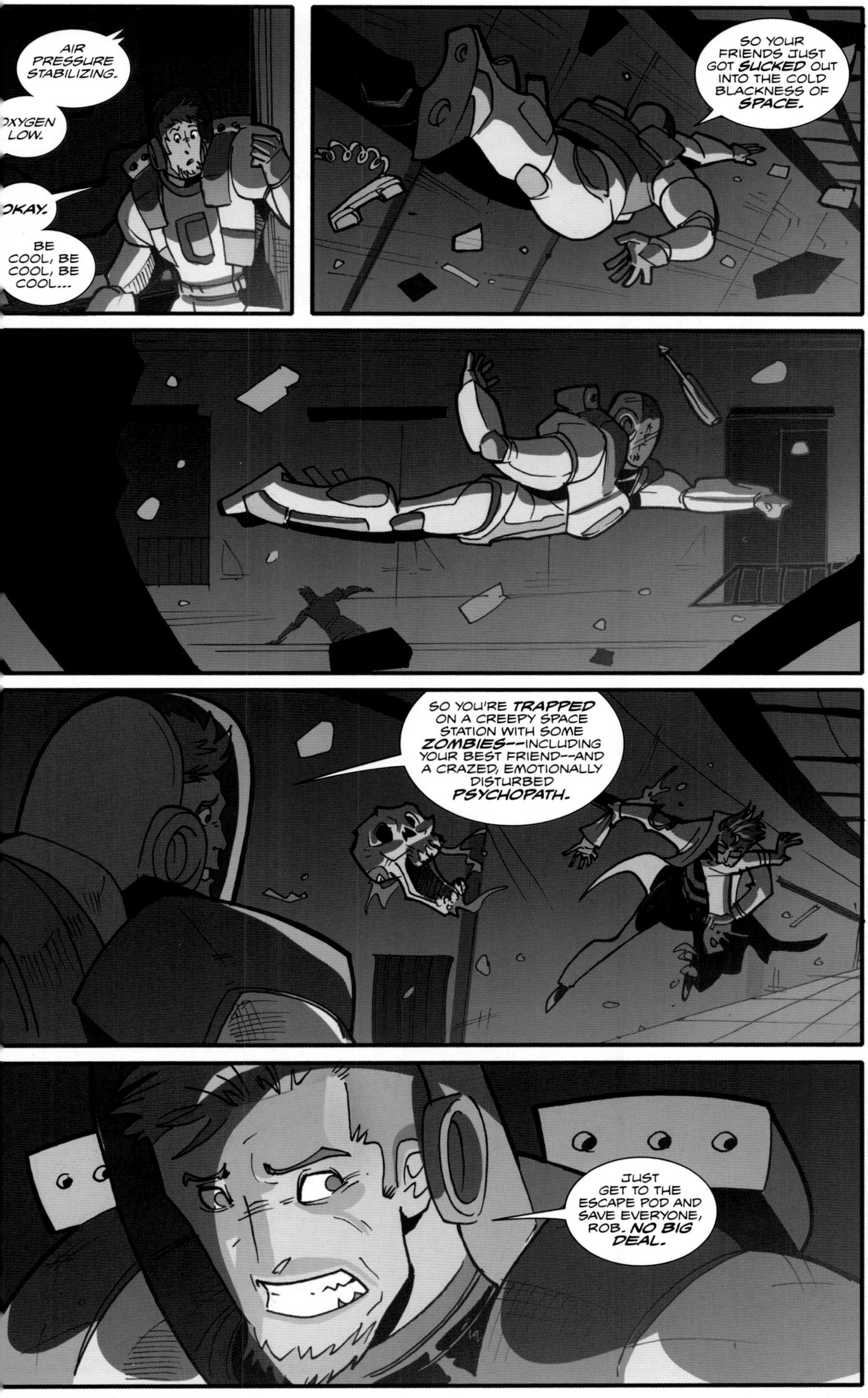
AIR PRESSURE STABILIZING.
OXYGEN LOW.
OKAY.
BE COOL, BE COOL, BE COOL...
SO YOUR FRIENDS JUST GOT SUCKED OUT INTO THE COLD BLACKNESS OF SPACE.
SO YOU'RE TRAPPED ON A CREEPY SPACE STATION WITH SOME ZOMBIES--INCLUDING YOUR BEST FRIEND--AND A CRAZED, EMOTIONALLY DISTURBED PSYCHOPATH.
JUST GET TO THE ESCAPE POD AND SAVE EVERYONE, ROB. NO BIG DEAL.

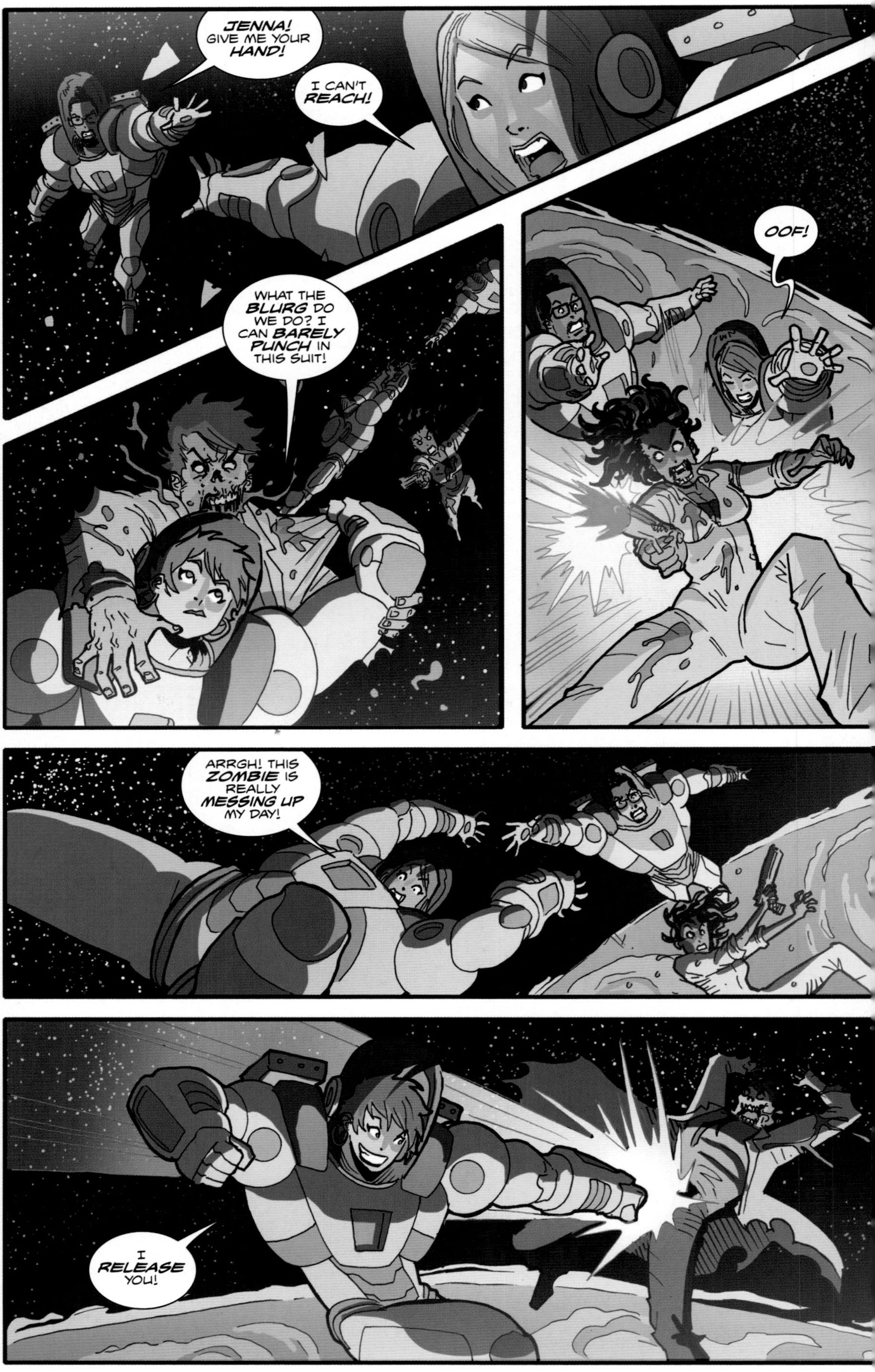
JENNA! GIVE ME YOUR HAND!
I CAN'T REACH!
WHAT THE BLURG DO WE DO? I CAN BARELY PUNCH IN THIS SUIT!
OOF!
ARRGH! THIS ZOMBIE IS REALLY MESSING UP MY DAY!
I RELEASE YOU!

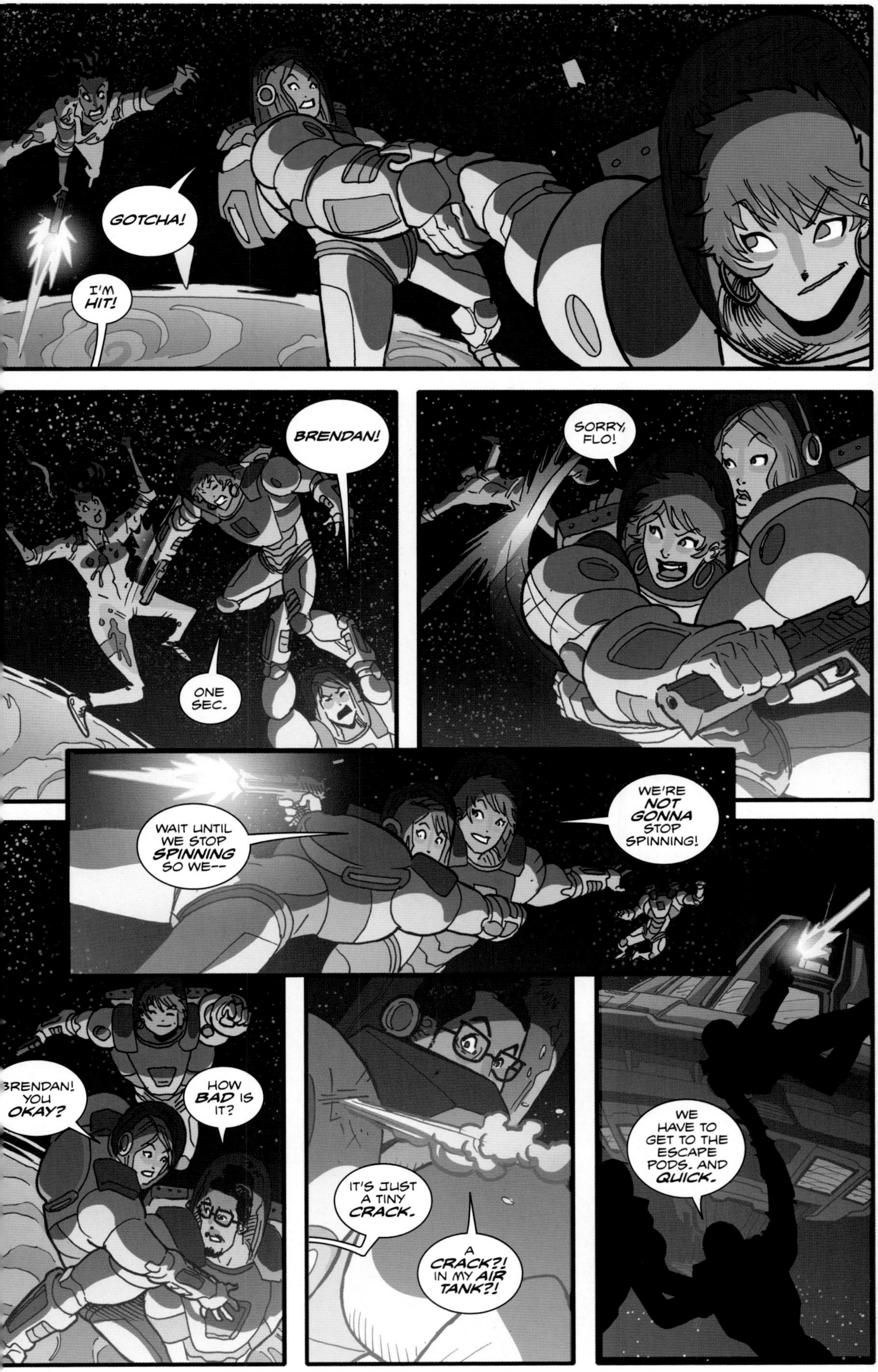
GOTCHA!
I'M HIT!
BRENDAN!
ONE SEC.
SORRY, FLO!
WAIT UNTIL WE STOP SPINNING SO WE--
WE'RE NOT GONNA STOP SPINNING!
BRENDAN! YOU OKAY?
HOW BAD IS IT?
IT'S JUST A TINY CRACK.
A CRACK?! IN MY AIR TANK?!
WE HAVE TO GET TO THE ESCAPE PODS. AND QUICK.

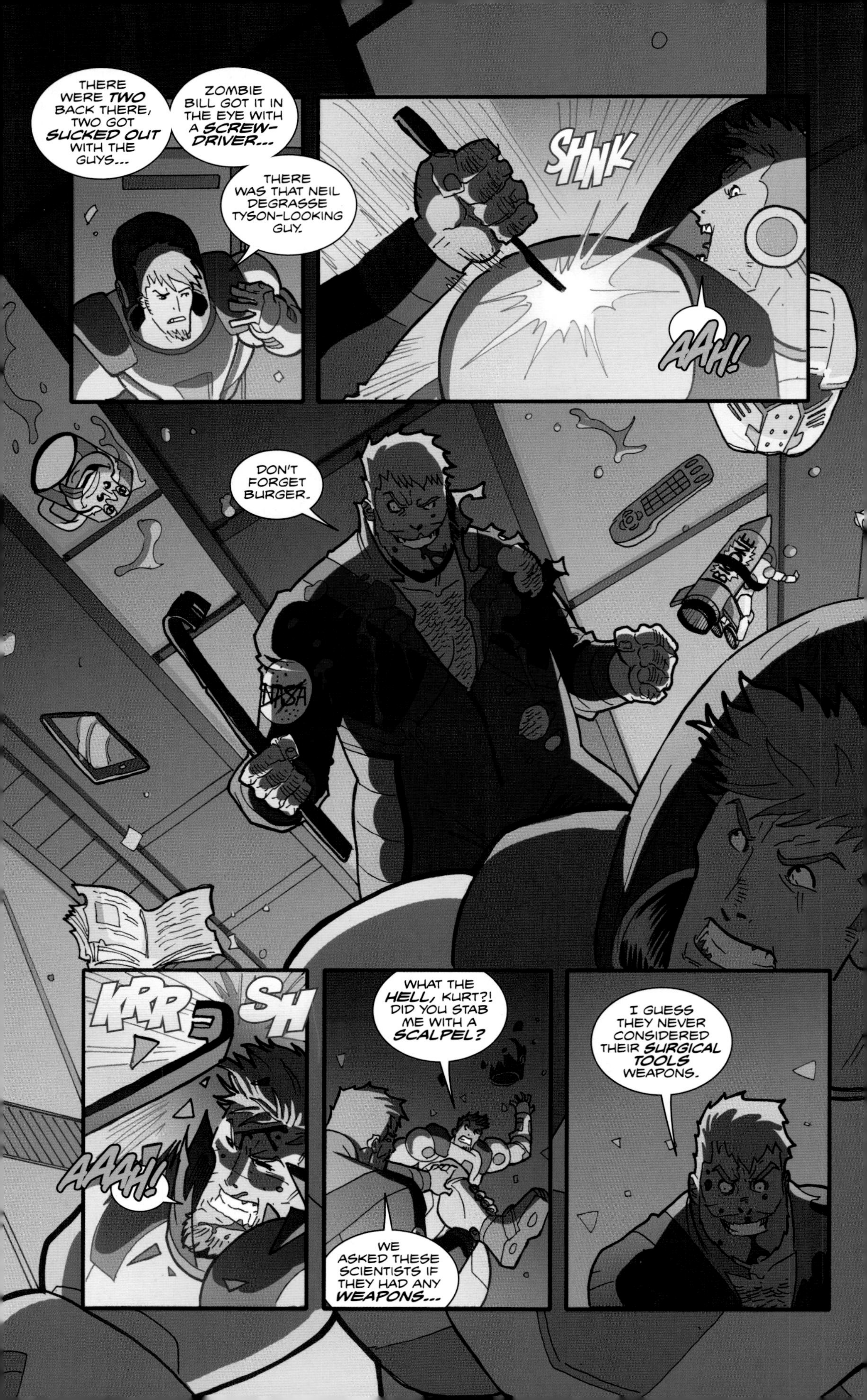
THERE WERE TWO BACK THERE, TWO GOT SUCKED OUT WITH THE GUYS...
ZOMBIE BILL GOT IT IN THE EYE WITH A SCREW-DRIVER...
THERE WAS THAT NEIL DEGRASSE TYSON-LOOKING GUY.
SHNK
AAH!
DON'T FORGET BURGER.
NASA
KRR
SH
AAAH!
WHAT THE HELL, KURT?! DID YOU STAB ME WITH A SCALPEL?
WE ASKED THESE SCIENTISTS IF THEY HAD ANY WEAPONS...
I GUESS THEY NEVER CONSIDERED THEIR SURGICAL TOOLS WEAPONS.

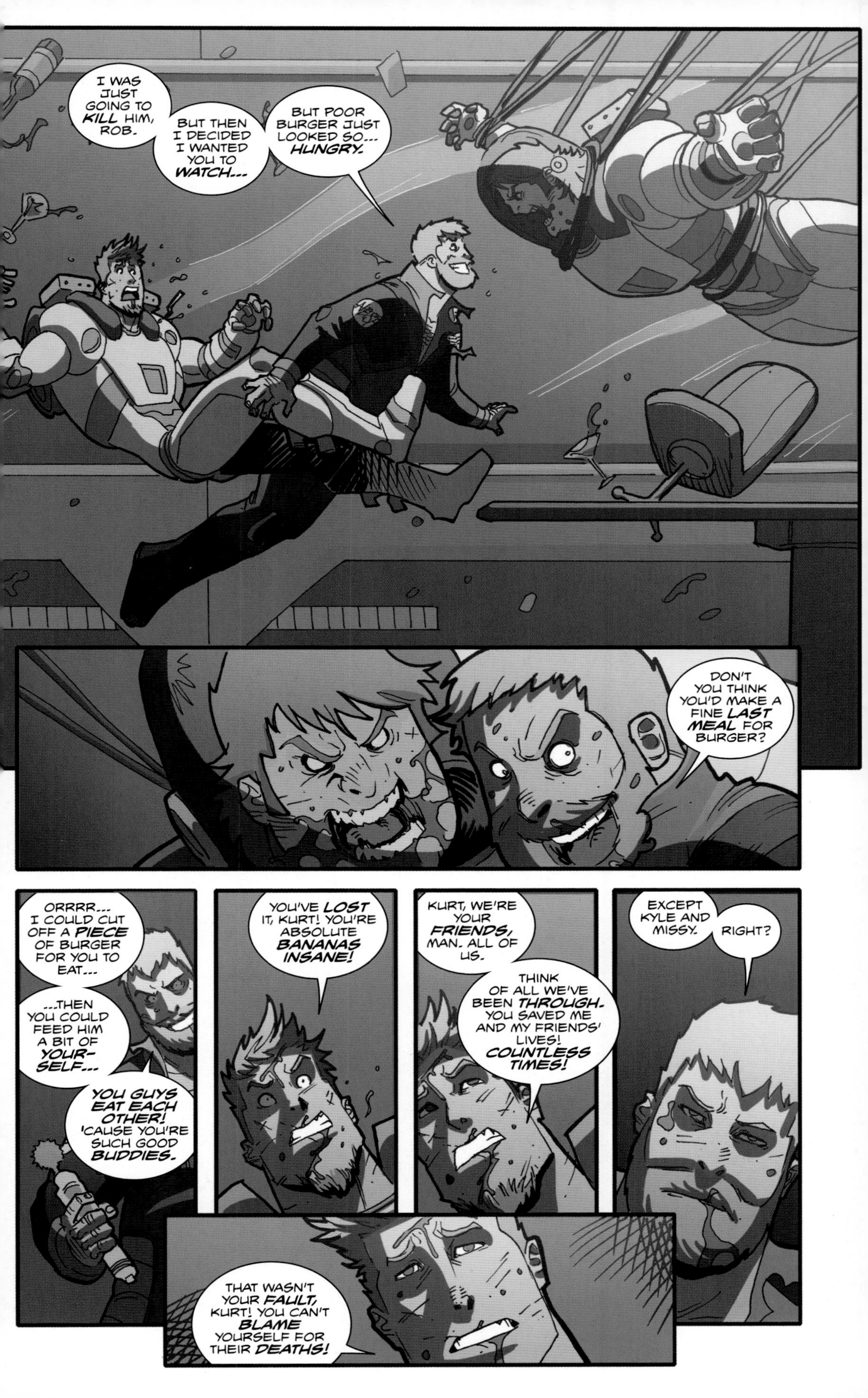
I WAS JUST GOING TO KILL HIM, ROB.
BUT THEN I DECIDED I WANTED YOU TO WATCH...
BUT POOR BURGER JUST LOOKED SO... HUNGRY.
DON'T YOU THINK YOU'D MAKE A FINE LAST MEAL FOR BURGER?
ORRRR... I COULD CUT OFF A PIECE OF BURGER FOR YOU TO EAT...
...THEN YOU COULD FEED HIM A BIT OF YOUR-SELF...
YOU GUYS EAT EACH OTHER! 'CAUSE YOU'RE SUCH GOOD BUDDIES.
YOU'VE LOST IT, KURT! YOU'RE ABSOLUTE BANANAS INSANE!
KURT, WE'RE YOUR FRIENDS, MAN. ALL OF US.
THINK OF ALL WE'VE BEEN THROUGH. YOU SAVED ME AND MY FRIENDS' LIVES! COUNTLESS TIMES!
EXCEPT KYLE AND MISSY.
RIGHT?
THAT WASN'T YOUR FAULT, KURT! YOU CAN'T BLAME YOURSELF FOR THEIR DEATHS!

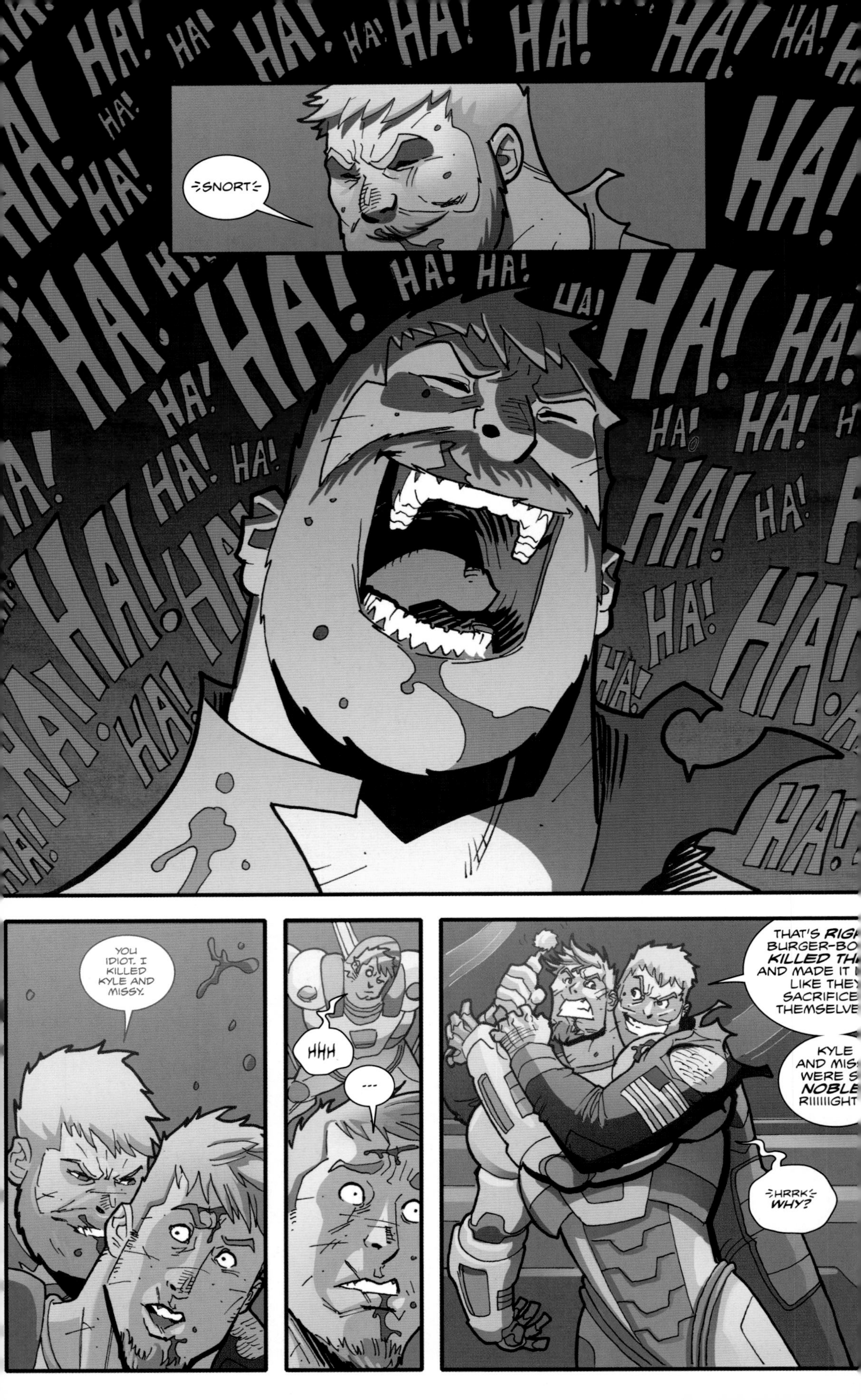
HA! HA! HA! HA! HA! HA! HA! HA! HA!
SNORT
HA! HA! HA! HA! HA! HA! HA! HA! HA!
YOU IDIOT. I KILLED KYLE AND MISSY.
HHH
...
THAT'S RIG BURGER-BO KILLED TH AND MADE IT LIKE THEY SACRIFICE THEMSELVE
KYLE AND MIS WERE S NOBLE RIIIIIIGHT
HRRK WHY?

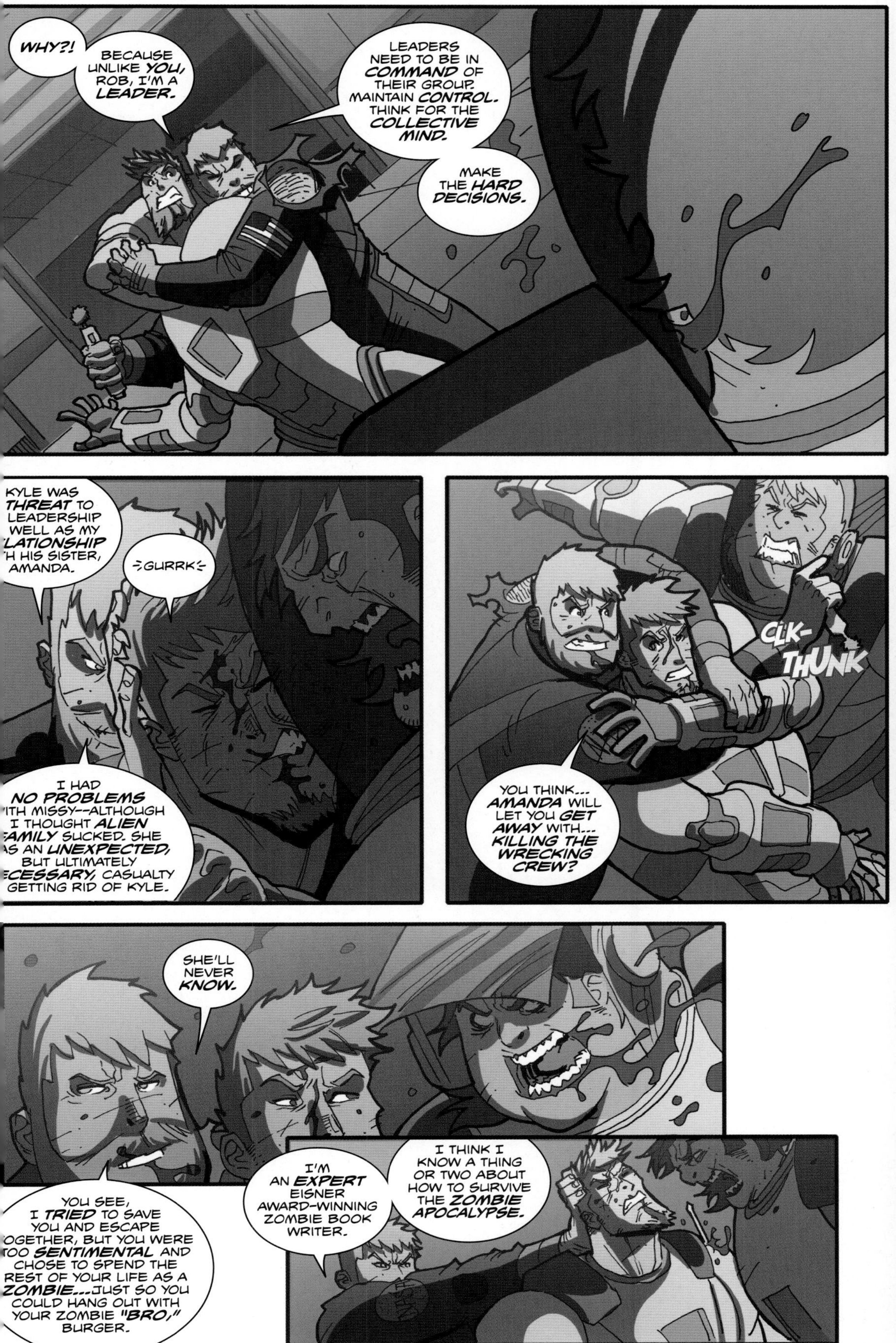
WHY?!
BECAUSE UNLIKE YOU, ROB, I'M A LEADER.
LEADERS NEED TO BE IN COMMAND OF THEIR GROUP. MAINTAIN CONTROL. THINK FOR THE COLLECTIVE MIND.
MAKE THE HARD DECISIONS.
KYLE WAS THREAT TO LEADERSHIP WELL AS MY LATIONSHIP TH HIS SISTER, AMANDA.
GURRK
I HAD NO PROBLEMS ITH MISSY--ALTHOUGH I THOUGHT ALIEN AMILY SUCKED. SHE AS AN UNEXPECTED, BUT ULTIMATELY ECESSARY, CASUALTY GETTING RID OF KYLE.
CLIK-THUNK
YOU THINK... AMANDA WILL LET YOU GET AWAY WITH... KILLING THE WRECKING CREW?
SHE'LL NEVER KNOW.
YOU SEE, I TRIED TO SAVE YOU AND ESCAPE OGETHER, BUT YOU WERE OO SENTIMENTAL AND CHOSE TO SPEND THE REST OF YOUR LIFE AS A ZOMBIE...JUST SO YOU COULD HANG OUT WITH YOUR ZOMBIE "BRO," BURGER.
I'M AN EXPERT EISNER AWARD-WINNING ZOMBIE BOOK WRITER.
I THINK I KNOW A THING OR TWO ABOUT HOW TO SURVIVE THE ZOMBIE APOCALYPSE.

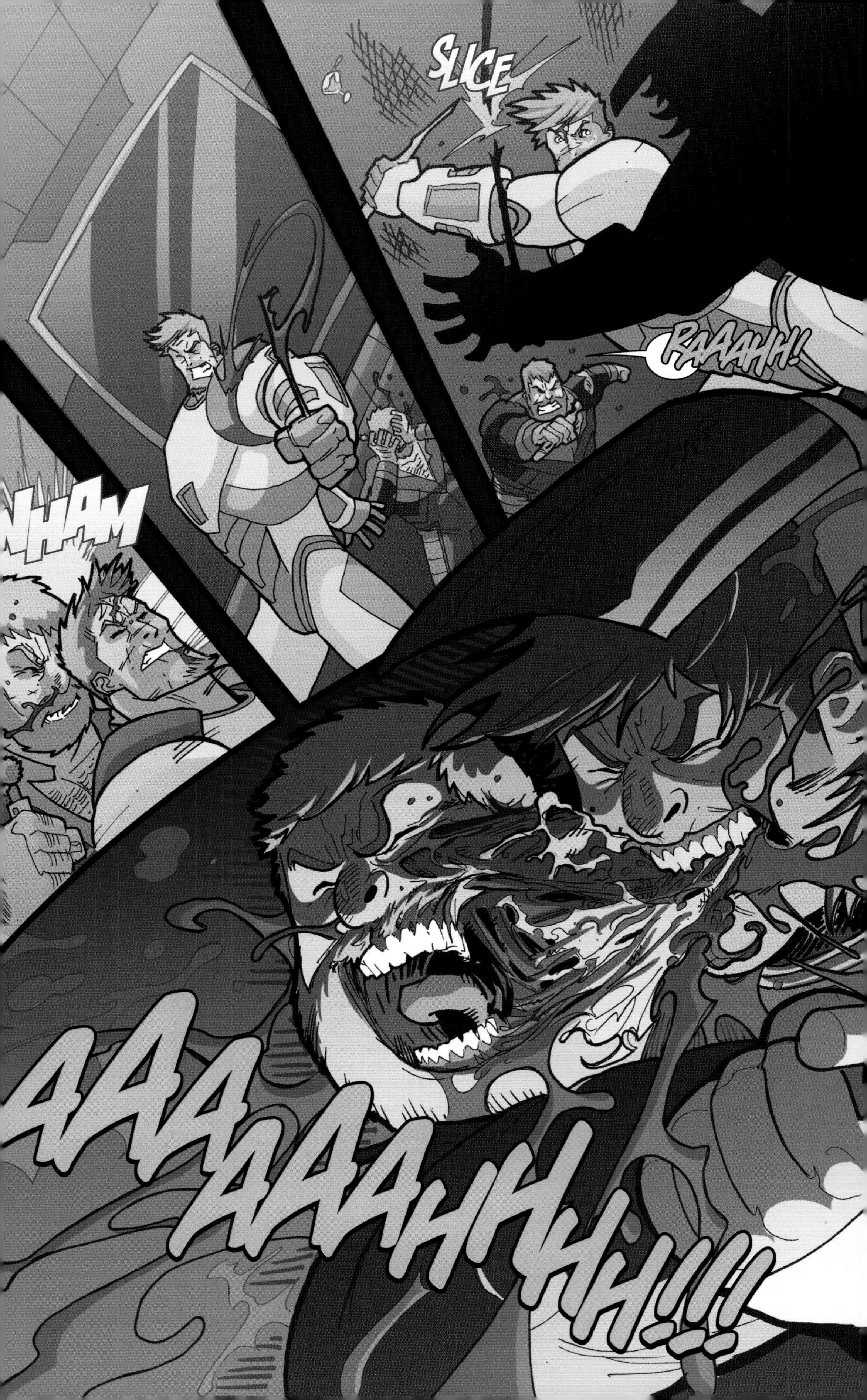
SLICE
RAAAHH!
WHAM
AAAAAAAHHHH!!!!

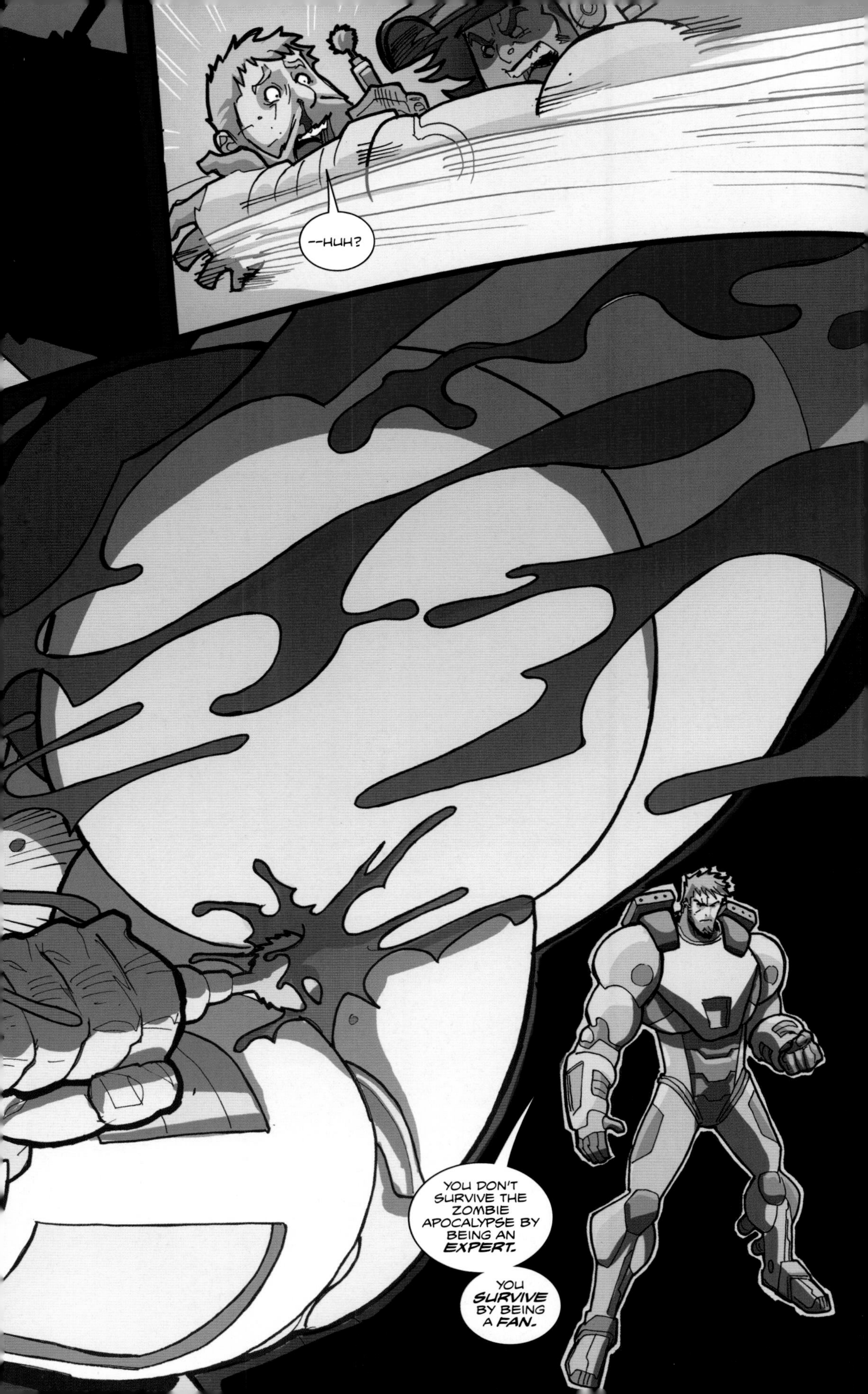
--HUH?
YOU DON'T SURVIVE THE ZOMBIE APOCALYPSE BY BEING AN *EXPERT.*
YOU *SURVIVE* BY BEING A *FAN.*

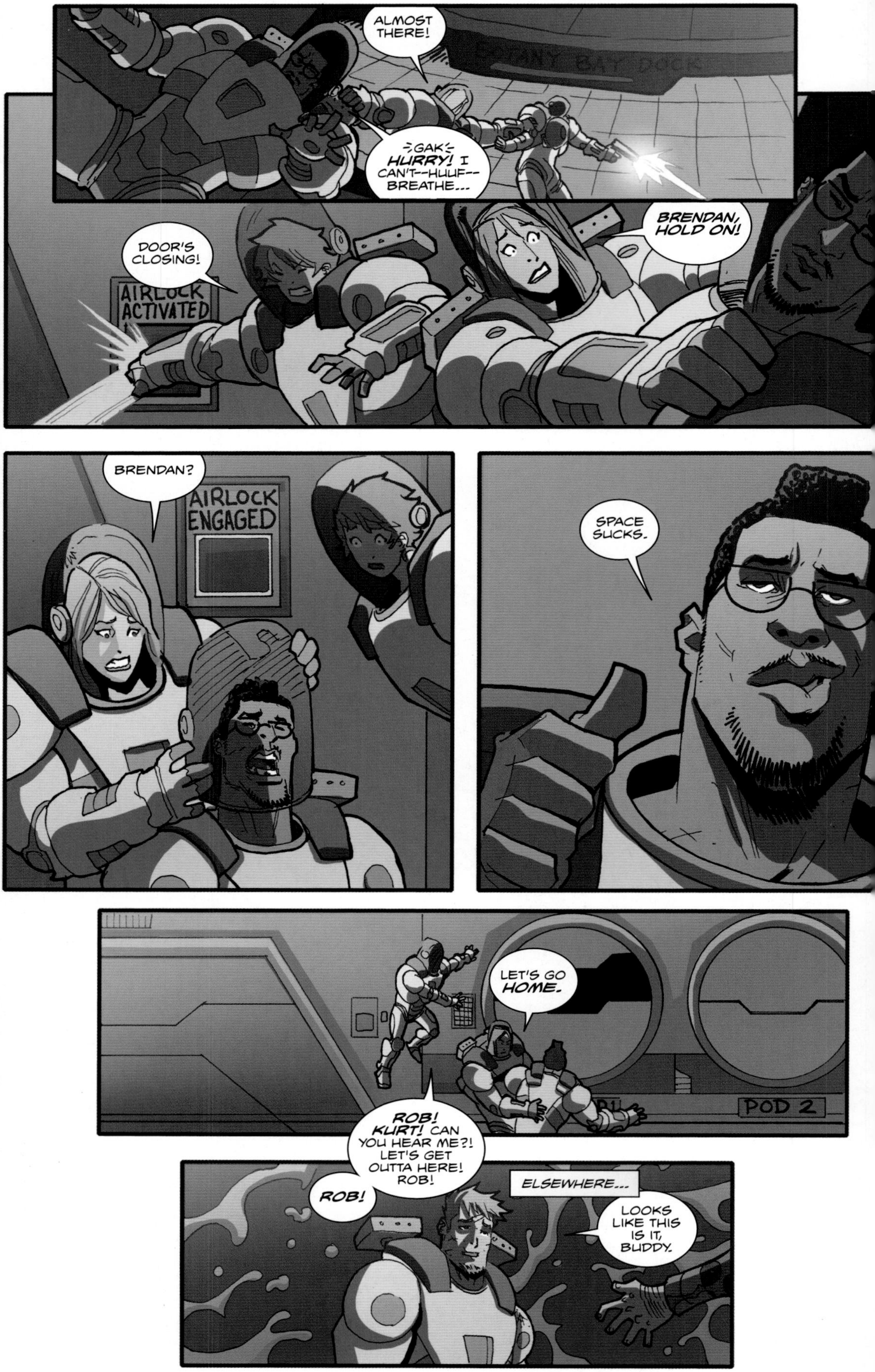
ALMOST THERE!
BOTANY BAY DOCK
=GAK= HURRY! I CAN'T--HUUF-- BREATHE...
DOOR'S CLOSING!
AIRLOCK ACTIVATED
BRENDAN, HOLD ON!
BRENDAN?
AIRLOCK ENGAGED
SPACE SUCKS.
LET'S GO HOME.
POD 2
ROB! KURT! CAN YOU HEAR ME?! LET'S GET OUTTA HERE! ROB!
ROB!
ELSEWHERE...
LOOKS LIKE THIS IS IT, BUDDY.

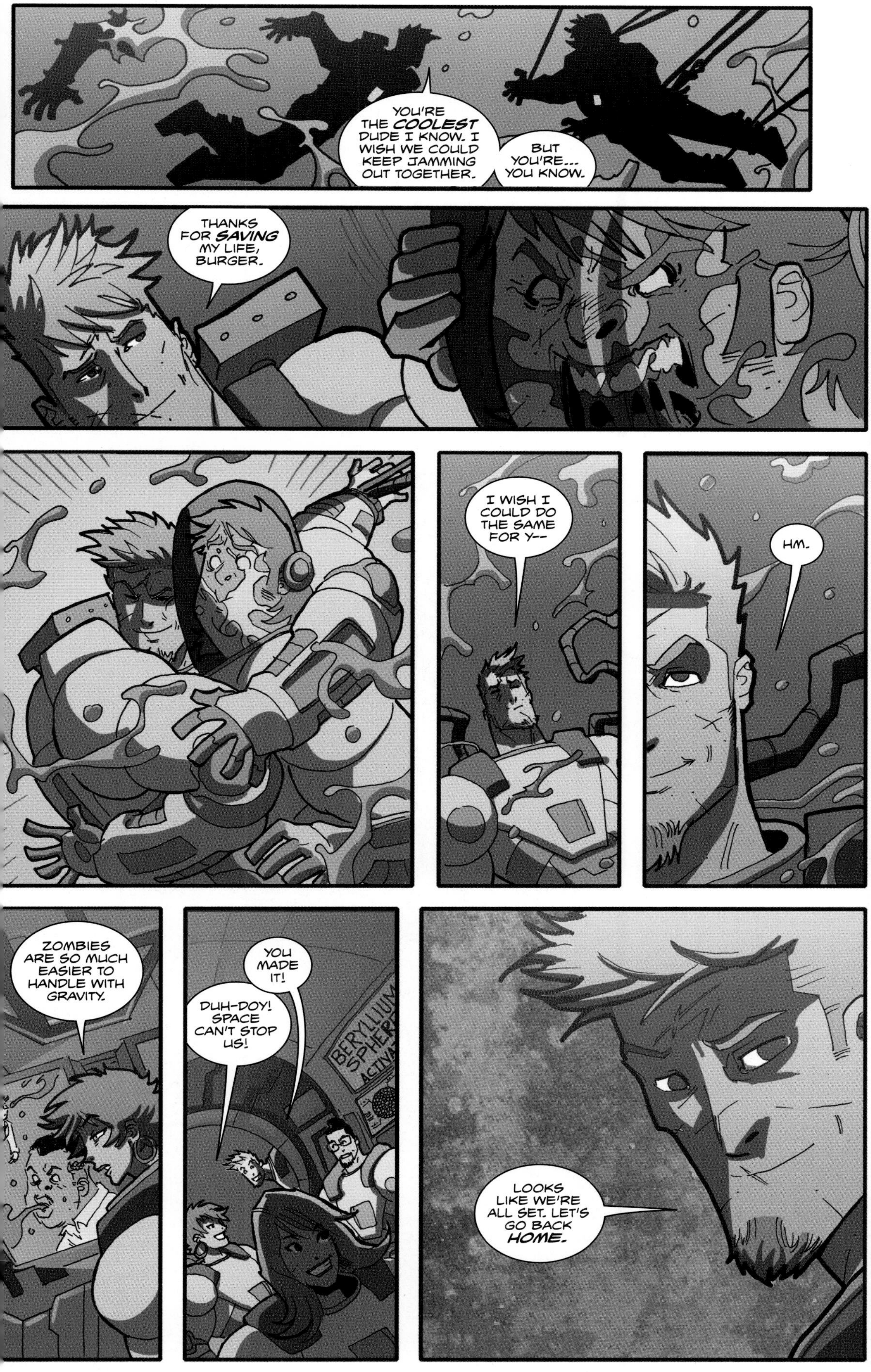
YOU'RE THE COOLEST DUDE I KNOW. I WISH WE COULD KEEP JAMMING OUT TOGETHER.
BUT YOU'RE... YOU KNOW.
THANKS FOR SAVING MY LIFE, BURGER.
I WISH I COULD DO THE SAME FOR Y--
HM.
ZOMBIES ARE SO MUCH EASIER TO HANDLE WITH GRAVITY.
YOU MADE IT!
DUH-DOY! SPACE CAN'T STOP US!
BERYLLIUM SPHERE ACTIVA
LOOKS LIKE WE'RE ALL SET. LET'S GO BACK HOME.

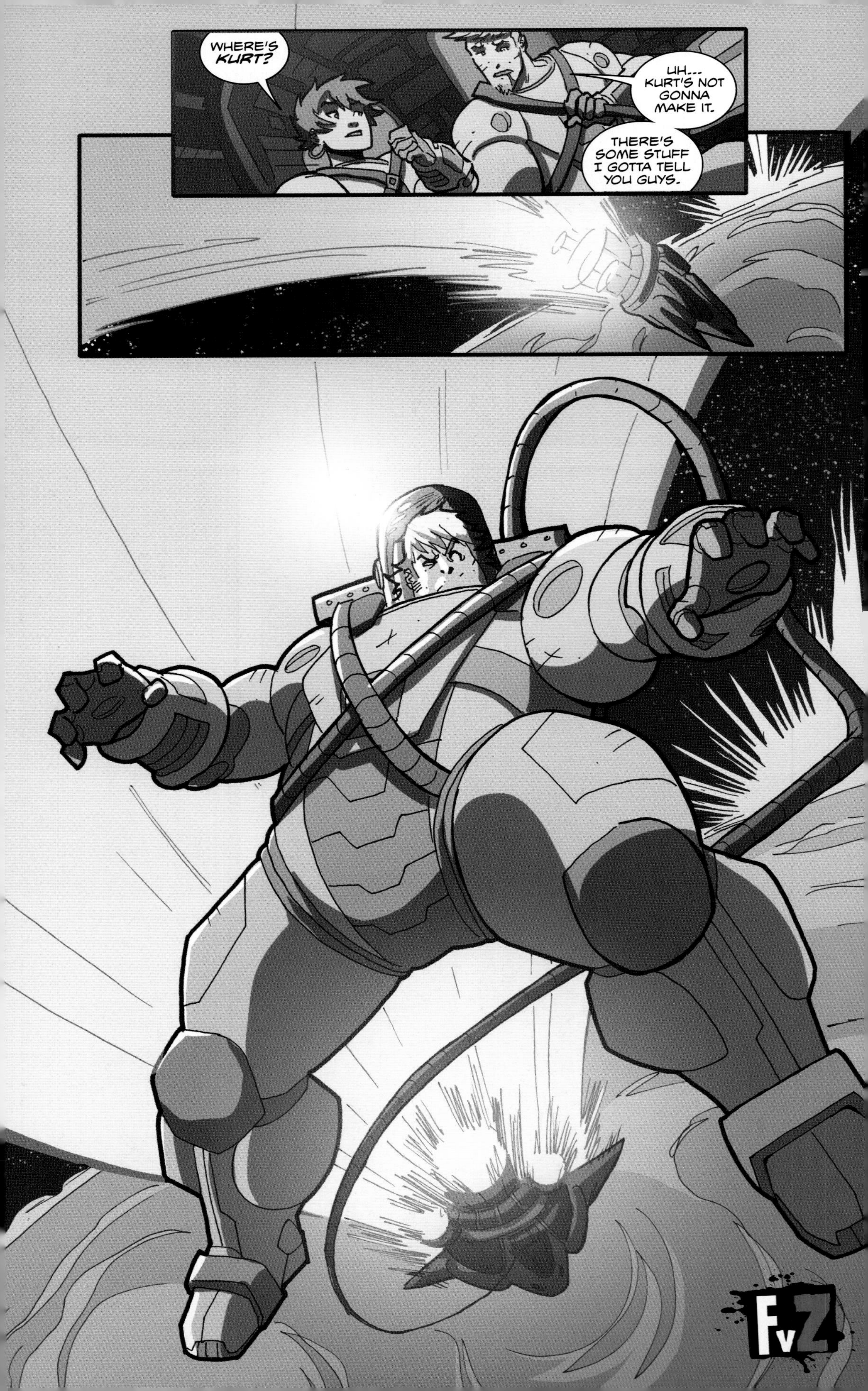
WHERE'S KURT?
UH... KURT'S NOT GONNA MAKE IT.
THERE'S SOME STUFF I GOTTA TELL YOU GUYS.
FvZ

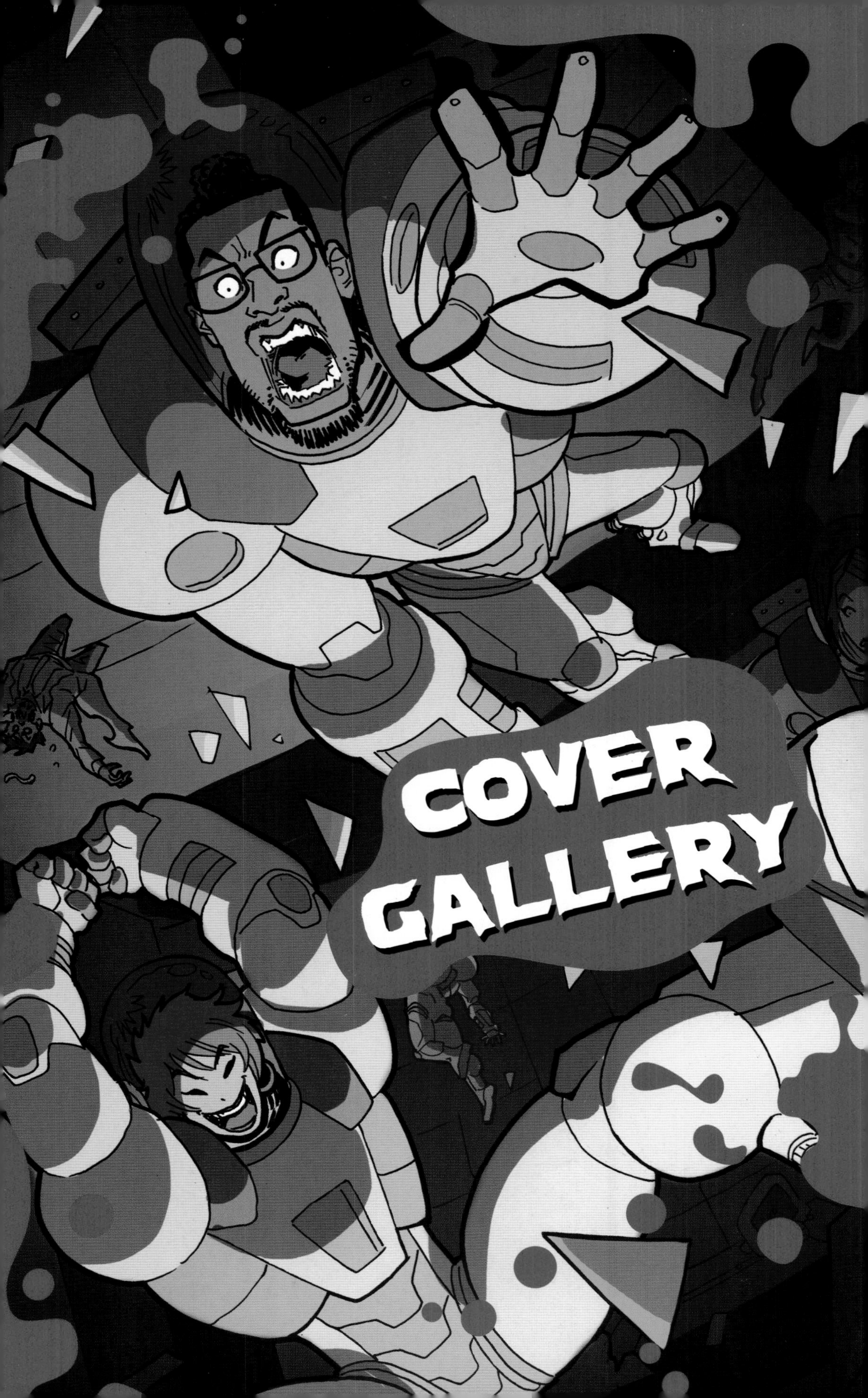
COVER
GALLERY

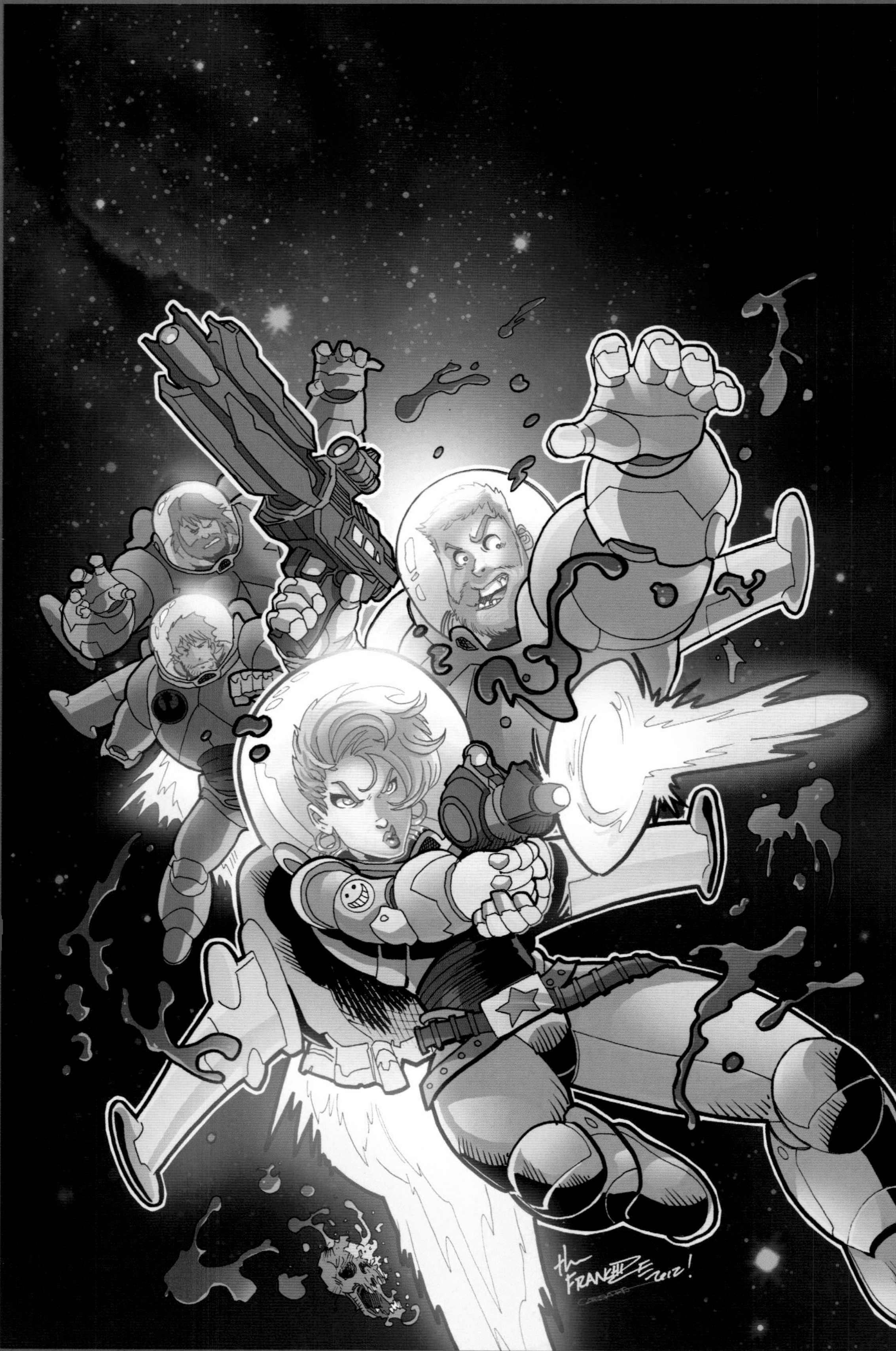

ISSUE THIRTEEN: JERRY GAYLORD
WITH COLORS BY GABRIEL CASSATA

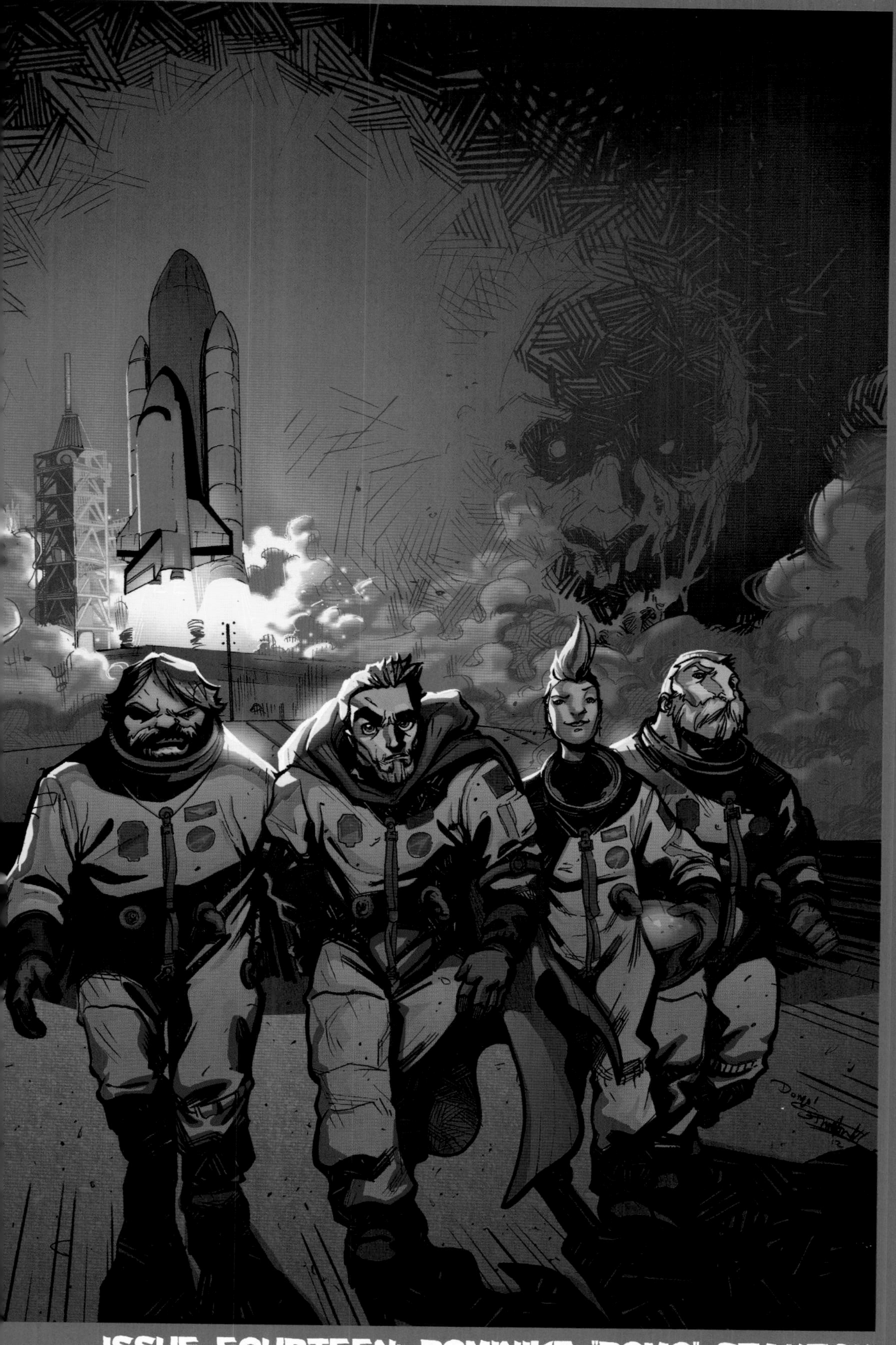

ISSUE FOURTEEN: DOMINIKE "DOMO" STANTON

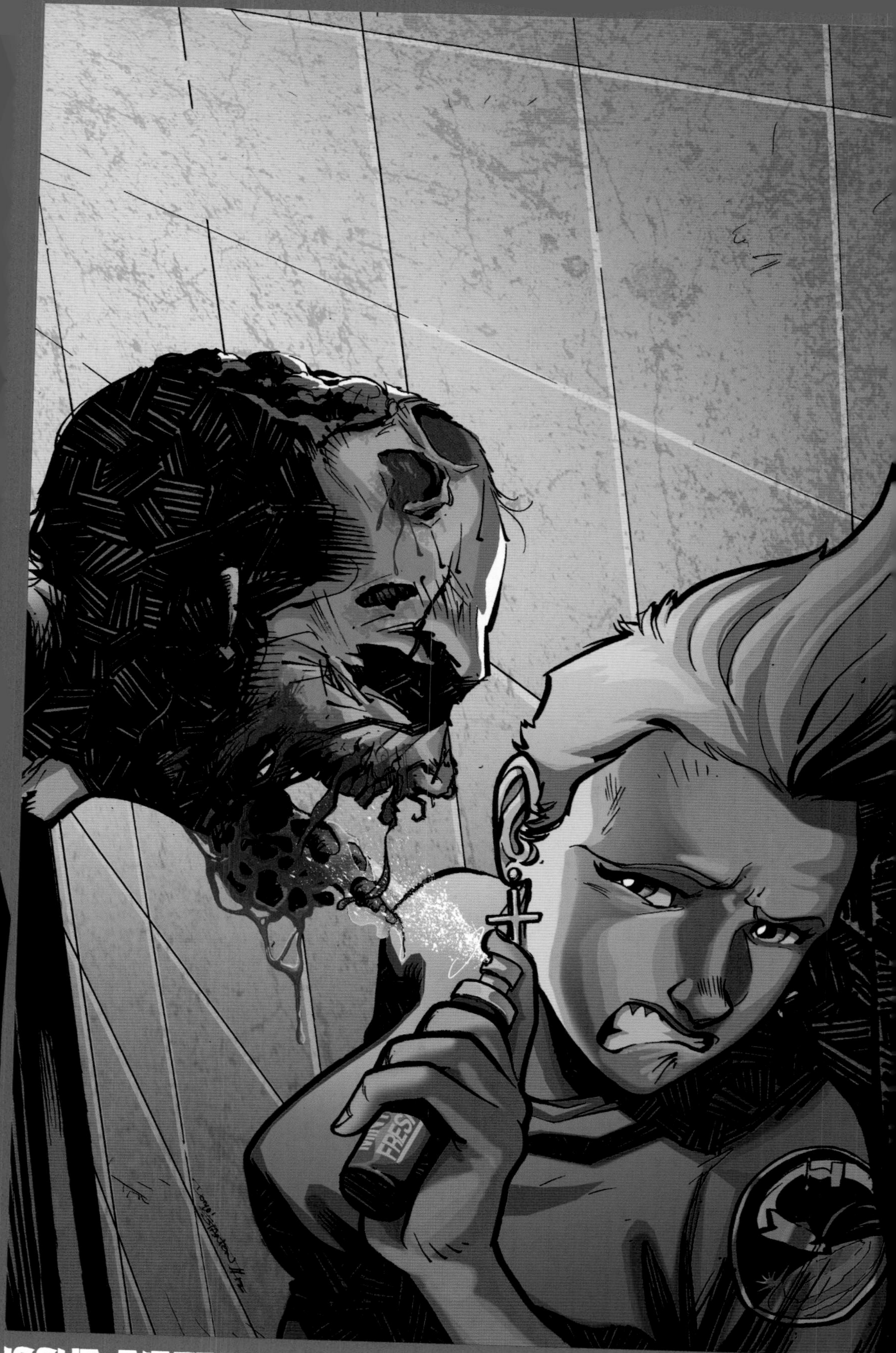
MINT FRESH

ISSUE FIFTEEN: DOMINIKE "DOMO" STANTON

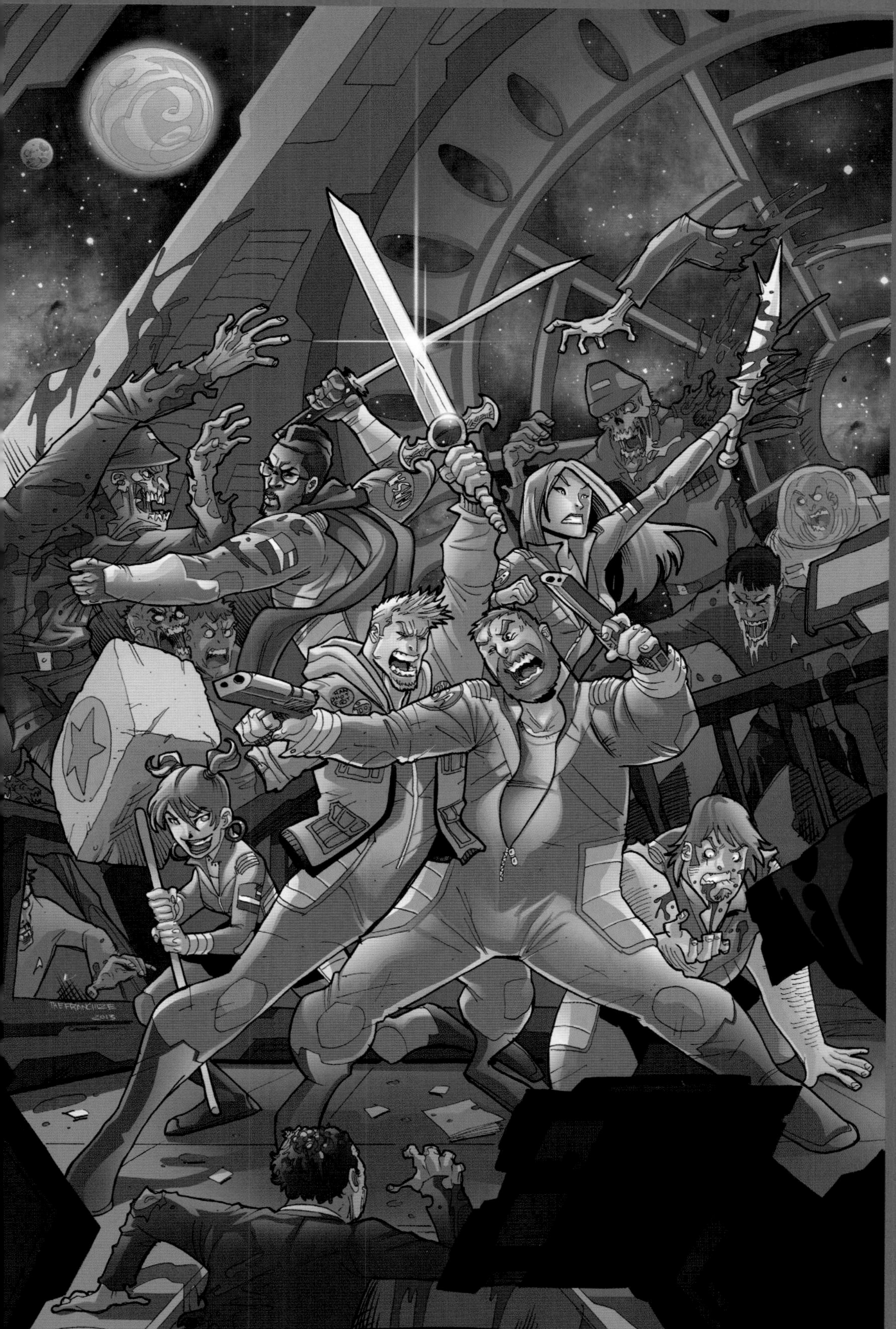

ISSUE SIXTEEN: JERRY GAYLORD
WITH COLORS BY GABRIEL CASSATA

DECOMPOSING FvZ

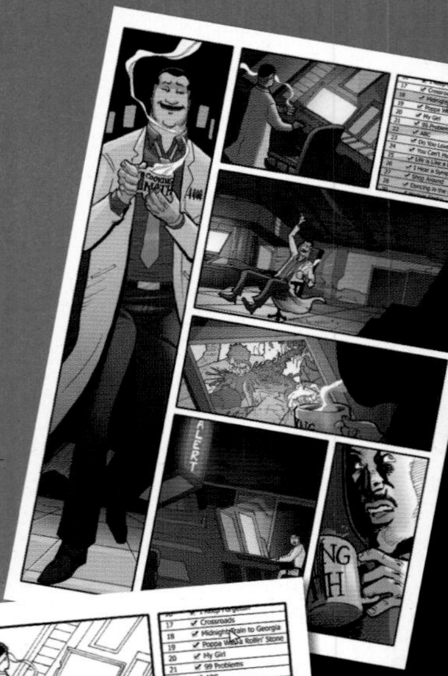

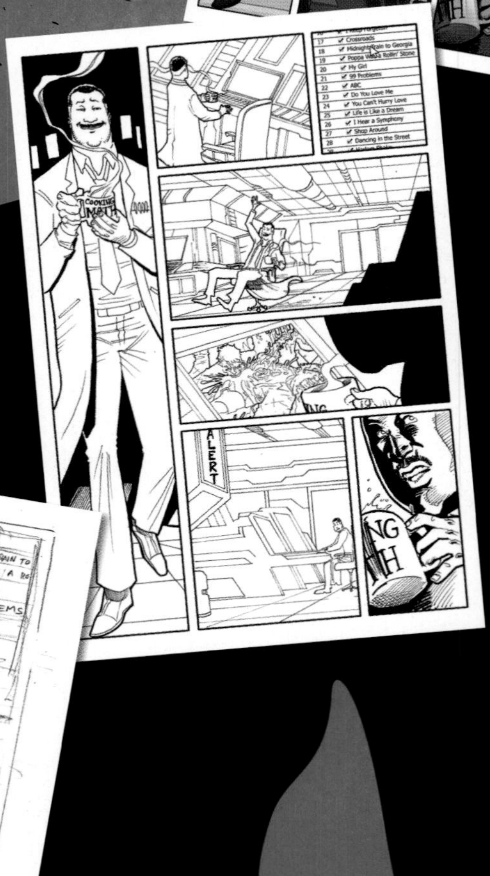

17 Crossroads
18 Midnight Train to Georgia
19 Poppa Was a Rollin' Stone
20 My Girl
21 99 Problems
22 ABC
23 Do You Love Me
24 You Can't Hurry Love
25 Life is Like a Dream
26 I Hear a Symphony
27 Shop Around
28 Dancing in the Street
COOKING MATH
ALERT

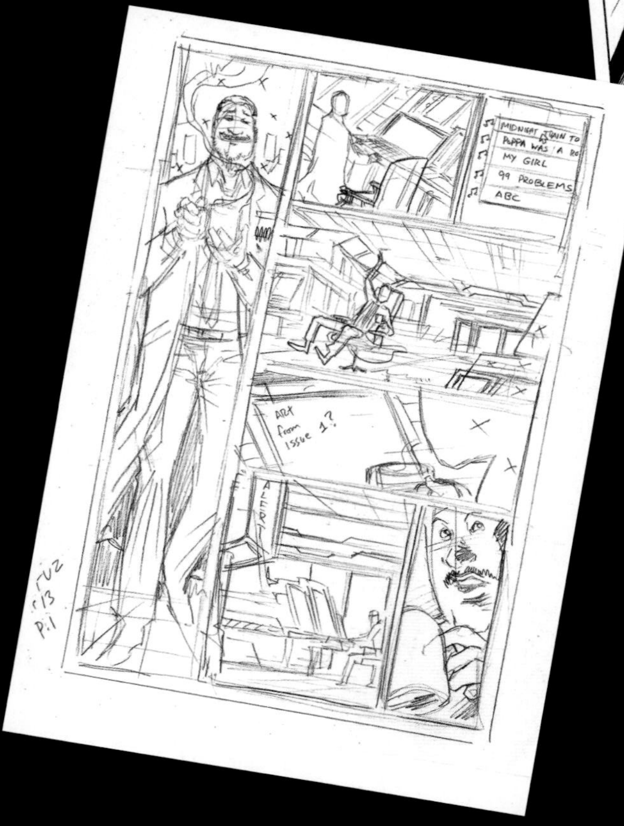

MIDNIGHT TRAIN TO
POPPA WAS A RO
MY GIRL
99 PROBLEMS
ABC
Art from Issue 1?
ALERT
FvZ #13 P.1

ISSUE THIRTEEN
PAGE ONE

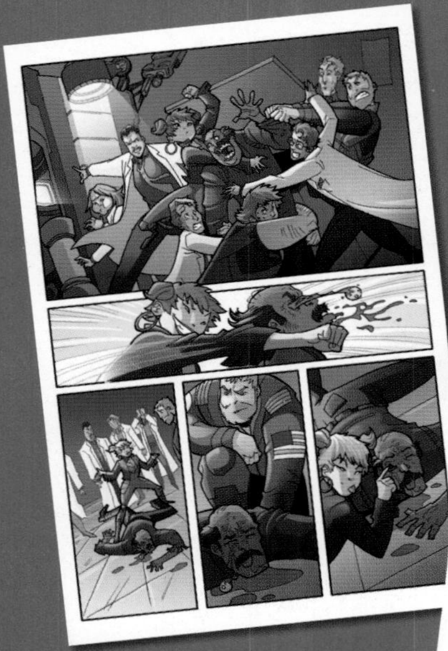

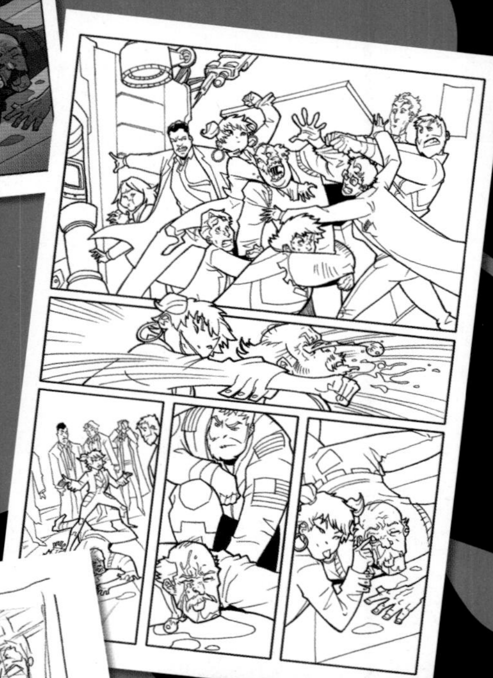

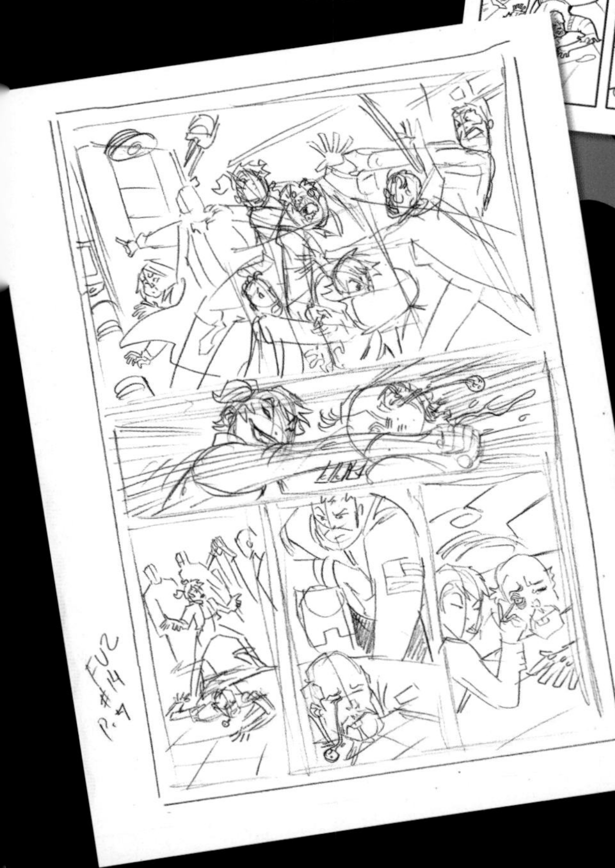

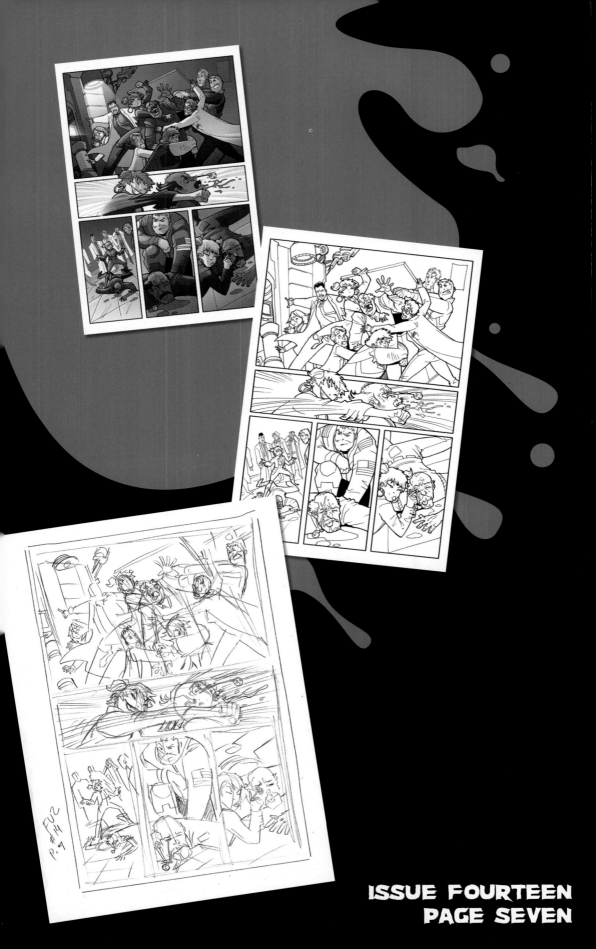

ISSUE FOURTEEN
PAGE SEVEN

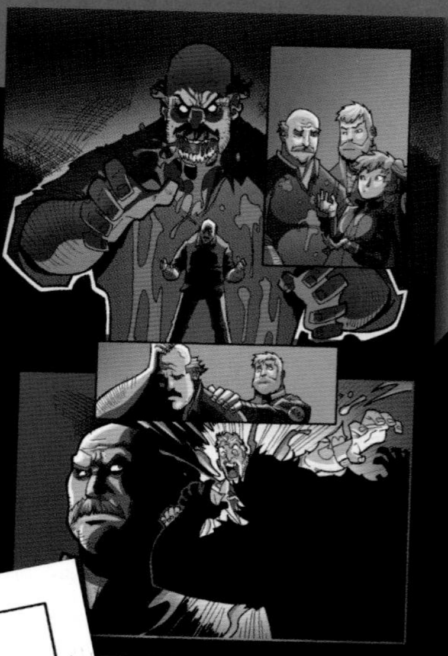

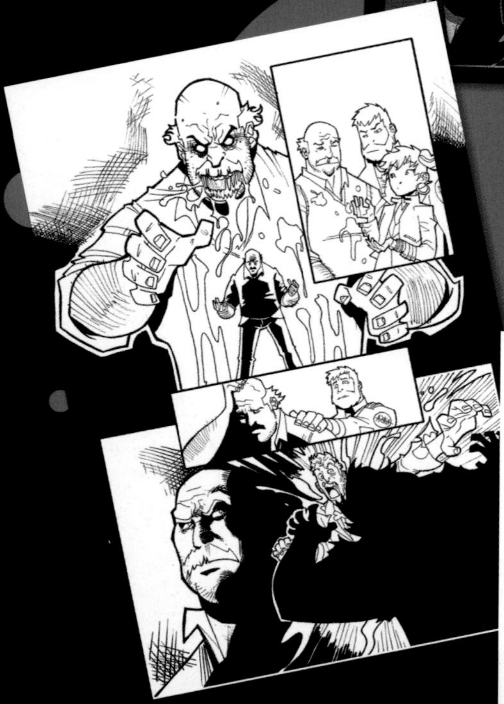

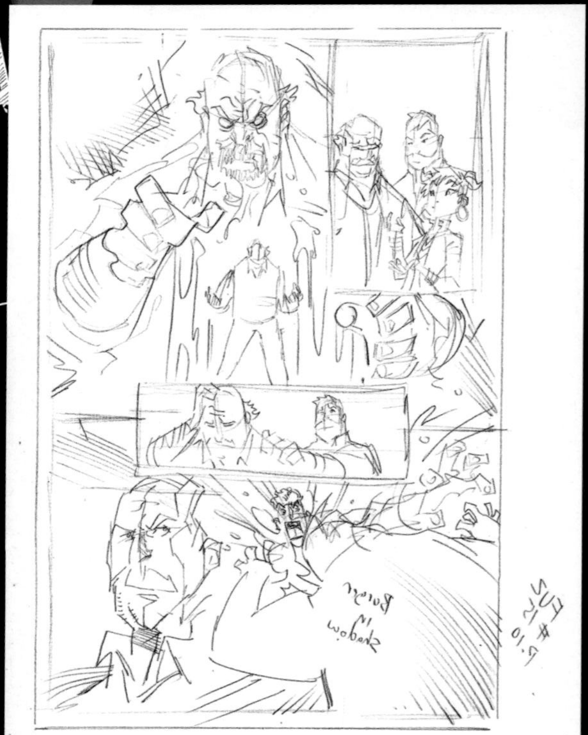

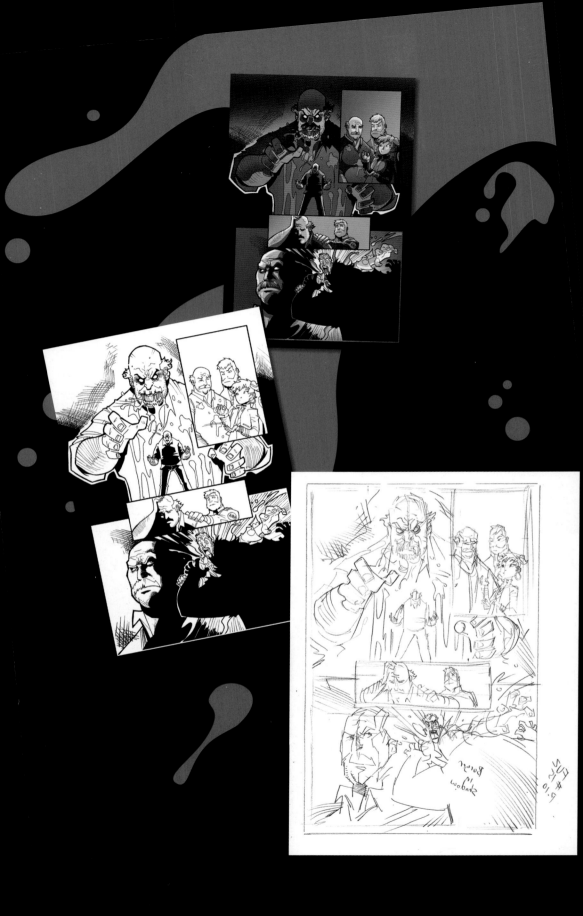

ISSUE FIFTEEN
PAGE TEN

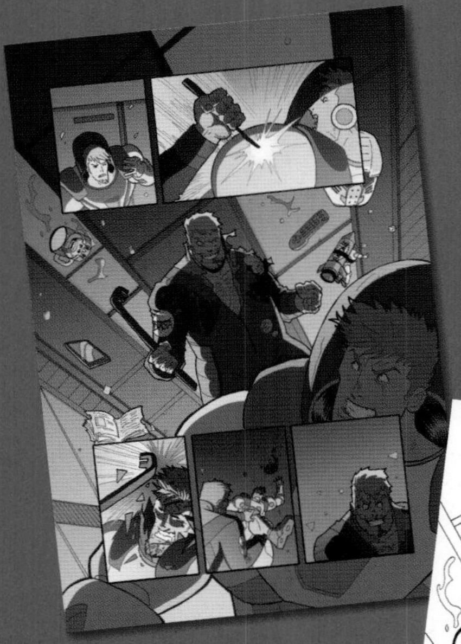

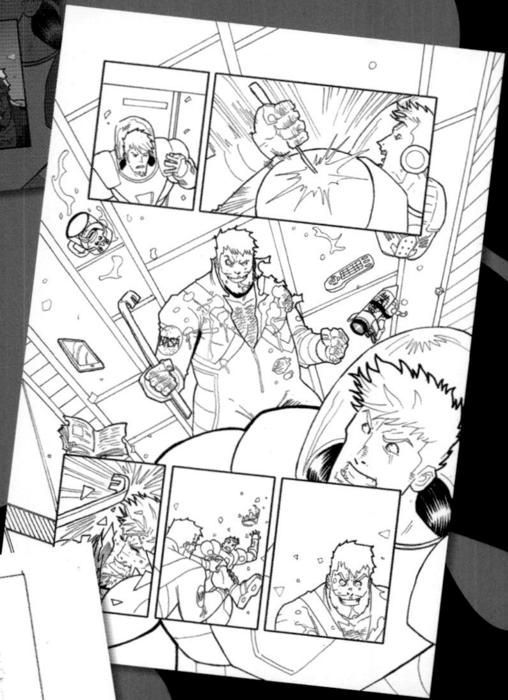

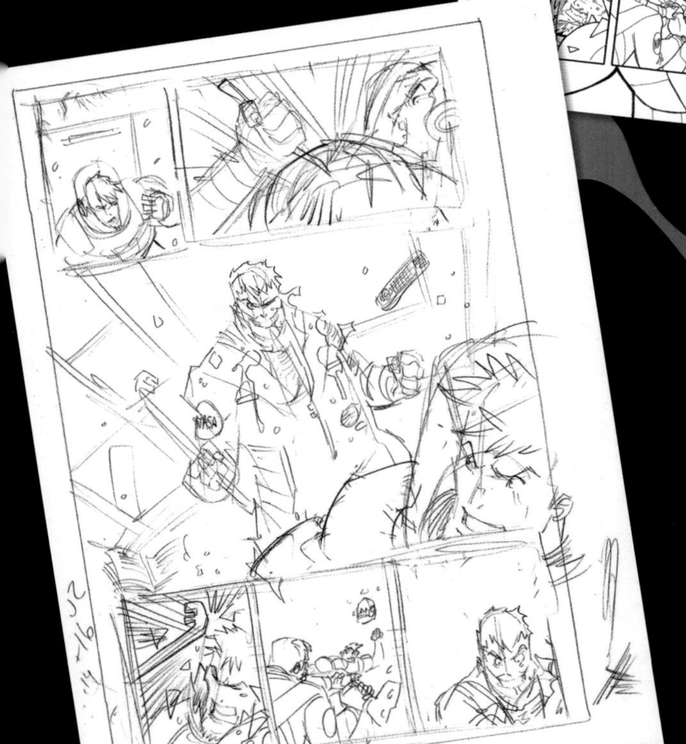

ISSUE SIXTEEN
PAGE FOURTEEN

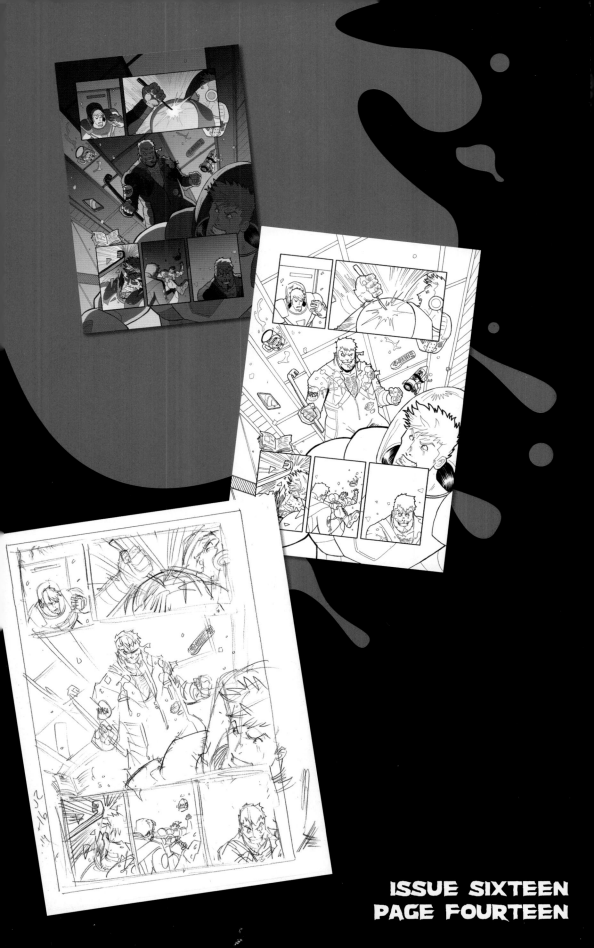

FvZ MAIL

FAN SKETCHES BY JERRY GAYLORD

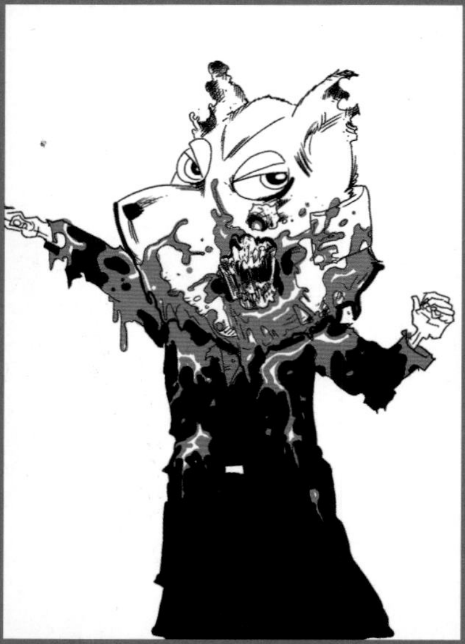

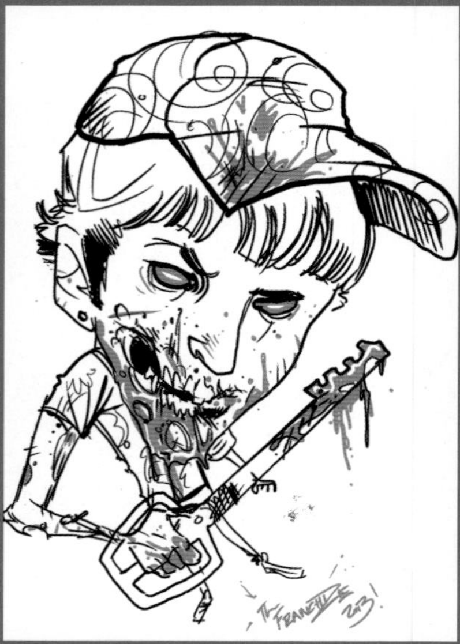

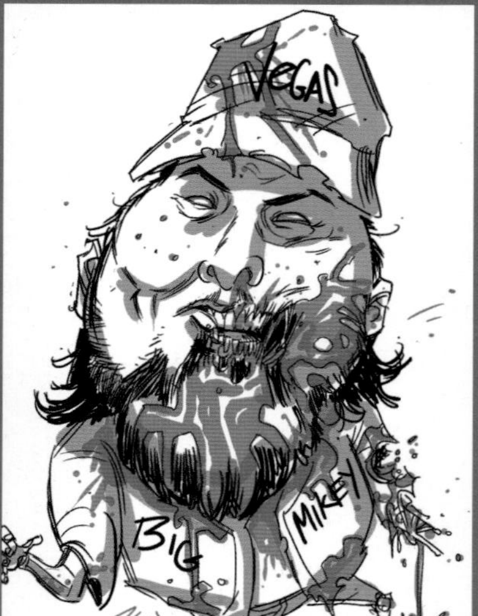
VEGAS
BIG
MIKEY

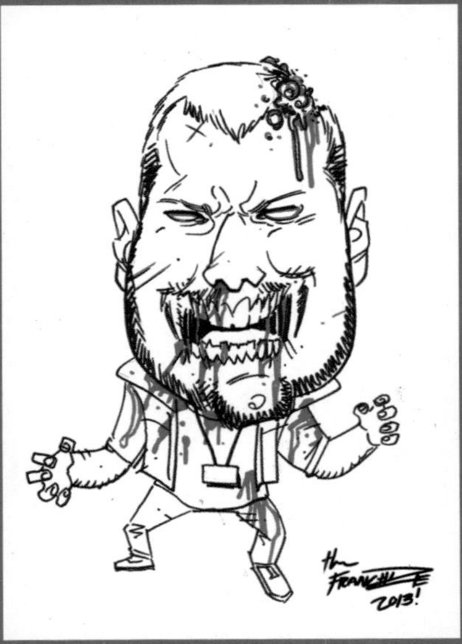
the FRANCHIZE 2013!

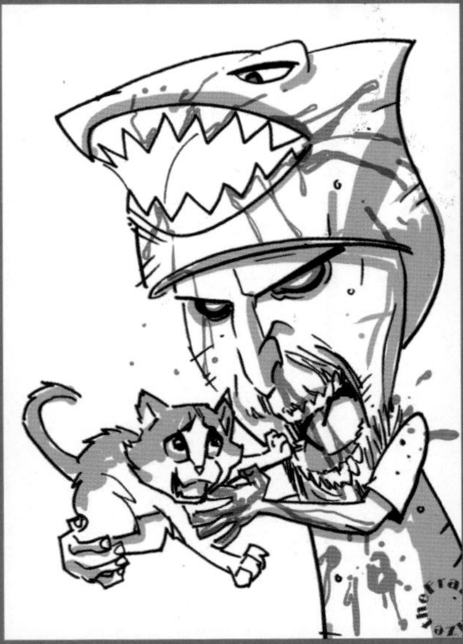

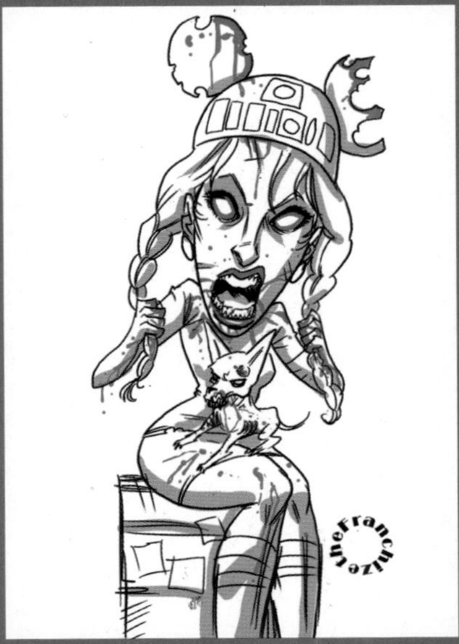
theFranchize

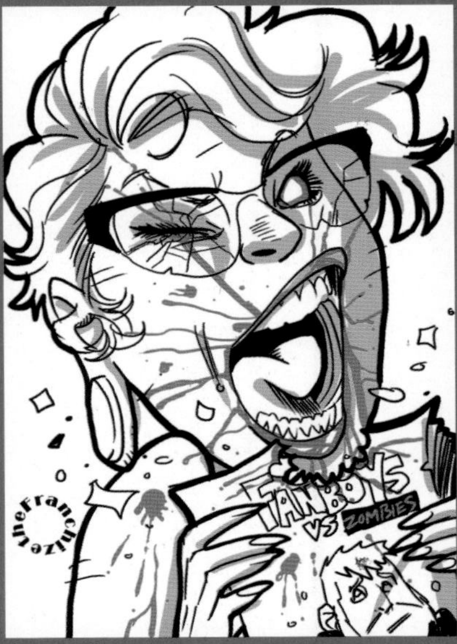
theFranchize
FANBOYS VS ZOMBIES

COMING SOON!

FANBOYS™
VS. ZOMBIES

VOLUME FIVE
4 STORIES OF THE APOCALYPSE